LAST WORDS
OF THE EXECUTED

LAST WORDS
OF THE EXECUTED

ROBERT K. ELDER

With a Foreword by Studs Terkel

THE UNIVERSITY OF CHICAGO PRESS
Chicago and London

ROBERT K. ELDER, a journalist and author, lives
in Chicago. He teaches journalism at Northwestern
University and can be found on the web at
www.robelder.com.

The University of Chicago Press, Chicago 60637
The University of Chicago Press, Ltd., London
© 2010 by Robert K. Elder
All rights reserved. Published 2010
Printed in the United States of America

18 17 16 15 14 13 12 11 10   1 2 3 4 5

ISBN-13: 978-0-226-20268-6
ISBN-10: 0-226-20268-2

Library of Congress Cataloging-in-Publication Data

Elder, Robert K.
    Last words of the executed / Robert K. Elder ; with a
foreword by Studs Terkel.
        p. cm.
    Includes bibliographical references and index.
    ISBN-13: 978-0-226-20268-6 (cloth : alk. paper)
    ISBN-10: 0-226-20268-2 (cloth : alk. paper) 1. Last
words. I. Terkel, Studs, 1912–2008. II. Title.
PN6328.L3E43 2010
082—dc22

                                              2009038402

♾ The paper used in this publication meets the minimum
requirements of the American National Standard for
Information Sciences—Permanence of Paper for Printed
Library Materials, ANSI Z39.48-1992.

FOR STUDS TERKEL,
FRIEND AND MENTOR

1912–2008

CONTENTS

Studs Terkel

Every thoughtful person at one time or another has had a fantasy about the last words he or she would say in approaching death. It might be toward the end of a lingering illness, a sudden accident, or murder. As for me, last words can be in the form of an epitaph. Mine's a simple one: "Curiosity did not kill this cat."

In Robert K. Elder's remarkable, deeply moving assemblage of last words, his informants are all inmates of death row. And who are the most likely interpreters of last words? Those who know the time, the place, and circumstance of their deaths.

Elder, as an assiduous journalist, has collected these final thoughts. Before I chose just a few of Elder's selections, I thought of Delbert Lee Tibbs. He was an African American theologian who, while hitching rides in the South on a vacation, was accused of the rape of a white woman and the murder of her friend. It was an all-white jury, and the trial was something of a farce. He was patently innocent, but he was convicted and remained on death row for over two years, until the Florida Supreme Court acquitted him.

Here are some of Tibbs's thoughts while in prison: "I believe that life is endless. We can't talk about life without talking about death. We can't talk about death without talking about life."

He quotes the Dalai Lama. He was reading the Bible, the Old and New Testaments; he was reading the Bhagavad-Gita. He quotes

Krishna: "This body wears out, like garments. And when a garment wears out, you take it off, and you lay it down, and you pick up another and put it on."

"When I meet people today now, if they try to make a big deal about me having been on death row, I sometimes gently remind them that we're all on death row," Tibbs says. "The difference is that here the state's gonna do it, and at some point you're gonna know the date and the hour, but that's the only difference. I mean, if you're walking around here, *shit*—you're on death row 'cause you're going to have to *leave* here. You're going to lay down and they're going to throw dust in your face."

He goes on: "If you really want to punish a guy, lock him up on death row for twenty or thirty years. After five years, he'll probably beg you to put him in the chair or strap him to the gurney."

What this book does is record and celebrate the final thoughts of some of Tibbs's colleagues on death row. This book's approach is an apolitical one, if that is possible. My own opinion is this: We are the only industrial country in the world that still maintains the death penalty. We are the only industrial country in the world that does not have universal health insurance. One represents death; the other represents life. Can it be that we are a necrophilic people? In order to prove we are not we would, of course, have to abolish the death penalty.

Some of the comments from this collection are from those who admit to the crime and beg forgiveness. Some are funny. This one is from a Dallas football fan: "What about those Cowboys?!" (William Prince Davis, September 4, 1999).

Some are resigned: "No sir, I just want to pray a chant, do what you have to do" (Timothy Lane Gribble, March 15, 2000).

Many deliver similar messages that could be boiled down to these heartfelt statements: "I am innocent, innocent, innocent. Make no mistake about this: I owe society nothing. Continue the struggle for human rights. . . . I am an innocent man, and something very wrong is taking place tonight" (Leonel Torres Herrera, May 12, 1993).

But there are better quotes here.

"You all brought me here to be executed, not to make a speech. That's it" (Charles Livingston, November 21, 1997). In many cases it's as simple and sharp as that. A great deal of these are sacred thoughts. Even those who may have been innocent speak of the kindness in all people. That's the remarkable part.

Indeed, several of the inmates' last words provide the strongest arguments I've heard for rehabilitation.

"The act I committed to put me here was not just heinous, it was senseless," said Napoleon Beazley (May 28, 2002). "But the person that committed that act is no longer here—I am."

He goes on: "Give those men a chance to do what's right. Give them a chance to undo their wrongs. A lot of them want to fix the mess they started, but don't know how. The problem is not in that people aren't willing to help them find out, but in the system telling them it won't matter anyway. No one wins tonight. No one gets closure. No one walks away victorious."

In tackling this book, Robert K. Elder is a journalist in the noblest tradition, getting at a certain truth. And the truth may come from the most rejected members of our society, the most reprehensible, and yet the humanity is still there. In some cases, it's casual. In some cases, it's dramatic. In some cases, it's ecclesiastical. In some cases, it's secular.

Perhaps there will come a time when a book such as this will no longer be needed but will be remembered as a history of a prehistoric time. It's all moving stuff.

What I will remember best about this book is its poetry—the actual poetry in the speech of people at the most traumatic moment of their lives.

Note: Terkel, a Pulitzer Prize–winning oral historian and recipient of the Presidential National Humanities Medal, interviewed Delbert Lee Tibbs in his book *Will the Circle Be Unbroken? Reflections on Death, Rebirth, and Hunger for a Faith* (New Press, 2001).
During the editing of this book, Terkel passed away at age ninety-six.

INTRODUCTION

Sometimes we remember nothing more than someone's last words.

Take, for example, Revolutionary War patriot and spy Nathan Hale, whose statue I walked by every day on my way into the *Chicago Tribune* offices. We remember little of him but how he left this world.

"I only regret that I have but one life to lose for my country," is how history records his last words.

The final words of the famous and infamous have been collected since antiquity because they speak to a primal curiosity and spark introspection: what does one say on the edge of oblivion? In America, the cult of last words remains particularly strong. Orson Welles's masterpiece *Citizen Kane* preys upon and fuels this primal pull, when an investigator is hired to make sense of a newspaper magnate's enigmatic deathbed utterance: "Rosebud." "Maybe he told us all about himself on his deathbed," suggests one character in the film.

Last words matter for one simple reason: they cannot be taken back. We expect last words to be poignant, a résumé or summation of life experience. Sometimes they are, sometimes they are not. We want them to reveal secrets. But they very seldom do.

On his last night, Louis Toombs played cards with his jailer until almost midnight. Convicted of first-degree murder in 1902, Toombs (also known as Thombs) had more than a month to ponder his final words. On the gallows, he said: "I am about to pay the penalty for a most atrocious crime. I am innocent. My only hope is that the lapse of time will purge my wife and child of the disgrace that is now being brought upon them."

Almost a hundred years later, in Texas, Dennis Dowthitt—convicted of rape and murder—had nine years to think about his parting words. When his time came, he said: "I am so sorry for what all of you had to go through. I can't imagine losing two children. If I was y'all, I would have killed me. You know? I am really so sorry about it, I really am. I got to go sister; I love you. Y'all take care and God bless you."

While other books have recorded the last words of the rich, respected and famous, *Last Words of the Executed* documents the final thoughts of the most discarded, reviled members of our society. It's an oral history of the overlooked, the infamous and the forgotten—who nonetheless speak to a common humanity with their last act on earth. This is the history of capital punishment in America, told from the gallows, the chair, and the gurney.

This book is divided into five chapters according to modern methods of execution, but these were not the only legal methods used. However, very few last words were documented in accounts of more peculiar executions. For example, no quotes from executed soldiers Patrick Dungraven and James McNaugton (1778) were printed in Rivington's *New York Gazette*, which reported that the men were crucified as harsh warning to potential deserters. The account has come in for some skepticism and has been dismissed as propaganda in some scholarly circles, given the newspaper's anti-American stance in British-occupied New York. One contemporary source speculates that the men were "probably shot."

But other forms of capital punishment have more certain historical precedent in the United States, in both pre- and postcolonial times. These included drowning, burning alive, garrote (strangulation), and, in one case, execution by tomahawk. Moreover, crimes other than murder drew capital sentences—among them horse theft, aggravated assault, piracy, rape, sleeping on sentry duty, treason, counterfeiting, forgery, arson, and highway robbery.

The more gruesome executions seemed to have been reserved for slaves and members of ethnic minorities, notably Native and African Americans. In 1708, slaves identified as "Indian Sam" and three other unnamed "blacks" were executed for the ax murder of their master, his wife, and their five children on Long Island. "Sam was gibbeted alive in a barbed cage," according to one modern source. *Gibbeted* meant left to hang in chains or in a metal cage in public. A female accomplice was slowly "roasted alive." Their last words, if they were given the opportunity to speak any, have not been recorded.

Read in a roughly chronological order and by method of execution, these final words reveal a cultural shift. As execution moved from a very open spectacle with public square hangings to a very intimate event behind prison walls, last words became less formal and more plainspoken. At the same time, modern quotations show an increased political awareness—some inmates use their last breath to rage against capital punishment. But it's not all political. Once men (mostly men) addressed the crowd with pleas of innocence, moral advice, or spiritual guidance; now they are more likely to address individuals, to apologize personally, or to proclaim their innocence to the victim's family.

Studs Terkel likens these final words to poetry, and for this there is historical precedent. Perhaps the best example of this is "Tichborne's Elegy," a poem attributed to Chidiock Tichborne, a young Catholic who plotted against Queen Elizabeth. It's said he wrote the following lines the night before his execution:

My prime of youth is but a frost of cares,
My feast of joy is but a dish of pain,
My crop of corn is but a field of tares,
And all my good is but vain hope of gain;
The day is past, and yet I saw no sun,
And now I live, and now my life is done.

My tale was heard and yet it was not told,
My fruit is fallen and yet my leaves are green,
My youth is spent and yet I am not old,
I saw the world and yet I was not seen;

My thread is cut and yet it is not spun,
And now I live, and now my life is done.

I sought my death and found it in my womb,
I looked for life and saw it was a shade,
I trod the earth and knew it was my tomb,
And now I die, and now I was but made:
My glass is full, and now my glass is run,
And now I live, and now my life is done.

Japanese nobility, Zen monks, and samurai also wrote "death koans" or death poems dating back to the fourteenth century and earlier. The poems, written just before the moment of death, were often not only a reflection of the dying person but also words of wisdom left behind for the living. Poet and Buddhist nun Nomura Boto (1806–67) left this poem, which echoes Nathan Hale:

Though moss
will overgrow
my useless corpse,
the seeds of patriotism
shall ne'er decay.

The monastery and the samurai, however, were noble institutions, held in high regard. Their lives, as well as their deaths, were honored. This, understandably, has not been the case for death row inmates. Our interest in the last words of the executed places us in a paradox, a moral and cultural quandary. If these are the most outcast, disgraced members of our society, why do we record their thoughts at all? Why does recording them remain a cultural value? We, as a society, have collected more final words from prisoners than from poets, politicians, saints, and celebrities combined. Why? It's partly pragmatic. These are scheduled meetings with one's Maker, easy to document. (Death isn't always predictable in the hour it arrives and often has stolen the final thoughts of our most revered figures. Albert Einstein's last words were lost because his nurse didn't speak German.)

The ritual recording of last words exists in a largely Christian framework. In early Christian history, last words were taken down as a show of spiritual mercy, a last chance for the condemned to repent and save his soul. From the fifteenth to the nineteenth centuries, speeches from the scaffold were mass-produced in pamphlets and prayer books that served as guides to dignified religious dying. The ritual also performed a legal function: in many countries, a "dying declaration" enjoyed a legal precedent as evidence.

Of course, another function of preserving a final statement is also political, a last chance for the condemned to confess guilt and to prove the government and its courts as fair and just.

Even William Shakespeare forwarded the belief that the executed would not die with a lie staining his or her soul. He expounds upon this in *Richard II*, act 2, scene 1:

O, but they say the tongues of dying men
Enforce attention like deep harmony:
Where words are scarce, they are seldom spent in vain,
For they breathe truth that breathe their words in pain.
He that no more must say is listen'd more
Than they whom youth and ease have taught to glose;
More are men's ends mark'd than their lives before.

What can we learn from a modern collection of last words? Those sentenced to die have three pieces of information the rest of us don't: the time and manner of their death and the knowledge that their last words will be recorded. *Last Words of the Executed* is an examination and record of what the condemned chose to do with that opportunity. Through reading, we gain a window into their dying thoughts, catching a glimpse into their lives, their crimes, and the world they inhabited.

Without passing judgment or taking a political stance, *Last Words of the Executed* seeks simply to document the final moments of these lives. Their messages range from awe inspiring to horrific; they are calls for peace and cries against injustice. Just as often, these final words are accepting, confessional, and consoling. Still others can be venomous, rage-fueled diatribes. Almost all statements fit into at least one of the well-known stages of grief: denial, anger, bargaining, depression, and acceptance.

Some prisoners' final words are short and almost lyrical, others rambling and incoherent. Many inmates spend their last moments raging against the death penalty itself. Some are philosophical, as was Robert Harris in 1992 when he quoted from the film *Bill & Ted's Bogus Journey* on his way to the gas chamber: "You can be a king or a street sweeper, but everyone dances with the Grim Reaper." Still others are confessional and repentant. In 1986, Charles William Bass simply said: "I deserve this. Tell everyone I said goodbye." Only a few statements are completely bizarre. Aileen Wuornos, executed for murder in Florida in 2002 and subject of the movie *Monster*, parted with "I'd just like to say I'm sailing with the Rock and I'll be back like *Independence Day* with Jesus, June 6, like the movie, big mothership and all. I'll be back."

The most touching selections are often quotes that reveal a sense of community. Sometimes, the most alienated people in society find connection with not only their fellow prisoners but also their wardens, their chaplains, and the officers who guard them. "The only thing I want to say is that I appreciate the hospitality that you guys have shown me and the respect; and the last meal was really good. That is about it. Thank you guys for being there and giving me a little bit of spiritual guidance and support," said James Collier in 2002, just before being put to death in Texas.

In order to keep this from being a catalog of horrors, the gruesome details of some executions and the even more gruesome details of the prisoners' crimes are provided sparingly, for context only. This book seeks to focus attention on the words themselves—not to create a rogues' biography or an excuse for morbid rubbernecking.

While I've strived to make this an apolitical volume, there's no ignoring the passionate debate over the death penalty in the United States. In fact, many of the executed quoted here used their last breaths to proclaim their innocence and protest capital punishment. Roger K. Coleman, executed by the state of Virginia in 1992 for the rape and murder of his sister-in-law Wanda McCoy, is one example. As guards strapped him into the chair, Coleman declared: "An innocent man is going to be murdered tonight. When my innocence is proven, I hope Americans will recognize the injustice of the death penalty, as all other civilized nations have."

An entire anti–capital punishment movement sprang up around

Coleman's case nationwide, until a DNA test in January 2006 put him at the scene of the crime and confirmed his guilt. His lawyer and his supporters were in shock. James C. McCloskey, a Christian activist who investigates wrongful convictions, felt betrayed. "How can somebody, with such equanimity, such dignity, such quiet confidence, make those his final words even though he is guilty?" he asked.

Of the sixteen thousand–some men and woman put to death on these shores since precolonial times, only one man has been posthumously pardoned after a wrongful execution. In Nebraska, William Jackson Marion was tried twice in the 1880s for the murder of John Cameron, a good friend. Both times, juries convicted him. On March 25, 1887, a crowd gathered to watch Marion hang and hear any last words.

He said, "Well, gentlemen, I suppose you are all waiting to hear what I have to say. You are waiting patiently to hear me make some confession. You have been waiting some time, some years, some months, some weeks, thinking to get a full confession out of me. No man has anything to show where I have confessed that I have committed any crime. I confess that I am a sinner, the same as any other law-abiding citizen or church member. I've made no confession to nobody, and I've got no confession to make."

The headline in the next day's *Nebraska State Journal* read "Pays the Penalty . . . Refuses to Make a Confession to the Last." But more than four years later, one man proved Marion's innocence—John Cameron himself, who reappeared alive and well. He was astonished: "I didn't even know Marion was in trouble. I never dreamed of such a thing. There was never any ill feeling between us."

It still took the state of Nebraska exactly one hundred years to pardon Marion posthumously.

I don't include these anecdotes as pro or con statements on capital punishment. But this history makes the last words of the condemned even more worth pondering. Texas death-house chaplain Rev. Carroll Pickett, who later became a death penalty opponent, was haunted by the question "Do the innocent die differently than the guilty?" Perhaps we will never know. But we keep collecting last words, keep honoring the ritual.

CHAPTER
ONE

THE NOOSE

In the two days before Augustus Johnson's 1878 execution, thousands flocked to Rome, Georgia, to witness the event: the *New York Times* recorded that they came by "steam-boat, railroad, wagons until finally there were at least 10,000 persons present." Johnson, who was white, faced the gallows for the murder of a "colored" man, Alfred M. Carver; details of the crime do not survive in newspaper accounts. Two weeks prior Johnson had converted to Catholicism; he was "clean shaved and drank whisky freely." Escorted to the gallows by one hundred guards, Johnson ascended the scaffold and said:

Ladies and gentlemen: This is Gus Johnson, who you have heard of as a bad man. Some think I am a monster. My father was a colonel in the rebel army and bore a good name. I am to die for killing a negro 14 miles down the Coosa River. I am sorry I killed him. Deputy Sheriff Sharp has been with me a good deal. I think a heap of him. He has his duty to perform, and I do not think less of him for it. Jim Jinkins, Sheriff of the county, is a good man. His wife is a good woman and has been a friend of mine.

I have always been a bad boy. I have killed four men in my life. I can swear to two. I have friends in the crowd who would rescue me, but I want them to let me hang. Cicero Echols, John Beard and Bob Milliean killed Squire Foster, a colored man. They would have been hanged, but they bribed the solicitor with $25, and the case was not pressed.

Johnson then said good-bye to his friends, and at 1:50 p.m. he dropped seven feet through the trap door. The fall did not break his neck. Johnson strangled to death for eighteen minutes and was cut down after twenty.

Hanging is America's oldest method of execution, imported from Britain, and also the simplest. It required only a sturdy rope and a high perch—usually a tree or scaffold bar—strong enough to support a human body. In the best circumstances, the fall broke the condemned person's neck. Some, however, like Johnson, dangled and kicked until they suffocated. In more than a few instances, others were decapitated by the force of the drop.

Prisoners knew these horror stories all too well, and their final statements reflect this. In 1852, in California, convicted thief James Robinson yelled at the sheriff: "You don't know anything about hanging men!" He then instructed the sheriff to move the knot under his left ear, a more effective placement. Then, as the wagon moved from under his feet: "Oh God! Have I got to die?"

History does not record how quickly he died.

But the presence of a crowd was more influential on last words than almost any single factor. As in Johnson's case, there's a sense of oration, of ritual and even public theater. Further, final statements in front of assembled masses facilitated dialogue, as the condemned often spoke directly to audiences and elicited responses. This changed, of course, as scaffolds came to be built behind prison walls and capital punishment was taken out of the public eye.

Rainey Bethea, age twenty-two, was the last person in the United States to face an official public execution. In 1936 the young African American was hanged in Owensboro, Kentucky, for the murder of a seventy-year-old white woman. The county had the choice of carrying out the hanging in public or in private and chose the former without explanation. No last words survive.

By the 1930s the noose had been largely replaced as a method of capital punishment by the gas chamber and the electric chair. But as late as 1996 it was in use in Delaware. Billy Bailey was convicted of the 1979 murder of Gilbert and Clara Lambertson, though he claimed until his death that he did not remember shooting the elderly couple because he had been drinking heavily that day. Delaware constructed a fifteen-foot-high gallows specifically for Bailey's execution. Bailey had chosen hanging over lethal execution because, he said, "the law is the law."

Be it known to all this day, that we suffer not as evil doers, but for conscience['] sake; this day we shall be at rest with the Lord.

MARMADUKE STEVENSON, convicted of disobeying banishment, Massachusetts Bay Colony. Executed October 27, 1659

Stevenson (sometimes spelled Stephenson) was a plowman in England until he took to a religious calling. He left his family and traveled to Barbados. Eventually, in Rhode Island he met William Robinson, with whom he traveled to the Massachusetts Bay Colony to protest a law banishing a new religious order called Religious Society of Friends, or Quakers. Stevenson was banished himself and, when he later returned to the colony, sentenced to die. He was hanged in the Boston Common, the first of three known as the "Boston martyrs."

This is the day of your visitation, wherein the Lord hath visited you. This is the day the Lord is risen in his mighty power, to be avenged on all his adversaries. I suffer not as an evil doer. Mind the light that is within you; to wit the Light of Christ, of which He testified and I am now going to seal with my blood. Now ye are made manifest; I suffer for Christ in whom I live and in whom I die.

WILLIAM ROBINSON, convicted of disobeying banishment, Massachusetts Bay Colony. Executed October 27, 1659

Robinson was a Quaker living in Rhode Island. Upon hearing of the nearby Massachusetts colony's law exiling members of his religion, he went with several others to protest the law and was arrested and exiled. After he violated the terms of his exile, he was executed.

Upon being asked to resume her exile:

Nay, I cannot; for in obedience to the will of the Lord God I came, and in his will I abide faithful to the death.

When told she was responsible for her own execution:

Nay, I came to keep blood-guiltiness from you, desiring you to repeal the unrighteous and unjust law of banishment upon pain of death, made against the innocent servants of the Lord, therefore my blood will be required at your hands who willfully do it; but for those that do it in the simplicity of their hearts, I do desire the Lord to forgive them. I came to do the will of my Father, and in obedience to his will I stand even to the death.

Being asked by a pastor to repent:

Nay, man, I am not now to repent.

Upon being asked if she wished for an elder to pray for her:

I know never an Elder here. . . . I desire the prayers of all the people of God. . . . I know but few here. . . . Nay, first a child, then a young man, then a strong man, before an Elder of Christ Jesus.

Finally, when someone from the crowd asked if she'd been in Paradise:

Yea, I have been in Paradise several days and now I am about to enter eternal happiness.

MARY DYER (AKA MARY DIER OR MARIE DIER), convicted of disobeying banishment, Massachusetts Bay Colony. Executed June 1, 1660

Dyer was already an unpopular figure in the colony for her support of Anne Hutchinson, who was banished for heresy—notably her belief that God spoke not through clergy but to individuals directly.

A Puritan, Dyer later converted to Quakerism, feeling God had called her to return to Boston. She was given a last-minute reprieve twice, the second with a sentence of banishment. Instead, she chose to be executed for violating the terms of her exile. Today, her statue sits outside the Massachusetts State House over the inscription "Witness for religious freedom."

For bearing my testimony for the Lord against deceivers and the deceived, I am brought here to suffer. Lord Jesus, receive my spirit.

WILLIAM LEDDRA, convicted of disobeying banishment, Massachusetts Bay Colony. Executed March 14 (sometimes recorded as March 24), 1661

Despite the executions of three fellow Quakers in the colony, Leddra had refused to stop preaching. He was the last Quaker to hang in Boston and is sometimes recognized as a fourth "Boston martyr."

I have been among drawn Swords, flying bullets, roaring cannons, amidst all which, I knew not what Fear meant: but now I have appreciations of the dreadful wrath of God, in the other World, which I am going into, my Soul within me, is amazed at it . . .

I pray God that I may be a warning to you all, and that I may be the last that ever shall suffer after this manner: In the fear of God I warn you to have a care of taking the Lord's name in vain. And have a care of that sin of Drunkenness, for that sin lead[s] to all manner of sins and wickedness . . . as I am a dying man, and to appear before that Lord within a few minutes that you may take notice of what I say to you . . .

UNNAMED RINGLEADER, convicted of treason and mutiny, Massachusetts Bay Colony. Executed 1673

Neither his name nor the details of his crime survive this "ringleader," only his last words.

I had rather go to an Ale-house than to any Church. Pray Young People take warning by my shameful end: keep the Sabbath truly. . . . I have had great Oppression upon my Spirit since I was in this prison and I thought I should never repent or confess, until Almighty God softened my hard heart and gave me grace to repent. I beg all good people to joyn in prayers with me, I have great need of your prayers.

THOMAS LUTHERLAND, convicted of murder, colonial New Jersey. Executed February 23, 1692

Lutherland, a carpenter, was hanged for strangling merchant John Clark, then stealing his goods. The undecided jury invoked the "law of the bier": Lutherland was forced to touch Clark's rotting corpse. It was believed that a corpse would bleed when touched by its murderer, and Clark's did not, but Lutherland broke down on the spot and confessed to his crime anyway. "When I touched the murdered Corpse of John Clark, I was afraid the Blood would have flown in my face," he said.

It should be noted that another source claims that Lutherland was executed in Pennsylvania; yet another insists he was put to death in 1691.

I am no more a witch than you are a wizard, and if you take away my life, God will give you blood to drink.

SARAH GOOD, convicted of witchcraft, Massachusetts Bay Colony. Executed July 19, 1692

After Good's first marriage failed, she moved to Salem and remarried. Some townspeople disliked her and accused her of casting evil spells and attacking a woman at knifepoint.

Good and fellow accused witches Rebecca Nurse, Susannah Martin, Elizabeth Howe, and Sarah Wildes were executed together on Salem's Gallows Hill. When urged by Rev. Nicholas Noyes to confess, Good called him a liar, then delivered her final, now famous last words.

Paraphrased account from Robert Calef, later a critic of the witch trials:

[Burroughs] made a clear Speech for the clearing of his Innocency, with such Solemn and Serious Expressions, as were to the Admiration of all Present. [Burroughs then perfectly recited the Lord's Prayer, which] drew Tears from many.

GEORGE BURROUGHS, convicted of witchcraft, Massachusetts Bay Colony.
Executed August 19, 1692

It was believed that witches could not say the Lord's Prayer, thus the tearful crowd reaction. Burroughs's recitation caused concerns that "the Spectators would hinder the Execution." But as soon as Burroughs hanged, Rev. Cotton Mather told the crowd that the prisoner was "no ordained Minister" and "the Devil has often been transformed into an Angel of Light."

. . . And now I have forsaken God, he has forsaken me, and I acknowledge he has been just in leaving me, for that I have gone from bad to worse, till for my sins I am now to die. . . . whereas I have been charged with and tried for burning my master's barn, I now declare as a dying man that I did not do it. . . . I acknowledge I deserve to die, and would confess especially my drunkenness and Sabbath-breaking, which have led me to this great Sin for which I now die.

JULIAN, convicted of murder, Massachusetts Bay Colony.
Executed March 22, 1733

Julian, slave of John Rogers of Pembroke, confessed to killing his master but denied accusations of burning his master's barn. When Julian fled authorities, a reward was posted, and a bounty hunter captured him. On the way to returning Julian, his captor stopped to eat, leaving the runaway slave standing outside the diner. He again fled, and when the chase led into a neighboring cornfield, Julian stabbed the bounty hunter. Shortly thereafter he was captured and hanged.

Julian may have been John Julian, pilot of the pirate ship *Whydah*.

How are we condemned by the Covenant of Works, and relieved by the Covenant of Grace.

PATIENCE BOSTON, convicted of murder, colonial Maine. Executed July 24, 1735

Boston did not intentionally kill her baby. She was released for lack of proof and because her confession had been alcohol fueled. However, Boston decided to murder another child to validate her claims; she did so by holding a boy under water until he drowned. Her written confession was printed and sold by S. Kneeland and T. Green near the prison in Falmouth, Maine. Other sources list her day of execution as July 31.

In the presence of God, the possessor of heaven and earth, I lift up my hands and solemnly protest I am innocent of what is laid to my charge. I appeal to the great God for my non-knowledge of Hughson, his wife, or the creature that was hanged with them [Peggy Carey, a prostitute]. I never saw them, living, dying, or dead; nor ever had I any knowledge or confederacy with white or

black, as to any plot; . . . and I protest that the witnesses
were perjured; I never knew them but at my trial.

REV. JOHN URIE, convicted of conspiracy, colonial New York.
Executed August 29, 1741

Urie was a clergyman and a schoolteacher who was accused of having incited a group of slaves into arson and robbery. The Hughson he references was a tavern owner who was also convicted of inciting arson. Hughson and Urie were both hanged when New York was gripped by a wave of paranoia that its slaves were seconds away from overthrowing their masters. The colony ended up hanging eighteen slaves and burning eleven who were implicated in the conspiracy, as well as hanging four white people: Urie, Hughson and his wife, and a prostitute who frequented Urie's bar. The order to execute the slaves read in part, "You have grown wanton with excess of liberty and your idleness has proved your ruin."

I heartily thank the good Ministers who have frequently
visited me, and prayed for me. I heartily forgive my enemies. And I sincerely fly to the Blood of Jesus Christ
which is able to atone for my innumerable iniquities
and cleanse me from the Pollution of Sin.

WILLIAM WELCH, convicted of murder, Massachusetts Bay Colony.
Executed April 11, 1754

Welch's relatives in Ireland attempted to curb his reputation for trouble by sending him to America, where they hoped he would reform. But little changed. Welch was soon wanted for theft and for stabbing a man who had pursued him. Later in life, Welch was caught by Darby O'Brian, who wanted to collect reward money. Welch offered him more money than the reward, then murdered O'Brian after the two achieved an agreement. Welch's account was recorded in *A Chronicle of Welch's Confession and Last Words*, published in Boston in 1754.

I die in the 30th year of my age, and desire all young Men and Children to take warnings by my untimely End. I die a Protestant according to the Principles of the Lutheran Church, desiring the Prayers of all my Spectators and Hearers.

In a letter to his victim's father:

Dear Mr. Jacob Woolman: I am now confined in the Dungeon in Irons for the barbarous and willfull [sic] Murder I have committed on your Son, without the least provocation, and every hour since I am praying to Almighty God to pardon my Weakness . . . Now I most humbly pray you and your Wife will forgive me as it lies so heavy on my Conscience, and send one Word as soon as possible! I am certain I shall die . . . but while Life remains, I include you and Family in my Prayer for your prosperity in this World and eternal Felicity in the World to come.

HENRY HALBERT, convicted of murder, colonial Pennsylvania. Executed October 19, 1765

Halbert followed in his father's footsteps as a wigmaker. After marrying and plying his trade, he was accused of stealing money. According to Halbert, the accusation was false and drove him to murderous desperation, during which he killed a young boy.

. . . And as to the Woman who was my reputed Wife, she died with a Lie in her mouth, but I freely forgive those who swore to her false Declarations. I acknowledge myself to have been a notorious Sabbath-breaker, and would warn all young People against that heinous

Crime. I ask forgiveness of all Men whom I have . . . injur'd, and pray they will forgive me, so I hope for Forgiveness of God.

JOSEPH LIGHTLY, convicted of murder, Massachusetts Bay Colony. Executed November 21, 1765

Lightly had married after lying to his betrothed about owning property and having money. When she discovered his deception, the marriage soured. Lightly became angry at what he claimed was her "adulterous behavior" and killed her.

I acknowledge that I had a fair and impartial [trial] and that the Sentence I received was very just. I am now in the 39th year of my Age, and I die an unworthy member of the Church of Rome, I sincerely bewail the errors of my past life, and hope for mercy in the next. I shall conclude with exhorting you to pray for yourselves, and at the same time to petition heaven to have mercy upon my poor soul.

JOSEPH ANDREWS, convicted of piracy and murder, colonial New York. Executed May 23, 1769

Andrews and fellow shipmate Nicolas Johnson attempted to take over the schooner *Polly*. They killed three passengers, the first mate, and the captain with an ax, then threw the cabin boy overboard. The duo spared the helmsman, whom they needed to steer the ship. When their captive jumped ship in the West Indies, he reported the killers, who were later apprehended. Andrews was "hanged in chains" on Liberty Island.

The Lord shewed me, that I had nothing in me that could commend me to God . . . and as I am shortly to die a shameful death, which I brought upon myself, by reason of living so long without God in the world, yet I would die this death, in the condition I am now in, rather than live in this world, to be carnally minded, as usual. I die now to live eternally. Glory be to God for his free grace bestowed on me, vile sinner. I die, though, most unworthy of the title, one of the Israel of God and an heir of glory.

FRANCIS BURDETT PERSONAL, convicted of murder, colonial New York.
Executed September 10, 1773

Personal had fallen ill and could not work, so his wife, a former prostitute, reverted to her old trade to support them. However, even after Personal recovered his wife continued to spend considerable time away from home. One night she did not come home and her husband went searching for her. Finding her in the company of two men, Personal bludgeoned one of them, Robert White, to death. These last words are taken from an account of his life sold by a printing office in New Haven, Connecticut. Another account describes Personal, age twenty-six, as his wife's pimp.

I only regret that I have but one life to lose for my country.

NATHAN HALE, convicted of espionage, colonial New York.
Executed September 22, 1776

An American spy during the Revolutionary War, Hale pretended to be a British loyalist but was captured after his true identity was revealed. The standards of the time dictated that spies be hanged as illegal combatants. While these are reported to be Hale's last words, they bear significant resemblance to a line from *Cato*, a play by George Addison that was popular at the time: "What a pity it is/That we can die but once to serve our country."

. . . Don't you imagine that men of liberal education are more intriguing, and do more frequently deceive the world then illiterate farmers? And will you not allow that there are as many bad clergymen, in proportion to their number as any other left? As this is my opinion, why should I request their advice or prayers, in preference to other?

THOMAS GROSS, convicted of murder, Connecticut. Executed 1788

Former solider Gross confessed to killing his wife. After his death sentence, Gross seemed composed for a considerable time but then turned "irrational": he became angry, abused clergy, and claimed that he was Jesus Christ.

. . . This is the first time since my condemnation that I thought what it was to die. The shock was terrible . . . what a night of horror was the next night! . . . [The doctor] perceived that agony of my soul and asked me some questions of the state of my mind . . . and [I poured] my heart out to him . . .

I had fortunately concealed my real name, that I might return, like the prodigal, to my parents, and live a life devoted to God and their comfort.

JOSEPH TAYLOR, convicted of violent assault and robbery, hanging (possibly unsuccessful), Massachusetts. Executed May 8, 1788

Taylor was part of a gang of thieves who mugged a man in broad daylight. As Taylor and his accomplices fled, the man started screaming for help. Since the man was mugged on a public highway, Taylor was convicted of capital highway robbery and was hung in a gallows constructed at the scene of the crime. The execution appears to have been unsuccessful, however, for a doctor advised Taylor on how to cheat death on the gallows. Taylor wrote about the experience: "My first feeling after the shock of falling, was a violent strangling and the oppression for want of breath, this soon gave way to a pain in my eyes, which seemed to be burned by two balls of fire which appeared before them which seemed to dart on and off like lightning, settling ever and anon my shoulders, as if they weighed one hundred ton, after one terrible flash, in which the two balls seemed to join in one, I sunk away without pain, like one falling asleep."

He also describes being revived by the doctor: "Making two hours and forty-three minutes after I was turned off, he perceived signs of life in me, by a small motion and warmth of my bosom. . . . I cannot describe the intolerable agony of that moment. Ten thousand stranglings are trifling to it."

Some accounts record that Taylor actually died on the gallows, while others insist he fled to Sweden.

I cannot forget to return my thanks to the Gentlemen and Ladies of the town of Dover, who so humanely petitioned his Excellency and council, for a short respite of my execution—may they enjoy long and uninterrupted happiness here, and may the best of Heaven's blessings await them hereafter. Nor must I neglect the same testimonials of kindness I have received from them during my confinement. I now recommend my soul to the all-merciful Creator of all Worlds and all Creatures, most ardently imploring the forgiveness, of may manifold transgressions, and that the redeemer would most graciously receive me to the arms of his everlasting mercy, when I leave the world.

ELISHA THOMAS, convicted of murder, New Hampshire. Executed June 3, 1788

Thomas was headed to Portsmouth when he stopped by a friend's house and went to have a few drinks with them. In a bar brawl, he killed—he insisted unintentionally—Peter Drowne, a friend who tried to intervene while Thomas was fighting another man. More than six thousand people showed up to see Thomas hang.

I likewise return my hearty thanks to the several Ministers of the town who have attended be [sic] since I have been under sentence: also to a number of other kind friends, for the care they have shewn to me both for soul and body . . . may God reward them all for their kindness to me. And now, into the hands of Almighty God I commit my soul, relying on his mercy, through the merits and mediation of my Redeemer, and die an unworthy member of the Presbyterian Church, in the 29th year of my age.

RACHEL WALL, convicted of highway robbery, Massachusetts. Executed October 8, 1789

Pennsylvania native Wall left home to marry a man her parents didn't approve of. Reportedly, the man was a thief who schooled his new bride in his trade. Wall faced the gallows for robbing a Miss Bender.

I declare that I ever had a great aversion to stealing and telling lies, and think them to be great crimes. I always meant to tell truth, and never stole, except taking a few apples from orchards may be called so.

SAMUEL FROST, convicted of murder, Massachusetts. Executed October 31, 1793

Before he was fourteen years of age, Frost killed his father, who had mistreated his mother. The young teen hit his father in the head with a shovel, then continued to strike his skull. He went to jail for a time but was released and moved from home to home. Eventually, he stayed with a man identified as Captain Allen, upon whom he repeated his crime: Frost beat him to death with a garden hoe.

And now, as a dying man, I recommend to the charity of Christian neighbors, my distressed wife Lydia, who I leave with two small children, destitute of everything to help themselves with, and she big with child. And I desire the prayers of all good people to God for them and myself.

EDMUND FORTIS, convicted of rape and murder, Maine. Executed September 25, 1794

Fortis was born into slavery in Virginia. After running away from his master, he wandered around the country. He encountered Pamela Tilton, whom he raped and then, strangely, began escorting home. Fortis's worry about being exposed drove him to kill and bury her. This account was printed in a booklet called *Last Words and Dying Speech of Edmund Fortis*, which was published and sold in Exeter, New Hampshire.

I most solemnly declare with my dying breath . . . that
I am innocent, and unknowing to the death of Thomas
Read the Guinea, Negro [that I die for]. . . .
   And now having settled my worldly affairs I shall close
and prepare to depart in peace. I've kissed this paper—
and bid it convey the kiss to you my love: and now my
dear Sally, I bid you—oh heavens! I bid you my dear
wife! Not the Farewell of a day, month, nor year—but an
eternal farewell—I earnestly beg your prayers for me
and may God protect, preserve, prosper, and bless you,
is the dying prayer of your dotingly fond husband . . .

ABRAHAM JOHNSTONE, convicted of murder, New Jersey.
Executed July 8, 1797

Johnstone was born a slave in Delaware but earned his freedom by
throwing himself in between a knife and his master. Sometime later
he was accused of killing a man named Tom in a brawl, for which he
faced the gallows. The full forty-seven-page booklet of his lengthy
speech and a final letter to his wife was printed the same year.

When I think how I have sinned against the great God,
my heart breaks and tears run from my eyes . . . I forgive every body, and hope that God will have mercy on
me. Now in the 28th year of my age, I commit my spirit
in to the hands of a merciful . . . God and hope he will
receive me for his great mercy's sake. I die in peace with
all mankind, and beg that all people will take warning
by my awful end.

STEPHEN SMITH, convicted of arson and burglary, Massachusetts.
Executed October 12, 1797

A slave born in Virginia and owned by William Allen, Smith ran away from his master and robbed houses. He claimed that his father was a religious man but his mother encouraged him to steal. In Boston he was indicted for arson and robbery, then sentenced to death.

Written:

Your husband is dying happy! For you I lived, for you I die! I hear you groan! I hope you may yet be recovered! If you are, live till it is God's will to take you, and prepare to meet me in a better world!

Your dying husband,
J. O. Beauchamp

JEREBOAM O. BEAUCHAMP, convicted of murder, Kentucky.
Executed July 7, 1826

Beauchamp murdered Kentucky legislator Solomon P. Sharp after the state representative denied paternity of a child by Anna Cooke, whom Beauchamp wed after the birth of the child. Rumors circulated that Sharp claimed the child was a mulatto and the product of a Cooke family slave. Vowing to avenge his wife's honor, Beauchamp stabbed Sharp to death at his home.

But this was not the end of the tragedy. While awaiting execution, Beauchamp was joined in his cell by his wife, at her request. Despite two suicide attempts, the couple was allowed to stay together. On the day of execution, both he and Anna stabbed themselves. The above note was written to Anna as Beauchamp was hauled to the gallows, before he could bleed to death. Anna died of her wounds.

This incident, known as the Beauchamp-Sharp Tragedy, inspired Edgar Allan Poe's unfinished work *Politian* and novelist Robert Penn Warren's *World Enough and Time*.

It's in God's hands now.

NAT TURNER, convicted of murder, Virginia. Executed November 11, 1831

Born a Virginian slave in 1800, Turner witnessed a solar eclipse, which he took as a sign from God that he should strike out against slavery. From childhood Turner believed he was "intended for some great purpose." In 1831 in Southampton, Virginia, he led one of the largest U.S. slave uprisings, in which more than fifty-five whites and two hundred slaves died. Turner hid in the woods for more than two months after the revolt but was hanged, beheaded and skinned two weeks after his capture. Reportedly, fifty-five slaves were executed by the state in retribution for the revolt.

I swear to you, sheriff, I'm an innocent man. I have never been to the Thompson house, and I never saw Mrs. Thompson on the day that she was murdered. I believe that there were two of them—two men—who did the murder that I've been wrongly accused of.

Even if I did know their names, I'd swing before I would have their blood upon me.

JOHN STONE, convicted of murder, Illinois. Executed July 10, 1840

Stone, age thirty-four, was the first man publicly executed in Chicago. He was accused of raping and murdering Lucretia Thompson, which he denied. Stone was escorted by two hundred horsemen to a lakeshore gallows at the back of Myrick's Tavern. It did not go as planned. Stone's drop from the scaffold was only four feet, and he died of strangulation.

Lord Jesus, have mercy on my soul. God bless you. I hope I shall be better off.

My dear fellow citizens—I now stand here before you to die, and I hope and believe my soul will be saved, I trust my God has forgiven me. You must all beware of Rum; for rum has been the cause of placing me here to meet this awful fate. I warn you all not to touch the intoxicating bowl, for it will eventually get the advantage of you all. I am sorry to die under the gallows but the laws must be carried out, and die I must, remember what I say, Rum has done it all, and I hope all who are here will be taking warning by it. God bless you all, may God have mercy on my soul, and receive me into his kingdom. Good-by, God bless you and my friends.

Farewell! All, mind what I tell you, and let Rum alone. [Then, turning toward the sheriff,] I may meet you in heaven. I hope I shall. I thank my friends. I thank the good and worthy Sheriff and others for what they have done for me, God bless the Sheriff, and heaven bless you all, good-by.

AARON STOOKEY, convicted of murder, New York.
Executed September 19, 1851

Stookey, forty-two, owned a shabby pub on Little Water Street in Manhattan's notorious Five Points district. A knife fight broke out when he tried to forcefully expel a disruptive drunk, Zeddy Moore. When their skirmish ended, only Stookey remained standing. The sheriff said, "Stookey, this is one of the most painful duties I ever performed, but I am forced to do my duty, so good-by, and may God bless you. I hope you will be happy in the other world." Six hundred people attended Stookey's hanging.

Here we go, pals, 'round and 'round.

JAMES WILSON, AKA MOUNTAIN JIM, convicted of grand larceny, California. Executed November 28, 1851

Wilson asked that he be allowed to place the noose around his own neck, a request that was denied. There were rumors about his true identity; one claimed that Wilson's name was a pseudonym for Noah James, a survivor of the infamous Donner Party.

One witness wrote in his diary that Wilson "spoke for more than half an hour by the watch I had in my hand. You could hear his voice three blocks away, and I have never heard more blasphemies that those he uttered." Few facts about Wilson's crime survive. He asked that the press "do him justice."

I committed the deed and now I'm paying for it. If I had to do it over again I would. I leave my written words for you all to read.

CREED TURNER, convicted of murder, Oregon Territory. Executed December 4, 1851

There was never a point after Turner was arrested that he regretted killing—the only thing he felt bad about was that he couldn't kill himself. Turner spent his last week writing his autobiography and proclaiming his innocence. Visitors during his last few days reported hearing him muttering about how the courts had not done him justice and an innocent man was going to die. Turner died for the murder of E. A. Bradbury and denied "being as bad as the people seemed to think him," according to an article in the *New York Times*.

Mr. Sheriff, you are a good man, and I have nothing to say, except that I protest my innocence. In my last dying words, I say I am innocent! I am innocent! I am innocent! Justice in this country is bad. I was not guilty, and the Jury did wrong in convicting me.

OTTO GRUNZIG, convicted of murder, New York. Executed February 27, 1852

Though he emphatically maintained his innocence to the very end, Grunzig died for poisoning his wife, Victorine, in order to enjoy his mistress's company unencumbered. He later blamed the murder on his mistress, Margaretta Lohrenz.

Grunzig thought he would be unable deliver a final speech on the scaffold, so he had Rev. Verren deliver this statement for the execution:

"My poor friend Grunzig does not feel able to speak, and wishes me to say a few words for his cause. He says he is going to die in a few moments, and he wants the world to know he is innocent, he says he was always taught and knows that if man spills the blood of a human being, his must be spilled also, and he says he never poisoned Victorine Grunzig, his wife. He begs me to say that Margaretta Lohrenz is the murderer of his wife, and that, in a few months, or a year, she will come forth and confess the crime to the world. He says he always loved his wife and cherished her, and when he found he had been doing wrong by living with a concubine, he at once resolved to lead a different life, and endeavored to do so by discarding Margaretta.

"He also says he is extremely grateful and thankful to the clergy, for their kind and attentive visits to his cell, during his incarceration within these walls, and also to Mr. Edmonds, warden, and keepers Jackson and Crosby, under whose immediate charge he has been since the first day of his arrest.

"I myself thought him innocent months ago, weeks ago, days ago, hours ago, and even up to the present moment, and he now tells me in his dying words that he is innocent. I hope he will walk straight forward to the gallows with the courage he now exhibits. Grunzig wants me to thank his countrymen for what they have done for him, and he bids them a long life and a happy one. He knows they all took an active part in his ease, because they all believed him innocent. Grunzig requests me to say that he offers thousands of thanks to the humane Sheriff Carnley, for his sympathy and feeling shown him.

"Some of the people have called him a Catholic, but I assure them that he dies in the Protestant faith, as are also his father and mother, sisters and brothers, all of whom are living at Berlin, in Prussia."

When asked how he felt:

I feel like an innocent man.

WILLIAM B. SHEPPARD, convicted of murder, California.
Executed July 28, 1854

When Henry Day would not grant Sheppard permission to marry his daughter, prosecutors said, Sheppard stabbed him in the abdomen. He died. But Sheppard maintained his innocence, claiming that a stranger attacked both men and then leaped into the wharf to escape. Tried and found guilty twice, he went to the gallows, where an estimated audience of eight to ten thousand sent him off with "rude jests" and "rabid laughter."

Make the time as short as you can, for I am fainting.

WILLIAM H. LIPSEY, convicted of murder, California.
Executed November 3, 1854

Lipsey, a miner by trade, was convicted of stabbing a man in the chest in an argument turned brawl in a "public house serving liquor." As he left the store, Lipsey expressed pride in his actions, saying while wiping his bloody blade on a post: "I stuck it into him that far and made him quake." Despite his early bravado, Lipsey was "almost carried" to the gallows.

As his legs were shackled in irons:

That's right—shoe this old hoss well—he's got a hard road to travel.

To the crowd:

I want all of you to take warning by me. See what whisky and bad women have brought me to. I have been to a good many hanging scrapes myself, and thought it was great fun, but I never thought I'd be hung myself. This is the work of Capt. Whisky. I am willing to die for the life of the man that I took. Talk of pleasure—I have tried all kinds of it, about shanties drunk, and everywhere else, but I have had more real pleasure up in that old jail, than ever before in all my life; and chains on my legs— big, heavy chains at that. I just took off this old coat, and whipped Satan clean out, fair. I've made my election sure, I think. Yes, sir, I think my election is sure.

Someone in the crowd called out, "If you are safe, I don't think there is much danger for the rest of us."

I am perfectly willing to die. The man you have got in jail for aiding me is perfectly innocent, and ought to be let go; but that Blair deserves all I've got. He was as much to blame as I was. . . . Yes; I hate this world and my own life and I'm going to leave it. I'll be in Paradise before sundown. Now, farewell, farewell, meet me in the other world. I want to see you all in Heaven. Whisky brought me to this—I expect you along in a few days.

Farewell, all my friends.

STEPHEN SHORT, convicted of murder, Kentucky. Executed January 19, 1855

An inebriated Short shot a Mr. McFarland, his employer at Clinton Furnace, who had fired Short's son and, according to a newspaper report, "endeavored to keep his hands from drinking whisky."

The Blair mentioned in his final speech was, according to Short, the man who told him to shoot.

Short spent the time before his execution hanging rats in his cell and "speculating on the analogy between the death struggles of these animals and men." More than six thousand people were present to witness the double execution of Stephen Short and fellow murderer William Hanning, who parted with "I haven't got anything against any man in the world. I hope nobody's got anything against me now."

Susan, receive me; I will soon be with you.

JEREMIAH V. CRAINE, convicted of murder, California. Executed October 26, 1855

Though married with four children in Kentucky, Craine had an affair with eighteen-year-old Susan Newnham. Craine, who believed in spiritualism, said his relationship with Susan was "sanctioned by heaven." This did not stop Craine from shooting Susan several times, claiming that she pleaded that they make a suicide pact to escape gossip and her family's anger about their relationship. Craine was stopped from committing suicide the next day. At his execution, Craine read an address to the assembled crowd, calling Susan his "wife." He was allowed to sing a song he wrote to the tune of "The Indian Hunter's Lament," in which he described his wish to die.

For God's sake, don't do that again.

DANFORTH HARTSON, convicted of murder, California. Executed July 15, 1857

Hartson (aka Sailor Jim) claimed self-defense in a fight that followed his argument with "estimable citizen" John Burke, whom he knocked to the ground and then shot in the chest. Burke was able to make a full statement, naming Hartson as the murderer, before he died. Hartson's last words came after he slipped through the noose and fell through the trap door.

I wish to speak a few words to my German countrymen. You all see what the temptings of the devil have brought me to, and I wish you to be warned by my fate. Keep away from bad company, and let liquor alone. Do not covet the money of others, and do not let your wish for money lead you into crime. I implore you to get religion, to go to church, and to pray to God, for there is more rejoicing in Heaven over one sinner who repents than ninety-nine that need no repentance. Be warned by me, and do not commit sin. Amen.

ALBERT STAUB, convicted of murder, Illinois. Executed April 20, 1858

Originally from Switzerland, twenty-two-year-old Staub immigrated to the United States ten months before his execution for the murder of Peter Lauermann. According to a *Chicago Tribune* article, Staub killed Lauermann either for his horse and team or because of a political argument that turned physical. On the gallows, he spoke for five minutes in German. The above quotation is a translation "in substance" by a reporter at the scene.

No, I am ready at any time; but do not keep me needlessly waiting.

JOHN BROWN, convicted of treason, Virginia. Executed December 2, 1859

Brown, a controversial figure in American history, has been called both a mass murderer and "the man who killed slavery." Brown, a stalwart abolitionist, was brought to trial for his raid on Harper's Ferry, a town in what is now West Virginia, then a federal arsenal. His attack had resulted in the deaths of five men.

A popular marching tune of the time was set to lyrics, which included the line "John Brown's body lies a-mouldering in the grave. His soul is marching on!" This song became "John Brown's Body" and was later adapted into the "Battle Hymn of the Republic," with its popular "Glory, glory, hallelujah" bridge.

Though the above are Brown's last words (another variation is "No, but don't keep me waiting longer than necessary"), he is better remembered for his final speech to the court that sentenced him. Though it contradicts Brown's own tactics and his advocating of violent insurrection to bring an end to slavery, Ralph Waldo Emerson paired it with the Gettysburg Address and named them the two greatest American speeches.

Brown said:

I have, may it please the court, a few words to say.

In the first place, I deny everything but what I have all along admitted: of a design on my part to free the slaves. I intended certainly to have made a clean thing of that matter, as I did last winter, when I went into Missouri and there took slaves without the snapping of a gun on either side, moving through the country, and finally leaving them in Canada. I designed to have done the same thing on a larger scale. That was all I intended. I never did intend murder, or treason, or the destruction of property, or to excite or incite slaves to rebellion, or to make insurrection.

I have another objection, and that it is unjust that I should suffer such a penalty. Had I interfered in the manner which I admit, and which I admit has been fairly proved—for I admire the truthfulness and candor of the greater portion of the witnesses who have testified in this case—had I so interfered in behalf of the rich, the powerful, the intelligent, the so-called great, or in behalf of any of their friends, whether father, mother, brother, sister, wife or children, or any of that class, and suffered and sacrificed what I have in this interference, it would have been all right. Every man in this Court would have deemed it an act worthy of reward rather than punishment.

This Court acknowledges, too, as I suppose, the validity of the law of God. I see a book kissed, which I suppose to be the Bible, or at least the New Testament, which teaches me that all things whatsoever I would that men should do to me, I should do even to them. It teaches me, further, to remember them that are in bonds, as bound with them. I endeavored to act up to that instruction. I am yet too young to understand that God is any respecter of persons. I believe that to have interfered as I have done, in behalf of his despised poor, I did no wrong, but right. Now, if it is deemed necessary that I should forfeit my life for the furtherance of the ends of justice, and mingle my blood further with the blood of millions in this slave country whose rights are disregarded by wicked, cruel and unjust enactments, I say, let it be done.

Before leaving her jail cell:

Don't let a crowd see me. I am willing to meet my God, but I don't want to have a crowd see me die. I die without having any mercy shown on me, or justice. I die for the good of my soul and not for murder. Your courts of justice are not courts of justice—but I will yet get justice, in heaven.

ANN BILANSKI, convicted of murder, Minnesota. Executed March 23, 1860

The only woman executed in Minnesota, Bilanski went through a lengthy trial over the poisoning death of her husband. Despite the state's attempts to make her hanging private, up to two thousand onlookers rushed the prison doors, and those who did not get in gained vantage points outside. Included in the crowd were some twenty-five to thirty women, some carrying children. Bilanski was accused of having an illicit affair with another man, and many believed that was her motivation for killing her spouse.

I feel deeply grateful to the people of New York and to all present who have had anything to do with me, for the sympathy they have expressed and the kindness they have extended toward me, and I ask God to bless and reward you all for your great attention. I feel sorry for the crime I have committed, but it was done under the influence of passion and without a design to do murder. I hope my wife and children will be taken care of by my friends, and that my disgrace will not fall upon them. I hope, too, that McHenry's wife and children will be looked to by my friends. I trust to receive the mercy of the Almighty.

JOHN CRUMMINS, convicted of murder, New York. Executed March 30, 1860

Crummins, a short-fused Lower Manhattan grocer, murdered a man in a lively confrontation that occurred in his own store. Wanting to secure his business, Crummins had banned a shoplifter, whom he esteemed worthless, from ever returning to the store. The slighted customer, a man by the name of Dennis McHenry, came back into the store to avenge his humiliation. Crummins, overwhelmed by the intense situation, stabbed McHenry with a bayonet. He was put to death six months after the killing.

Written:
You have deceived me. You told me that if we followed the advice of General Sibley, and gave ourselves up to the whites, all would be well; no innocent man would be injured. I have not killed, wounded or injured a white man, or any white persons. I have not participated in the plunder of their property; and yet to-day I am set apart for execution, and must die in a few days, while men who are guilty will remain in prison. My wife is your daughter, my children are your grandchildren. I leave them all in your care and under your protection. Do not let them suffer; and when my children are grown

up, let them know that their father died because he followed the advice of his chief, and without having the
blood of a white man to answer for to the Great Spirit.

HDAINYANKA (OR RDAINYANKA, TRANSLATED AS "RATTLING
RUNNER"), convicted of murder, Minnesota. Executed December 24, 1862

Hdainyanka's final words were written to his father-in-law, Chief
Wabasha. According to military tribunal accounts, Hdainyanka was
an instigator of raids on white settlements, even though he claimed
that he tried to stop the murders once they began.

He was recorded as saying, "I am for continuing the war, and
am opposed to the delivery of the prisoners. I have no confidence
that the whites will stand by any agreement they make if we give
them up. Ever since we traded with them their agents and traders
have robbed and cheated us. Some of our people have been shot,
some hung; others placed upon floating ice and drowned; and many
have been starved in their prisons. It was not the intention of the
nation to kill any of the whites until after the four men returned
from Acton and told what they had done. When they did this, all
the young men became excited, and commenced the massacre. The
older ones would have prevented it if they could, but since the trea-
ties they have lost all their influence. We may regret what has happened but the matter has gone too far to be remedied. We have got
to die. Let us, then, kill as many of the whites as possible, and let the
prisoners die with us."

---

*Each man called out his name, then the name of a friend, who called back, saying in
essence:*

I'm here! I'm here!

THIRTY-EIGHT DAKOTA INDIANS, AMONG THEM CUT NOSE AND BIG
EAGLE, convicted of murder, rape, and other crimes, Minnesota.
Executed December 26, 1862

These thirty-eight men were among the "most ferocious" followers of the Dakota (or Sioux) leader Little Crow; they were accused
of slaying approximately 490 settlers, including men, women, and
children, in a raid along the Minnesota frontier.

All of the 303 Sioux captured by General John Pope for the attack were sentenced by military court to death, but President Abraham Lincoln interceded and reduced the number to thirty-nine.
Thirty-eight were eventually hanged.

The *St. Paul Pioneer* described the scene and their "death wail"
just before the execution:

> All joined in shouting and singing. . . . The tones seemed somewhat discor-
> dant and yet there was harmony in it. Their bodies swayed to and fro and their
> every limb seemed to be keeping time. . . . The most touching scene on the
> drop was their attempt to grasp each other's hands, fettered as they were. . . .
> Three or four in a row were hand in hand, swaying up and down with the rise
> and fall of their voices. One old man reached out on each side but could not
> grasp a hand. His struggles were piteous and affected many beholders.
>
> We were informed . . . that their singing and dancing was only to sustain
> each other—that there was nothing defiant in their last moments. . . . Each
> one shouted his own name, and called on the name of his friend, saying in sub-
> stance, "I'm here! I'm here!"

Yes, tell our friends that we are being removed from
this world over the same path they must shortly travel.
We go first, but many of our friends may follow us in
a very short time. I expect to go direct to the abode of
the Great Spirit, and to be happy when I get there; but
we are told that the road is long and the distance great;
therefore, as I am slow in my movements, it will probably take me a long time to reach the end of the journey, and I should not be surprised if some of the young,
active men we will leave behind us will pass me on the
road before I reach the place of my destination.

Shaking hands with fellow Native Americans Red Iron and Akipa:
Friends, last summer you were opposed to us. You were living in continual apprehension of an attack from those who were determined to exterminate the whites. Yourselves and you families were subjected to many taunts, insults and threats. Still you stood firm in our friendship for the whites, and continually counseled the Indians to abandon their raid against the whites. Your course was condemned at the time, but now we see your wisdom. You were right when you said the whites could not be exterminated, and the attempt indicated folly; you and your families were prisoners, and the lives of all in danger. To-day you are here at liberty, assisting and feeding and guarding us, and thirty-nine men will die in two days because they did not follow your example and advice.

TAZOO (OR PTAN-DOO-TAH, TRANSLATED AS RED OTTER), convicted of murder, Minnesota. Executed December 26, 1862

History records Tazoo as a medicine man and juggler who faced the gallows for murder and the rape of a white woman, though he denied the charges of sexual assault.

I see it now, it is all bright.

HIRAM REYNOLDS, convicted of murder, hanged, Tennessee. Executed August 17, 1863

Hiram Reynolds had already proven himself a capable soldier as a veteran of the Mexican-American War. A widower with two children, he was court-martialed during his service in the Civil War, after he shot and killed Private Washington Mosier in a duel. Rev. John R. Adams, an army chaplain, rode with Reynolds as he was transported to the gallows in Nashville. Having been silent during most of the trip, Reynolds spoke his last words to Rev. Adams.

You may break my neck, but you won't break the seal of manhood.

THOMAS R. DAWSON, convicted of desertion and rape, Virginia.
Executed April 25, 1864

An Englishman who had served in the Crimean War, Dawson was already the recipient of both the Victoria Cross and the Cross of Honor. He had been serving in Company H, Twentieth Massachusetts Infantry, when he was convicted. "He was an excellent soldier," according to the infantry record, "intelligent and obedient." On the gallows, a misjudgment of rope length caused Dawson to hit the ground standing when he fell through the trapdoor. Panicking, the executioner grabbed the end of the rope "and jerked the prisoner upwards until death slowly came."

On the way to the gallows:
How beautiful the sunlight is! I never knew what its splendor was till now, when I look upon it for the last time.

On the scaffold:
I protest against the execution of this sentence. It is absolute murder—brutal murder! I die in the defense and service of my country.

When asked if he had anything else to say:
No! I beg you to make haste!

JOHN YATES BEALL, convicted of espionage, New York.
Executed February 24, 1865

In September 1864, Beall, a well-educated Acting Master of the Confederate navy, led a raid on the Great Lakes, in part to free rebel prisoners held at Johnson's Island on Lake Erie. He and several other men boarded the steamer *Philo Parsons*, "took possession of the steamer, threw overboard part of the freight, and robbed the clerk of the money in his charge, putting all on board under duress." Beall was branded a pirate and was hanged for spying and violations of the laws of war. He protested his innocence until his death.

I am a regular Confederate soldier, and have served in the Confederate army four years. I fought under General Buckner at Fort Donelson, and belonged to General Morgan's command when he entered Kentucky. I have assisted, and have taken many prisoners, and have always treated them kindly. I was wounded at Cynthiana and cut from my command. I have been in Kentucky ever since. I could prove that I am a regular Confederate soldier, and I hope to die for the Confederate cause.

MARCELLUS JEROME CLARKE (AKA SUE MUNDY, AKA MARCUS CLARK), convicted of guerrilla activity, Kentucky. Executed March 15, 1865

Enlisted in the Confederate Fourth Kentucky Infantry in 1861 at the age of seventeen, Clarke (or Clark) was a part of Morgan's Raiders from 1862 until Morgan's death in 1864. Clarke left the group to lead guerrilla warfare throughout Kentucky as the infamous Sue Mundy. According to the *Louisville Journal*, Clarke said "he was not guilty for one-tenth of the outrages that he had been charged with and that the *Louisville Journal* had done him a great injustice."

Clarke's words reflect the belief that the Sue Mundy persona was a creation of the *Louisville Journal* and meant to embarrass the Union.

Clarke left one final note to a loved one, whom the *Journal* describes as "a young lady of this State." It read: "My dear: I have to inform you of the sad fate which awaits your true friend. I am to suffer death this afternoon at 4 o'clock. I send you, from my chains, a message of true love; and, as I stand on the brink of the grave, I tell you I do truly, and fondly, and forever love you. I am, ever truly, yours. M. Jerome Clark."

Please don't let me fall.

MARY SURRATT, convicted of conspiracy to murder. Executed July 7, 1865

Surratt was convicted as a conspirator in the assassination of President Abraham Lincoln, along with Lewis Powell (alias Lewis Paine or Payne), David Herold, and George Atzerodt. The prisoners received their death sentences only the day before they were set to hang. Surratt was the first woman executed by the federal government. She was never allowed to testify at her own trial, in which she was accused of using her tavern as a meeting place for the conspirators. President Andrew Johnson signed her death warrant and was reputed to have said, "She kept the nest that hatched the egg." In some accounts of the execution, Powell said from the gallows, "Mrs. Surratt is innocent. She doesn't deserve to die with the rest of us."

I had made a request not to have my photograph taken, for fear my friends would recognize me. Somebody else made a request that it should be taken, and Chase [the sheriff] paid more attention to them than to me, and let them try to take it as I came out. You can see what kind of man this Chase is, and if I had a chance I would take his photograph d—d quick. I don't think they got a good one. So my friends will not know it. Perhaps my photograph will be the means of finding out who I am, but I doubt it d—dly. I have nothing more to say, and you may go on as soon as you please, for it is no consolation to me to be kept standing here in the cold.

HENRY WILSON, convicted of murder, New York. Executed December 22, 1865

A career burglar, Wilson was executed for slaying of Henry DeVoe, whose home he had been robbing. Wilson admitted to killing two other New Yorkers—Burr Burton in Syracuse and Mrs. Lewis in Lancaster—and told police he was the man wanted for a host of unsolved crimes. He went to the gallows three days before Christmas. A reporter for the *Rochester Democrat* censored Wilson's profanities, which appear to be derivations of *damn*.

I don't know as I've got anything to say; I am going to be hanged, and don't want to make a stump speech.

BARNEY OLWELL, convicted of murder, California. Executed January 22, 1866

Working for a hog farmer, Olwell was owed forty-two dollars, which his employer kept promising to pay him. After an argument Olwell shot him dead, later telling the arresting officer: "Any man who owed me money and did not pay me, I would kill him." Olwell was eventually granted a second trial after the court accepted evidence of insanity. He was again found guilty and sentenced to die. After Olwell delivered his last words, according to the *California Police Gazette*, a priest "leaned forward and whispered in his ear a mild rebuke for this seeming levity."

The time will come when my innocence will be proven, and then Bob Dodge will haunt you for his murder.

ROBERT S. DODGE, convicted of murder, California. Executed November 8, 1866

Borrowing a double-barrel shotgun, ostensibly to hunt quail, Dodge could not account for his whereabouts when a man who was quarreling with his brother was shot. Dodge went through two trials and during the second was found guilty of first-degree murder. In prison, he attempted suicide by taking opium.

Gentlemen, do you see this hand? Does it tremble? I never hurt a hair of that girl's head.

TOM DULA, AKA THOMAS C. DULA, convicted of murder, North Carolina. Executed May 1, 1868

The name Tom Dula was provincially pronounced "Tom Dooley," and his case was the basis for the murder ballad of the same name, made famous by folksingers—particularly the Kingston Trio in 1958. Few facts from the case, however, are reflected in the song lyrics and its famous bridge, "Hang down your head Tom Dooley . . ."

In May 1866, Dula and accused accomplice Ann Melton were arrested for the murder of Laura Foster in a sordid love-triangle scenario. It should be noted that these final words were quoted by Dr. Robert L. Isbell, who later wrote about the case. Dula's exact last words are not captured in the *New York Herald*'s account of the execution, except the reporter does mention that Dula made a lengthy speech. Melton was exonerated a few months after Dula's execution.

Gentlemen, I have a few remarks to make and I have left a statement with Mr. Byron G. Howard, from which you will learn, as citizens and my friends, some of those points which you are not posted on. Furthermore, I have left all I intend to leave. I have a statement to make further. I am not satisfied at the proceedings of the court, especially with the action of District Attorney and Mr. Peckham, the judge. Mr. Peckham is a man voted for by the people, with power and right to judge me to the best of his knowledge, and also all judges. I have got this to say: I think there were a good many gentlemen who were witnesses on this trial, whom Mr. Peckham did not allow to state such facts which would throw light on this subject as it should be.

First, I am not a lawyer, not an accomplished man. I have my own idea about this affair. I have seen their proceedings from the beginning. He came in with his mind poisoned by the people who prosecuted me; he came out like a lion braced up against me, having the evidence of these gentlemen with power and money to proceed in the case. I was a man supposing I should hear the truth and the facts, which any man with principles should speak. But on the contrary the witness brought forward papers and statements I never made.

Gentleman, what were they? Nothing but fabrication and lies; they can read my statement, which will throw light on the subject; they cannot rebut it very well; they said, "Here is a man with no friends and no money; we will give him something anyway." There was a coroner's inquest and other proceedings, the result of which was not stated. After getting through with the proceedings the judge came out like a lion, and went away a little more than a lion. Then he charged the jurymen on points with it was for the jury to decide. He said, "The pantry door was locked; Brown was the last one in the house who did it—you Brown."

Gentlemen, it was for you to say who did it, not for the man; after the jury had returned they could not agree on some point; gentlemen, what was the matter, the judge said to them, "Well, I will repeat it again: Brown was the last man in the house." There was a large amount of stuff, rubbish there, so many bushels, while the real fact was that there were only 6½ bushels. I don't state this as a fact which I know, but it was told to me by a nice, respectable man. A gentleman got up to say, "Was it any more stuff than would naturally be found in a place of that kind?" Hold on, I object to that.

Is that proper to judge a case in that way? A man ought not to be found guilty by one man. When the jury brought in a verdict that charged in favor of the people, not in favor of the prisoner, then the jury recommended me to the mercy of the court. Why, gentlemen, I haven't seen much mercy yet? Standing here with a rope around my neck, ready to draw me up when I get through with these few words? I have not seen much mercy yet—not much.

Then Mr. Welch, the District Attorney, had said, "Gentlemen of the jury, guilty or not guilty, give him six years in the state prison anyway." Oh, what a nice man he must be in his heart, anyway! What nice feelings he must have; then, after all this, he came to me in my cell and said, "Brown, how do you do; how do you do?" There were others there; I did not pay much attention to him.

To Sheriff Overhiser:

Do you object to my showing his manner when he said this? Well, no matter, I'll tell you how he did. He came up and took hold of me with both hands and said, "How do you do? I hope you'll forgive me." I should like to ask a question. If you're willing, I'll proceed further. "Well, Brown," the District Attorney said, "I am District Attorney. I had to do my duty, and they made such awful complaint against me that I had to do what I did, but I know you're not guilty."

He went down the stairs and I heard him tell my wife, "Well, he's not guilty." He said he was very sorry to see me in the condition I was in.

I forgive him, and I think that if it was in his power to do anything, I would not stand here now. I forgive all who were engaged in the prosecution and I hope God will forgive them as I do. I am even sorry for what I've said. I believe that Mr. Welch in his heart is sorry to see me here. I have merely stated what he told me. I forgive the Judge, Mr. Welch and all the witnesses in the case, and I hope they'd forgive me for what I have said.

In regard to Mr. R. E. Andrews, my lawyer, he defended me well, gentlemen. I was well defended. He labored hard for me. He never received any pay for all his labor. I'm very thankful to him and also to Mr. Overhiser for the good treatment he has given me since I've been in jail, and the good care and respect with which he has treated me, and have had all I deserved from him to comfort me. I thank all the gentlemen who have helped me in this matter.

Concerning this crime, I am not guilty of murdering the child; I am not guilty of setting the house on fire. I know nothing about it whatever, and I do not know as anybody did it any further than this, gentlemen—I was not wanted in Canaan Four Corners by one gentleman, and, gentlemen, there was one gentleman among the witnesses that took a good deal of interest in me. He knew the quantity of stuff and the amount of everything in that house, while there were twelve men there who did not, I do not lay up anything; this is what I have in my mind. He went and got stuff belonging to me and got in his own provisions without my consent.

Well, gentlemen, the Lord God Jesus Christ is the judge of all judges which you will know some day or other. He numbers your days, hours and minutes. You'll find I'm not guilty some day of the crime for which I am to be hanged till I am dead, dead, dead; as it is written in the paper that the Sheriff has read.

I suppose you are already sick of hearing such foolish, nonsensical talking. There's a future coming when you'll all be satisfied about Joseph Brown, and whether that's my true name. Mr. Peckham said I tried to cut all communications by railroad and telegraph, by changing my name. My name is Joseph Brown, and I had a half brother named R. Barney. When I went into partnership with him, he put on to his sign, "J. and" so as to make it read "J&R Barney."

Well, I owe no grudge to the gentleman who is to pull the rope. I forgive him from the bottom of my heart and I'll first make a little prayer to God, now I'll kneel down and give my heart and soul to God.

When the sheriff tried to help him to his feet:
Let me alone, I ain't done praying.

JOSEPH BROWN, convicted of murder, New York. Executed May 30, 1868

Brown and his wife Josephine, a working-class couple from Ohio, were accused of murder and defrauding a life insurance company. According to the prosecution, the Browns extended a travel invitation to a neighbor's young daughter, twelve-year-old Angie Stewart. Once in Cleveland, the Browns took out a five-thousand-dollar life insurance policy on the girl. Police found Stewart's charred body in a cabin rented by the couple. The Browns contended the fire started accidentally. Police investigators said the girl had been killed before the fire began and that the house had been deliberately burned in a poorly disguised insurance scam.

Brown left a posthumous statement that read as follows:

In regard to the crime, I am not guilty. I know nothing of its commission. I believe the death of the child was purely accidental. I am not guilty of the crime of murder; neither am I guilty of setting fire to the building. I have only to say in addition, that my greatest satisfaction is the belief that in the endless future all men will be satisfied of my innocence. Great stress has been laid upon the statement that my wife has compelled me, which is not so. I have generally managed my own affairs, having had the ability to do so. This statement is true, and I make it with a conscience that I am soon to answer at the bar of my Maker for all the deeds done in this life.

The sands of a brief existence have nearly run; my eyes are closing forever upon the beauties of this lesser world, to open, I hope and trust and pray, upon the splendor of a better. I bid all a last farewell.

GEORGE TRUMAN, convicted of murder, Maryland. Executed May 28, 1869

In his confession, twenty-year-old Truman said an "unnamed accessory" advised him to rob a clothing peddler on Frederick Road. When the man resisted, Truman beat him with stones until he lay bleeding on the ground. Truman took the man's boots, pants, hat, and carpetbag full of merchandise, and left him for dead. The next day, Truman found the man a short distance from where he had left him, conscious but unable to move. He returned to his uncle's home, where he lived, and brought his uncle's pistol back to shoot the peddler in the head.

The above quotation is part of a longer confession prepared by Truman.

Look at me! I no cry; I no woman; I man. I die brave!

JOHN BOYER, convicted of murder, Wyoming. Executed April 21, 1871

Son of a Frenchman and a Sioux Indian woman, Boyer was convicted of murdering two people he suspected of raping his mother and sister. At one point he escaped by simply walking out past a prison guard, but he was again arrested. Boyer's case drew much media attention as the first legal execution in Wyoming's history.

I have always wished not to die with my boots on; please pull them off.

ISSAC M. WEAVER, convicted of murder, California. Executed January 4, 1874

Weaver claimed he planned to "arrest" Adolph Walmer, after Walmer made threats against his former ranch boss. But Weaver was not a law enforcement official and, the local sheriff said, did not act under his authority. The pair had intertwining histories, as went the rumor, and Weaver was looking for an excuse to kill Walmer. At Weaver's request, his boots were removed.

Gentlemen, I am here to die, but I am an innocent man compared to that woman. She deserves death ten times more than I do.

MARSHALL MARTIN, convicted of murder, California.
Executed January 23, 1874

Martin's work supervisor was Valentine Eischler, whose marriage with wife Elizabeth was in the course of unraveling. According to Martin's testimony, Elizabeth seduced him and urged him to murder her husband. Eventually, Eischler died in an attack with an ax, with both parties claiming responsibility at different times. Elizabeth pleaded insanity and was sent to an asylum. Martin was convicted of first-degree murder.

It's worth noting that the *Chicago Daily Tribune* recorded slightly different last words: "Gentlemen: I want you all to understand that I am here to die; but I am an innocent man; I don't deserve this. The woman that caused me to do this deserves death a thousand more times than I do. That's all I have to say."

Martin's hanging was particularly gruesome, as recorded by the newspaper *Alta California*: "Although there was a drop of only six feet, the body dropped headless to the ground. His head rebounded a distance of six feet."

Statement to the crowd:

My Friends: You are now gazing upon a very unfortunate man, who is called forth to bid a final adieu to this cheating and sinful world. God of infinite mercy have compassion upon a poor sinner and save me from perdition. My friends, I desire to thank all the good people of Montana, and now ask God to bless you all and those dear ones so far away. I am now about to offer up my life. I make this statement to show you how unfortunate

I am and as a warning to you all, just as I go to that awful future, to meet my God. May God bless you all.

To the hangman:

I am ready, God have mercy on my soul.

WILLIAM WRIGHT WHEATLEY, convicted of murder, Montana, August 13, 1875

The jury recommended clemency in Wheatley's case after he turned in his coconspirators in the murder of Franz Warl. Neither the judge nor the territory's governor had the power to commute the sentence, however, and Wheatley was hanged against the jury's wishes. Wheatley's was recorded as the first legal hanging in the Montana territory.

I'm going to Jesus.

ALCEE HARRIS, convicted of murder, Louisiana. Executed November 26, 1875

Upon her husband's discovery of her affair with Tony Hellum, Mrs. Harris and Hellum decided that Mr. Harris needed to be killed. Mrs. Harris pretended to make peace with her husband and offered him a beer to celebrate their reconciliation. However, she had drugged the beer, and as her husband slept, Hellum proceeded to hack the man apart with an ax. The guilty pair both embraced Catholicism right before their executions and professed a belief that they were going straight to heaven. "Jerked to Jesus" read the headline in the *Chicago Times*—one of the most infamous newspaper headlines in history.

I must make a statement in regard to this matter. I feel it my duty to God and to man to do so. I am guilty of killing the two men. My soul is stained with blood and my punishment is just. I hope all will forgive me. I pray God to guide and prosper this country. I am the murderer of William Spence. And George W. Sisney. That is all I have to say.

MARSHALL CRAIN, convicted of murder, Illinois. Executed January 21, 1876

Crain, a twenty-year-old hired assassin, murdered Sisney and Spence in 1876. The double murder, labeled by the press the "Williamson County Vendetta," was part of a long-standing feud between the Bulliner and Henderson families of Carbondale, Illinois. Before Crain's execution, he was remanded to a jail in Marion County in order to avoid a lynching at the hands of an angry mob.

The *Chicago Tribune* noted: "He was born, raised, educated, married, committed his crimes and was executed within a radius of 10 miles."

Sheriff Emmerson, on behalf of John Daniels:

By request of the prisoner no prayers or remarks will be made. He wishes people to understand that he lived like a man and he would like to die like a soldier.

JOHN DANIELS, convicted of murder, Missouri. Executed January 3, 1878

Daniels hired Jesse R. Miller to accompany him to Johnson County, Missouri, on February 20, 1877. Daniels returned to his home alone on February 24 with Miller's personal property and horse team, which he claimed he had bought when Miller had decided to go on to Colorado. Miller was found with a cut throat and a fractured skull on the banks of Cedar Creek. The men had camped together February 22, and Daniels had driven away alone the next morning.

In a jailhouse interview, the night before his execution:

I had a square trial. Everything the witnesses said was pretty much true. I felt at the time that I ought to have done it, and afterward I felt I did wrong. I tell you it's a hard thing when a man brings it on himself, but whisky did it.

ISAIAH EVANS, convicted of murder, Louisiana. Executed May 10, 1878

"Isaiah Evans (colored)." That's all the *New York Times* revealed about the twenty-three-year-old man hanged for murdering an eighteen-year-old man. More than two thousand attended the execution. After a clergyman prayed, Evans's rope was adjusted, he fell, and his neck broke. He had admitted to intoxication the night he shot a man named Edward Bowen.

**I bid you farewell, my sister, likewise to this world of sin.
But 'tis hard, 'tis hard, my sister, to part from friends and kin.
To be led like a brute to the slaughter, to die by the hangman's hand.
To perish like a guilty felon, condemned by the laws of the land.**

GEORGE SHERRY, convicted of murder, Illinois. Executed June 21, 1878

After a night of drink, slaughterhouse coworkers Sherry, age twenty-one, and accomplice Jeremiah Connolly, nineteen, assaulted four people before hitting a young girl, Rose McConville. When her uncle Hugh McConville intervened, the men attacked him. One stabbed him just beneath his heart, and the assailants proceeded to kick him. He died. Arrested two days later, each man blamed one another, and they were hanged together. The murder was called by the *Chicago Tribune* "the most cold-blooded in the criminal annals of Chicago."

I have nothing at all to say. I will die like a Game Man. That is all I have to say.

MARTIN BERGIN, convicted of conspiracy to commit murder, Pennsylvania. Executed January 16, 1879

Prior to his execution, Bergin spent time with his wife and time in prayer, including a two-hour mass. After a final meal of bread, butter, eggs, and coffee, Bergin prayed some more before two priests escorted him by candlelight to receive his punishment. Bergin had killed a coal mine clerk in a murder-for-hire scheme to protect another man's secret.

I have a great deal I would like to say, but it would not be worth while to say anything. The State of Indiana to-day, in the sight of that Court-house, is doing an unjust thing to one of her citizens. I say, as I have said before to this people and to the world, I am innocent of the charge. When that drop fails and my life goes out, it will be eternal peace. I wish to say no more.

WILLIAM MERRICK, convicted of murder. Executed January 29, 1879

The jury took only eleven minutes to find Merrick guilty of murdering his wife, Julia A. Merrick. During the trial, it surfaced that he had arranged with the janitor of a medical college to deliver a body about the time of his wife's disappearance. He was seen buying a packet of strychnine in a saloon and, the next morning, leaving town with his wife in a buggy. That night, he drove around town "until his wife became cold enough to warrant delivery to the medical college," according to a *New York Times* article. Julia Merrick's nude body was later discovered in a ditch with the body of a baby boy with his umbilical cord still attached.

Mercy! Mercy! Mercy! Don't hang me! I can't die! I'm not ready to die! I don't want to die!

HENRY F. ANDREWS, convicted of burglary, North Carolina.
Executed May 16, 1879

The spring of 1878 became known as the "season of terror" in Chapel Hill, North Carolina, and Andrews was one of three men responsible. Andrews and his accomplices were accused of committing a "series of burglaries and attempts to violate the persons of young ladies." In the end, Andrews, once described as stout and athletic, met the noose in a fragile physical and emotional state.

I forgive my enemies.

ANDREW TRACY, convicted of murder, Pennsylvania.
Executed December 4, 1879

Tracy murdered his cousin after she refused to marry him. During his execution, Tracy's noose was not tied properly, and he fell seven feet to the ground. With his hands tied, Tracy was unable to catch himself, and he lost consciousness. When the sheriff picked him up, Tracy woke up and said his last words. They tied the rope around his neck, whereupon he fainted again and died without regaining consciousness.

All young men take warning and never be guilty of theft, however small, because they might deserve the small penalty I am about to suffer.
I have five minutes to live. I can think of Heaven in that time. While there is life there is hope.

After kicking off his slippers:
I will give them to the poor. The *Courier-Journal* cannot say I died with my boots on.

JOHN VANDERPIED, convicted of murder, Kentucky.
Executed February 25, 1881

The murderer of Rebecca Johnston, Vanderpied climbed the scaffold smoking a cigar. Although his full speech has not survived, it was reported that in it he maintained his innocence and read from the *Shelby Sentinel*, saying the newspaper misreported the story.

Folks, hear me, as I'se to be hanged. I'se free from any guilt about Nash Carter. I had a child by another man, but was smart enough to keep my husband from knowing it.

MATILDA CARTER, convicted of murder, North Carolina.
Executed January 13, 1882

Carter was sentenced to death for the murder of her much older husband, Nash Carter, after he voiced concerns about her acquaintance with a group of young men. While he was sleeping, prosecutors said, Mrs. Carter and three accomplices slipped a noose around Mr. Carter's neck and pulled. On the scaffold, fellow convicted murderer Joe Hay admitted to adultery with Mrs. Carter.

I read from Matthew, tenth chapter and twenty-eighth verse: "And fear not them which kill the body, but are not able to kill the soul and body in hell . . ."

My dying prayer on the gallows; I tremble for the fate of my murderers. This nation will go down in the blood. My murderers, from the Executive to the hangman, will go to Hell.

I am now going to read some verses which are intended to indicate my feelings at the moment of leaving this world. If set to music they may be rendered effective. The idea is that of a child babbling to his mamma and papa. I wrote it this morning about 10 o'clock.

I am going to the Lordy,
I am so glad
I am going to the Lordy,
I am so glad,
I am going to the Lordy,
Glory, hallelujah! Glory, hallelujah!
I am going to the Lordy.
I saved my party and my land, Glory, hallelujah,
But they have murdered me for it,
And that is the reason I am going to the Lordy,
Glory, hallelujah! Glory, hallelujah!
I am going to the Lordy.
Glory, hallelujah! I am with the Lordy.

CHARLES JULIUS GUITEAU, convicted of murder, Washington, DC.
Executed June 30, 1882

Guiteau spent his early years roaming the United States, working in as varied of fields as journalism, religious work, and law. He was arrested several times on charges of embezzlement and thievery, though no charges stuck. In 1881, he moved to Washington, DC, and demanded a foreign diplomatic office from President James A. Garfield, haunting federal buildings for a chance to speak to him. Guiteau purchased a revolver and shot the president in a train depot on July 2, 1881. Garfield hovered between life and death for eighty days, and when he succumbed, Guiteau was indicted for murder. His defense was insanity; throughout the court proceedings he repeatedly erupted in outrageous displays, which garnered him the nickname "the Hyena."

I have got nothing more to say. May God forgive you for murdering me. You are about to hang an innocent woman—innocent as the man that stands there [pointing at one of the deputies].

EMELINE MEAKER, convicted of murder, Vermont. Executed March 30, 1883

Meaker and her son Almon were convicted of poisoning Emeline's eight-year-old niece, Alice Meaker. The *Free Press* labeled the crime "one of the most cold-blooded murders known in history or fiction." Awaiting her execution, Meaker had the "ferocity of a wild beast," according to newspaper accounts. She attempted to set fire to one prison and made numerous attacks against the sheriff and attendants. She spent her remaining time knitting in her cell. Meaker became the first woman to be legally executed by the state of Vermont.

The *Washington Post* reported her full statement as "Good-bye, Mr. Hall; I have no more to say, only I forgive you for hanging me. May God forgive you all."

You young saints and sinners, take warning and let
whisky alone. It was whisky that brought me here. I did
not kill the man, it was whisky; but I am come here now,
and God has pardoned me. My way is clear before me.
I have nearly come up, and am now pulling myself into
the light of glory. . . . I advise all you saints and sinners
not to fool too much with whisky. Here I am, a hard-
working man, brought here by whisky. Steele told me
in the spirit that if could he come and speak for me he
would say a good word for me. I trust to meet you all
with my Jesus. . . . God bless you all.

HENRY DICKERSON, convicted of murder, Louisiana.
Executed September 7, 1883

Dickerson was drinking and gambling unsuccessfully with a group
of plantation and steamboat workers when he left the dice game
and met John Steele, "an uninterested passerby." After Steele refused to give him a dime, Dickerson shot him through the heart.
Dickerson escaped to spend eight days in a swamp but then, having
nearly starved, gave himself up. He later found religion in prison.

I am going to tell the truth before God. I am innocent
of the charge. I did not poison Leia Lewis, and I hope
to meet her in heaven. My kin people brought me to
this, and I want them to pray to meet me in heaven. I
have heard they said hanging was too good for me, that
I ought to be burned. Farewell all, I am going to die. I
hope this poor man will be released, as he is innocent
before God.

Turning to her sister on the scaffold:

I want to be buried by the side of my mother, but they will not allow it. They don't care what becomes of my body. Good-bye! Sister, good-bye!

MARGARET HARRIS, convicted of murder, Georgia. Executed October 19, 1883

Indentured servant Harris, age eighteen, was accused of poisoning the family she worked for in order to leave and live with David Dukes, her alleged accomplice, whom she referred to as "this poor man." Prosecutors said she first added the poison to coffee, which only sickened her mistress, widow Nancy Barnwell, and Barnwell's two grandchildren. She then added poison, procured from Duke, to rice, killing one of the grandchildren. A commutation was requested from the governor, but it was refused "as there has lately been a perfect avalanche of poisoning cases and an example needed to be made of it," according to the *Chicago Daily Tribune*. At the hanging, "In the Sweet By-and-By" was sung by the four clergymen attending. The condemned and spectators joined in the song.

On his execution day:

I am almost sorry you woke me up. I was having pleasant dreams. No! I can't tell you what they were, because I can't recall them. I only know that I was in a most delightful frame of mind.

ROBERT MARTIN, convicted of murder, New Jersey. Executed January 3, 1884

After ingesting a dangerous mix of medicinal morphine and alcohol, Martin had a fight with his wife. He shot at her and the infant in her arms, killing them both with a single bullet. Martin left behind a letter expressing his deep sorrow and guilt for his deed. He said that "the tragedy seems like a dream to him, and he did not know until the next morning what he had done."

Where is my little boy? Look at me, my son, and take warning.

EDWARD (ALIAS VALMAR RECTOR) RECTOR, convicted of murder, Louisiana. Executed January 4, 1884

Rector faced the gallows for the stabbing murder of Duncan Williams. He had previously been accused of slaying his stepfather. After he spoke these last words, Rector struggled and had to be subdued as his son wept "bitterly," according to a newspaper account. It was also recorded that "he fought hard and begged most piteously to be spared." Rector strangled to death for eighteen minutes after the trapdoor sprang.

What time is it? I wish you'd hurry up. I want to get to hell in time for dinner.

JOHN OWENS (AKA BILL BOOTH), convicted of murder, Wyoming. Executed March 5, 1886

Owens was convicted for murdering a man who hired him to work on his farm. Owens confessed to the killing but claimed he had done it in self-defense, after the man attacked him.

On the gallows:

Go ahead and do what you ____ please. Don't squeeze me to death, ____ you. It don't take a hundred men to hang me.

When asked for his last words:

None of your business. What in the ____ do you want to take a man's life in this way for, you ____ ____ cutthroats.
   Hurry up, old man, or Clark will want another drink

of whisky. If you don't look out, I may fall through and
sue the city for damages.

ALLEN J. ADAMS, convicted of murder, Massachusetts.
Executed April 16, 1886

Adams spent time as a whaler, moonshiner, and a prisoner of the
Connecticut State Prison before he murdered his boss, Moses B.
Dickenson, in 1875 and then disappeared for ten years. He turned
up again in Tennessee, where he was convicted for forgery. To avoid
the chain gang, he confessed to the murder and returned to Massachusetts for his March 16 hanging. Two days before his sentence,
Adams tried to cut his own throat. His execution was postponed
for a month while he healed. The man named Clark mentioned in
his last words was the sheriff. The blanks in his speech, presumably,
represent profanity the newspaper didn't wish to print.

Gentlemen, one and all, I am about to die for a crime of
which I am guilty and I am perfectly willing to go. I have
nothing to regret, but I am sorry that I, John Thomas
Ross, have to pay it all. As Marshall Frey knows, there
are others who are as much guilty as I am. I am glad I
have been brought to this and I am thankful to God for
bringing me here. I have no hard feelings against anyone. Had not God stopped me in my bad career I might
never have gotten here. I am going where there is no
trouble or sighing and where I will have rest forever. Let
me go. Lord Jesus, remember me.

Singing:

It is Good to be There
I do not Want to Leave that Happy Home

JOHN THOMAS ROSS, convicted of murder, Maryland.
Executed September 9, 1887

Ross smiled at the jury and "chuckled" when the judge read his sentence of death for the murder of Emily Brown. Ross hit her over the head and stabbed her through the heart in hopes of receiving payment for her body at the Maryland University of Medicine. The night before his execution, several other prisoners were allowed to enter his cell, and they sang camp melodies. "He went to bed smiling last night and woke up with a broad grin on his black countenance, which expression he wore until the black cap hid it from view," reported the *Chicago Daily Tribune*. His final words were taken from the hymn "I'll Soon Be at Home."

This is the happiest day of my life.

ADOLPH FISCHER, convicted of murder, Illinois. Executed November 11, 1887

An anarchist and labor union activist, Fischer was present at an organizing meeting the night before what has been called the Haymarket Square Riot, Haymarket Massacre, or Haymarket Tragedy. At this rally in Chicago's Haymarket Square, a few thousand people showed up to protest the killing of two workers the previous day, when police had broken up a clash between union workers and their replacements at a local reaper factory. In the square, someone threw a bomb that killed police officer Mathias J. Degan and incited a riot.

Officers fired into the crowd. Some accounts say police shot back at armed members of the gathering; others say it was unclear why the officers fired. The Chicago Herald newspaper estimated at least fifty civilian dead, while the Chicago Tribune reported, "A very large number of the police were wounded by each other's revolvers."

Seven more officers would die of wounds sustained during the incident. No single person was clearly proved to be the bomb thrower, but German immigrant Fischer was held responsible for the event, along with seven other men.

Haymarket became a symbol of the labor rights struggle and helped set May 1 as International Labor Day.

The time will come when our silence will be more powerful than the voices you strangle today.

AUGUST SPIES, convicted of murder, Illinois. Executed November 11, 1887

Spies was a German-born immigrant who eventually became the editor of the anarchist paper *Arbeiter-Zeitung*. On the day of the Haymarket Riot, he spoke on stage at Haymarket Square and was still on stage when the bomb was thrown. It has been reported that he began his speech with a clear statement of nonviolence. Despite clearly not being the thrower of the bomb, he was charged with being involved in the planning of the event.

In German:

Hurrah for anarchy!

GEORGE ENGEL, convicted of murder, Illinois. Executed November 11, 1887

Engel was one of the four men executed after being convicted of being involved in the bombing that started the Haymarket affair. Engel, a German immigrant, had traveled to the United States because of poor economic conditions in his country. Orphaned at a young age, he was forced to work for most of his life. He was testified against by other anarchists, who claimed he had come up with a plan to bomb police stations and other targets in the event of police aggression.

May I be allowed to speak? Oh, men of America! May I be allowed the privilege of speech even at the last moment? Harken to the voice of the people—

ALBERT PARSONS, convicted of murder, Illinois. Executed November 11, 1887

Parsons was an American-born anarchist who was forced to flee Texas in response to pressure from the Ku Klux Klan because of his interracial marriage. In Chicago, Parsons became a prominent labor activist and was a founding member of the International Working People's Association. Executed along with three other Haymarket activists, he was cut off in the middle of his last words as the hangman dropped the trapdoor from beneath the four men's feet.

In 1992, the site of the Haymarket incident was commemorated with a bronze plaque. It read:

A decade of strife between labor and industry culminated here in a confrontation that resulted in the tragic death of both workers and policemen. On May 4, 1886, spectators at a labor rally had gathered around the mouth of Crane's Alley. A contingent of police approaching on Des Plaines Street were met by a bomb thrown from just south of the alley. The resultant trial of eight activists gained worldwide attention for the labor movement, and initiated the tradition of "May Day" labor rallies in many cities.
Designated on March 25, 1992
Richard M. Daley, Mayor

Good-by for all my gentlemens [sic], good-by. I am going to die like a man; isn't that so gentlemen? [A friend called back: "That's so, that's so."]

JOSE RAMIREZ, convicted of murder, California. Executed December 2, 1887

In a Santa Clara County saloon confrontation over a woman, Ramirez and the much larger Fernando Acero exchanged harsh words that escalated into roughhousing and finally bullets. Only Acero, who fled the scene, was badly wounded. Both men were arrested, and Acero, whose wounds did not seem fatal at the time, made a "dying declaration" six days after the shooting, naming Ramirez the killer. He expired two days later. Ramirez was sentenced to die almost a year after he had shot Acero.

I wish you all a restful conscience and a useful life on this life on this earth. I hope when you come through this door you will bring some little child that has no father and mother on this earth for protection. That is all I have to say on this earth, Good-bye.

JOHN PATRICK HART, convicted of murder, Montana.
Executed February 10, 1888

Hart's mother died when he was nine months old, and his father died when he was fourteen, leaving him an orphan—presumably the "little child" he refers to. After the father of the young woman he was courting accused him of visiting brothels, Hart shot him. Following his trial, Hart told reporters that he felt justified in the murder because the victim had been trying to wrong him.

I killed the men. I do not regret [it], but they tell me it was wrong. If so, I am sorry. You see how I am here. Try and help my people. If so, tell them how I died, and warn them not to do as I did, or they may die, as I have to die. Be kind to my people and see that they do not want. I am glad you come and I thank you for being here and for what you have done for me. See that I am buried with my people.

PIERRE PAUL, convicted of murder, Montana. Executed December 19, 1890

Paul, a member of the Pend d'Oreilles Native American tribe, participated in the shooting of two white men. He addressed his final statement to two Native American chiefs who were attending his hanging. Afterward he said "Good night" to his defense attorney and then amended it to "Good-bye."

Written:

I acknowledge and deeply repent before God and my fellow men the awful crime that has brought me to this sad end. I do not seek to screen myself in any wise, yet my ignorance of God's word, my bad habits of card playing leading me into all manner of trouble, led me into this. So far was I gone in liquor that a few days before my great crime I attempted my own life but was hindered by merciful Providence. All these things I would warn young men to flee. When I came to this jail my heart was as hard as flint, but the warning of my father to make my peace with God, and my brother's entreaties, and the faithful labors of some kind Christian friends who have visited me in my trouble, have led me to seek God and to hope in his mercy, through the Lord Jesus Christ.

I rely upon the promise of God's word for forgiveness of all my sins, and if such a sinner as I have been is forgiven, I do not think that there is any man on earth but that may be forgiven if he turns to the Lord. I am grateful to all my friends for their kindness to me in these days, and my last thoughts are for my children, and that my fate shall be a warning to others.

[Signed] James M. Eubanks.

Spoken:

Oh, Jesus, I give myself to Thee; Thy will be done. I hope that this will be a warning to others.

JAMES M. EUBANKS, convicted of murder, California. Executed January 19, 1891

Eubanks shot his daughter, Ana, in the chest, then turned the shotgun on himself, but missed. Relatives' testimony revealed that Eubanks was a hard drinker who repeatedly abused his daughter and admitted, according to a female relative, to having an incestuous relationship with her that resulted in a pregnancy.

He wrote in his confession: "I am a nuisance to the world; so I leave it in disgust. But I could get along in it sometime yet if I had no children; so good-bye."

I have this to say: That I know nothing about the murder. The people bore false witness against me. I hired Mr. Platt to defend me and told him all I knew, but he turned against me and went over to the other side. That is the reason I am on the scaffold to-day. If I did the deed and knew what I was doing, I ought to be hanged for it, but I did not know what I was doing.

CHARLES WALL, convicted of murder, Pennsylvania. Executed March 8, 1892

A large crowd pushed past prison gates and some even jumped walls to stand in ankle-deep snow to see Wall hang. Wall, convicted of axing his wife in a field in front of her father, remained calm in his cell the morning of his execution. Prison guards were surprised by Wall's happy mood in the death cell and claimed that he was bothered only by the fact that his favorite horse had just died.

I only wish to say that the statement I have made about the crime with which I stand charged is true. I must say that since I have been here, no Protestant minister has come near me. When the priests came, they were kind to me, and I can only say that I die happy and a Catholic. That is all.

WALTER HOLMES, convicted of murder, Massachusetts. Executed February 3, 1893

Though raised a Protestant, Holmes converted to Catholicism as he awaited execution—an act that angered many people in the community. He walked to the gallows on a pair of crutches, then was nearly decapitated when the noose knot caught under his chin.

I had no malice against anyone.

PATRICK EUGENE PRENDERGAST, convicted of murder, Illinois. Executed July 13, 1894

Prendergast murdered Chicago mayor Carter Henry Harrison, a leader of the Columbian Exposition, or World's Fair, of 1893. The delusional Prendergast believed Harrison owed him a political appointment after he supported the mayor's reelection.

Famed legal mind Clarence Darrow took Prendergast on as his first murder case, but his insanity defense failed.

My heart is not bad. . . . I did not kill the cowboys; the Indian boys [White Faced Horse, Fights With, Two Two, and First Eagle] killed them. I have killed many Indians, but never killed a white man; I never pulled a gun on a white man. The great father and the men under him should talk to me and I would show them I am innocent. The white men are going to kill me for something I haven't done. I am a great chief myself. I have always been a friend of the white man. The white men will find out sometime that I am innocent and then they will be sorry they killed me. The great father will be sorry, too, and he will be ashamed. My people will be ashamed, too. My heart is straight and I like everybody. God made all hearts the same. My heart is the same as the white man's. If I had not been innocent I would not have come up here so good when they wanted me. They know I am innocent or they would not let me go around here. My heart knows I am not guilty and I am happy. I am not afraid to die. I was taught that if I raised my hands to God and told a lie that God would kill me that day. I never told a lie in my life.

CHIEF CHA NOPA UHAH, convicted of murder, South Dakota. Executed December 28, 1894

Sioux chief Cha Nopa Uhah, or Two Sticks, led a small band of Ghost Dancers in raiding a herd of cattle close to South Dakota's Pine Ridge Reservation. When tribal police attempted to arrest the band, the Ghost Dancers opened fire and succeeded in killing all but one of the police officers. According to authorities, they then returned to the cattle ranch and killed four cowboys. Eventually, a group of more than fifty chiefs agreed that Two Sticks was the instigator of the altercations, and they gave him up to the state of South Dakota. Upon seeing the gallows, he said. "Washta you bet," meaning "Good you bet."

Good-bye, boys. Here goes a brave man!

ANTHONY AZOFF, convicted of murder, California. Executed June 7, 1895

Azoff and two others were taken by surprise when attempting to rob the South Pacific Train Station Depot. Three officers sprang from an empty boxcar, informed ahead of time of the robbery. While running to escape, Azoff fired wildly, fatally wounding Detective Len Harris in the abdomen. A five-hundred-dollar reward was place on his head before he was finally captured. Later Azoff spoke with a reporter, telling him that he actually liked prison. "This is better than scrapping for a living outside any day," he said. "Before I came here I had a dread of the place. Instead I have a fine room, dry and clean and white as snow. And such beds! It's almost worth hanging to have a nice, soft place to lie in."

No, let her go. Tighten her up, old son, tighten her up!

CLAYBERG PUGH, convicted of murder, Montana. Executed July 1, 1895

Many observers thought that Pugh was eager to die. He openly mocked his attorney's efforts to commute his sentence for killing a train conductor, and he refused to sign the petition that circulated asking the governor for clemency. When the sheriff told him that they could set the execution anytime between 10:00 a.m. and 2:00 p.m., Pugh responded, "Make it as soon after 10 as possible and let's have it over with."

Gentlemen, it was said that I killed Richards over a girl. That is not so. It was pure passion. I had thought the man wanted to take everything away from me and now I am to pay for his life. Good-bye.

JOSEPH CADOTTE, convicted of murder, Montana. Executed December 27, 1895

According to rumor, Cadotte shot his hunting partner, Oliver Richards, in the middle of an argument about hunting proceeds and a pretty girl who preferred Richards to Cadotte. Cadotte later claimed that Richards drew a knife on him during the fight. During his trial, the prosecuting attorney pointed to a birthmark around Cadotte's neck that looked like a rope burn and said, "Nature evidently intended the man to die. He was born to be hung."

Gentlemen: I did the deed. I killed George Wells, and I do not want any one to suffer for it. But the Lord has forgiven me of all my crimes. All I have to say is, I did not want to die. This may be a lesson to some one. I see

a lot of you around here who may have young boys coming up, and this may prevent them from coming where
I am today.

To Eugene Tousley, a prison official:
You may have a boy and I want you to watch him and
see that he does not come to where I have today. I am
ready to die.
I am trusting in Jesus.

HENRY FOSTER, convicted of murder, Illinois. Executed January 24, 1896

Foster was attempting to rob another man when Wells ran into the
street from a saloon to stop him. Foster fired two shots, killing Wells
almost instantly.

Gentlemen, I have very few words to say. In fact, I would
make no remarks at this time except that by not speaking I would appear to acquiesce in my execution. I only
wish to say that the extent of my wrong-doing in taking
human life consisted in the death of two women, they
having died at my hands as the result of criminal op-
erations. I wish to also state here, so that there can be
no chance of misunderstanding hereafter, that I am not
guilty of taking the lives of any of the Pitezel family—
the three children and Benjamin, the father—of whose
death I was convicted, and for which I am to-day to be
hanged. That is all I have to say.

HERMAN WEBSTER MUDGETT, best known by his alias H. H. Holmes or
Dr. Henry Howard Holmes, convicted of murder, Pennsylvania.
Executed May 7, 1896

Holmes killed more than twenty people in his hotel on Chicago's
South Side and sold some of their remains to medical schools, ac-

cording to authorities. Perhaps it's understandable that Holmes instructed that his body be cemented into his coffin to fend off grave robbers after his execution. He had built his hotel to prepare for Chicago's World Fair, the 1893 World's Columbian Exposition, and many of his guests were his victims. Holmes was the "devil" in Erik Larson's book *The Devil in the White City.*

Put him in the bad box. [muttering] Put him in the . . .

JOSEPH WINDRATH, convicted of murder, Illinois. Executed June 5, 1896

Windrath muttered this phrase continually for several weeks before his execution. He was examined several times but was found each time to be mentally sound and responsible for the murder committed during the robbery of Carey Birch. The night before his execution, Windrath's wife made a final visit to his cell. "Don't you know me . . . ?" she asked. "Hang up Mannow. Put him in the bad box," Windrath replied. Mannow was the name of Windrath's accomplice, who testified against him.

Written:

My, dreAm,—1896
i, dremp'T, i, was, in, heAven,
Among, THe, AngeLs, Fair;
i'd, neAr, seen, none, so HAndsome,
THAT, TWine, in golden, HAir,
THey, looked, so, neAT, And; sAng, so, sweeT,
And, PLAY'd THe, golden HArp,
i, wAs, ABout, To, Pick An, ANgel, ouT,
And, TAke, Her, To, mY, HeArT,
BuT, THe, momenT, i, BegAn, To, PLeA,

i, THougHT, oF, You, mY, Love,
THere, wAs, none, I'd, seen, so BeAuTiFuLL,
On, eArTH, or, HeAven, ABove,
gooD, By, My, Dear, Wife, anD, MoTher
all, so, My, sisTers
RUFUS BUCK
youse Truley
i Day, of, JUly
Tu, THe, Yeore,
off 1896

H
O
L
Y
FATHER   Son
G
H
O
S
T
virtue & resurresur.rection,
RememBer, Me, ROCK, OF, Ages.

RUFUS BUCK, convicted of rape, Arkansas. Executed July 1, 1896

Buck was the leader of the Rufus Buck gang, a group of five men who worked together for only thirteen days. In that time, the gang allegedly committed numerous rapes and robberies; they were hanged for the gang rape of a farmwife named Rosetta Hassan. Buck's last words are not recorded, but after his execution, officials found the poem entitled "mY, dreAm" in his cell, written on the back of a picture of his mother.

My friends, I can't leave without saying something. You never can tell my feelings as I stand before you. It is sad indeed. Bad women are the cause of my being in this position. I am safe, as Christ Jesus has pardoned my sins. I soon will be somewhere in God's kingdom. Reflect before you get mad, and you will never commit crime. Just think of it! I am to be executed in the bloom of youth and good health! I committed the crime, and I am sorry. If I could only call it back!

With all due respect to women, I must say they have brought me to ruin. She deceived me and robbed me of my character and money. I was over persuaded by this woman. She had me in her power and worked her way in my heart, so that I felt I had rather be dead than alive. She is lying in the cold, silent grave, and tomorrow I also will be numbered with the dead. My soul will then be at rest. I implore you all to abstain from evil habits. Especially beware of bad women. No, I am through.

LOVETT BROOKINS, convicted of murder, Georgia. Executed April 16, 1897

Brookins, a teacher, met the gallows smoking cigarettes. Before the drop, he prayed and sang. The high-ranking Freemason received the death penalty for murdering his mistress, Leila McCrary, and a man named Sanders Oliphant.

A letter delivered to the press:
The poor young fellow I killed and the girl I loved and also killed, were victims of a moment's passion. I only wish that I could bring them back to life. The scaffold has no terrors for me. I rather welcome it. A man can

only die once. My time has come and I am content
with it.

HARVEY ALLENDER, convicted of murder, California.
Executed December 10, 1897

When Allender found that his longtime sweetheart Wilburga Feilner
was to marry an ice-cream cart driver, Venanze Crosetti, he stalked
both of them. After a few whiskeys one night, he drew a pistol and
shot them. With one bullet left, Allender attempted to shoot himself
in the head but only punctured his hat.

On the morning of August 18, 1897, Ida, my wife, took
a bucket and started to the well. My mother ran to me
and said, "Now, Hiram, is your time." I took another
bucket and followed her. We came to the well, and Ida
stooped down to dip her bucket of water. I threw my
weight against her and pushed her into the well. She
caught with her hands and feet on the sides of the well.
As she clung there, looking up into my face with such
a pleading, pitiful face, I thought that surely I had no
heart at all, for such pleading would have melted a
heart of stone. I stooped down, picked up a large stone,
and struck her on the head with all my strength. She
quivered for a moment and then dropped lifeless into
the water.

I did not wait to see if she sank, but went immediately to the house. In a minute or two mother came running into the house and told me that Ida was trying to
get out, and that she could do nothing. I went back to
the well and found her floating on the top of the water,
apparently lifeless. I took a plank and struck her on the

head and face several times; then pushed her under the water with the plank and held it on her a few seconds. Then she sank.

HIRAM HALL, convicted of murder, Tennessee. Executed April 13, 1899

Before confessing, in gruesome detail, to the murder of his wife, Hiram Hall coolly made his way to the gallows with a cigar hanging from his mouth. He claimed that his mother put him up to the deed because she didn't like his wife. Hall also claimed that his mother had encouraged him to kill his father, but Hall never followed through on that. Hall's mother abandoned him after his arrest, leaving his attempts to contact her unanswered. However, his father defended him and attended his execution.

Good-by, people. I gladly give my life for my sweetheart. I loved her.

WILLIAM WASCO, convicted of murder, Pennsylvania.
Executed January 9, 1900

The *Washington Post* ran a brief that read, in part, "The crime for which Wasco was executed was the murder of Annie Sestak, a comely young Hungarian girl, who had refused to marry him. He shot himself at the same time, but soon recovered from his wounds."

I am sorry for killing Gates. I was wrong. I don't know if I am forgiven. I may have to suffer in the next world. The priest tells me so, perhaps, but I am as sorry as I can be for it.

JOAQUIN ESLABE, convicted of murder, California. Executed April 23, 1900

Eslabe was a street vendor and friend to Charles E. Gates, whom
he killed in an alcohol-inflamed argument. While in prison, Eslabe
made an escape attempt aided by a woman who regularly brought
him fruit and other treats. When police searched his cell they found
a hacksaw. At his execution, Eslabe trembled as he climbed the scaffold but smiled as the black hood was placed over his head.

As the rope was placed around his throat:

Oh, I'll smother with that on. I've got electricity in my head now.

BENJAMIN SNELL, convicted of murder, Washington, DC.
Executed June 29, 1900

"A man of education and good family," Snell was convicted of murder after breaking in to the house of child Lizzie Weisenberger and
cutting her throat with a razor. Other prisoners shunned Snell, and
when Frank Funk heard that he was to be executed on the same day
and scaffold as Snell, he petitioned the courts to change the day.
President McKinley reprieved Funk for several days, and Snell and
Funk maintained "bitter hatred" until Snell's death.

Goodbye. Please dig my grave very deep. Let her go!

THOMAS E. "BLACK JACK" KETCHUM, convicted of murder, New Mexico.
Executed April 26, 1901

Train robbery landed Ketchum in a stockade with a rope around
his neck. He claimed that he wasn't the real Black Jack. He did,
however, boast that he had modeled his image on the real deal—
who was still enjoying his freedom—and had committed crimes of
his own. Ketchum claimed he'd hang for the crimes of both Black
Jacks. He even wrote a letter to President McKinley, begging for
mercy. Clemency did not come.

If I only knew my family would not be in want I could die in peace.

GEORGE DOLINSKI, convicted of murder, Illinois. Executed October 11, 1901

Dolinski's wife ended a visit with her parents and hurried across the Atlantic to prove that her husband was innocent of her murder. When she arrived, she discovered that she had been misinformed: it was for the murder of her brother-in-law Anton Lisle that Dolinski had been arrested. Reportedly, Dolinski had become infatuated with his wife's sister, Mrs. Lisle. Anton Lisle was found in a pasture with his throat cut and four bullets in his body. Dolinski claimed that he and his brother-in-law had fought about money and he was forced to shoot Lisle in self-defense.

The Chicago Daily recorded different last words: "I have got this to say. I am not guilty of killing that man. I—I—"

Boys, let me kneel and pray. I want to pray for all of you and send a message to my blessed little wife. I love her dearly and want you to tell her that I pray that you will have the papers print it. I pray for you, Charles Ricker, and for all of you. I never had a grudge against Sheriff Ricker; never in God's world. I never meant to shoot him. For God's sake don't choke me to death. Oh—

CHARLES FRANCIS WOODWARD, convicted of murder, Wyoming. Executed March 28, 1902

Imprisoned for the shooting death of Sheriff Charles Ricker, Woodward was taken from jail by "twenty-four masked men" and lynched from the scaffold that had been erected for his legal execution. He had been granted a stay of execution by the U.S. Supreme Court, but an angry mob seized him, demanding immediate justice.

Before his captors could spring the trap themselves, Woodward jumped from the gallows, hanging himself.

One person from the lynch mob pinned a card to Woodward's clothing that read: "Process of the law is a little slow, so this road you will have to go. Murderers and thieves beware—People's verdict."

Ain't losing your nerve, are you, Joe?

TOM HORN, convicted of murder, Wyoming. Executed November 20, 1903

Horn's last words were directed to County Clerk Joseph Cahill, who assisted him to his execution. Horn, sentenced to die for killing a fourteen-year-old boy, even helped adjust the noose in front of the forty witnesses. As a reverend prayed, Horn and another condemned man sang "Keep Your Hand upon the Throttle and Your Eye upon the Rail." A famous army scout, Indian fighter, and cattle detective, Horn was self-educated and served as a tracker for the party that captured the Apache leader Geronimo. He left behind a 160,000-word history of his career. Horn claimed innocence in the crime for which he went to the gallows.

No, I have nothing to say except that I am sorry and that I hope all my friends will profit by my experience. Good-bye friends, good-bye all. God bless you all.

JAMES MARTIN, convicted of murder, Montana. Executed February 23, 1904

Martin refused to tell the press his real name to keep his family from finding out that he was a murderer. Before his execution, Martin had his lawyer write a letter to his father that said that he was serving a brief sentence in jail but he was sick and not expected to survive. After the execution, it was revealed that Martin's family had known for some time of his situation and that prison authorities had decided not to tell him so as to spare his feelings.

After taking off her eyeglasses:

These are for my sister. Please see that she gets them.

MARY MABEL ROGERS, convicted of murder, Vermont.
Executed December 8, 1905

Rogers, age twenty-two, faced her execution "with the stoical calm-
ness she has maintained since her arrest." She had chloroformed her
husband Marcus and rolled him into a river to drown with the help
of "a half witted boy," Leon Perham. Granted two reprieves by the
state of Vermont, Rogers waited three years before her death sentence was carried out after a decree from the U.S. Supreme Court.

*Sheriff Taylor: Bill, for God's sake, if you are guilty, do not go before your Maker with
a lie on your lips.*

Baird: I am innocent.

W. C. BAIRD, convicted of murder, Tennessee. Executed May 24, 1907

Even at the moment of his death, Baird proclaimed his innocence.
He was labeled a wife killer but claimed that highwaymen had shot
his wife after the couple was stopped on the road near Fayetteville,
Tennessee.

Gentlemen, I presume you have come here to witness the execution of a murderer but while that is the word for my crime, I am not a murderer at heart. But the law requires my execution, and I am ready.

EDWARD DELEHANTE (AKA DELAHANTY), convicted of murder, California.
Executed December 6, 1912

Delehante was already serving a fourteen-year assault charge in
San Quentin when the murder took place. As the prisoners lined

up for breakfast one morning, Delehante stabbed two men, one of whom, William Kaufman, died from his wounds. Delehante's defense rested on the accusation that Kaufman had teased him to the point of madness.

Four perjurers sent me to this. I did not have a fair trial. I am a Socialist and would rather die than live under the present oligarchy. It was a long, hard fight I made, but I lost. I surrender, but am not conquered. I will take my medicine. There have been none in my family who would not take his medicine.

JOHN GOODWIN, convicted of murder, Arizona. Executed May 13, 1913

After he deserted the army at Fort Apache with his friend William Stewart, Goodwin killed two men who had gone to the San Carlos Reservation to hunt deer. One of the deer hunters had kicked Stewart's dog after it bit him. Goodwin and Stewart were sentenced to life imprisonment for the murders, but their lawyer thought he could reduce the sentence with a retrial. The new verdict led Goodwin to the gallows.

I will raise mine eye unto the hills, whence cometh my help . . .

ROSWELL C. F. SMITH, convicted of murder, Illinois.
Executed February 13, 1915

Smith killed a four-year-old girl, Hazel Weinstein, by luring her into an alley with candy and then strangling her with a strip of her dress. He returned the body to her home, where her parents immediately contacted the police. Called a "physical defective and degenerate" by the *Chicago Daily Tribune,* Smith received several mental health examinations but was found to have been mentally solvent at the time of the murder.

They can't kill a smile!

HARRISON GIBSON, convicted of murder, Montana.
Executed February 16, 1917

Gibson was one of a group of seven railroad workers who attacked and robbed three men on another train. Gibson, along with Lesley Fahley and James Foster, shot their victims after the robbery was over; the three were convicted and hanged together. Before the execution, a local newspaper quoted Gibson as saying: "Say, Mistah Sherrif, Ah've got a bad taste in my mouf this mawnin. There's a red apple down in my pocket and Ah'd like jess' one bite before Ah leaves. [Eats the apple.] All right, let's go."

Reportedly, Gibson had a huge smile on his face as they brought the black cap down over his head.

I shouldn't have killed those bank messengers. Maybe my death on the gallows will even the score.

EDWARD BLACKIE WHEED, convicted of murder, Illinois.
Executed February 15, 1918

While his accomplice fainted when taken to the gallows, veteran thief Wheed "kept cool and did some praying," according to the *Chicago Daily Tribune.* Wheed had killed two bank messengers with a sawed-off shotgun during a seven-thousand-dollar payroll robbery. He was captured "after a battle with several hundred policemen."

Are—they—really—going—to—hang—me? Don't—let—them. Save me. Jesus—Mary—Joseph. My little baby! My wife! . . . I'm—going—my—rest. Take—care—me. Where are you, Mr. Meisterheim [his jailer]? Talk to me.

Meisterheim: "Be brave, Frank. It'll be over in a minute."
Shake hands once more then. Are they—really going—to hang me?

FRANK CAMPIONE, convicted of robbery and murder, Illinois. Executed October 14, 1920

Part of the Cardinella Gang, Campione and company were responsible for more than four murders and 250 holdups and burglaries, according to authorities. The gang killed Albert Kubalanzo for $6.30. During the months he was in jail and on trial, Campione sang lullabies to his pillow night and day. Even when admitting that he had been feigning madness, Campione held the pillow. "I'll die happy if you let me keep this pillow with me," he said. "It reminds me of my baby son."

My last wish is that Sam Cardinella hang, too. He's responsible for me being here. He headed the gang. It is sweet to die for a mother, sister and a brother. I forgive all who have done anything against me. I want to thank the sheriff and the jailer and all who have been good . . .

NICHOLAS VIANA, convicted of murder, Illinois. Executed December 10, 1920

The nineteen-year-old Viana said that he had walked into a pool hall one day and a week later became a criminal. Viana murdered a saloon owner during a holdup. He spent his last hours with his mother singing "Mother o' Mine" at her request. On the way to the death cell he sang "Miserere."

Written, to Sheriff Charles W. Peters:

Dear Sir—Is this a fair proposition? You have been quoted often as saying that public hangings would be a deterrent to crime. I disagree with you. I think that hangings, in public or in the secrecy of the county jail, are barbarous and obscene. And yet, for the benefit of the hypocrites who say they believe as I think you really do, what do you say to this? I am the next on the executioner's list. I go Friday unless the Governor intervenes. I want all the people who are whooping it up for public executions for public example to see me go, if I do go. I don't think 5 percent of them will have the nerve to stick it out, but there will be less talk and more thinking afterwards. My suggestion on this is that if you must hang me, do it in Grant Park—and invite the world. Yours sincerely, Edward Brislane.

Spoken:

I am against this horrible form of murder by the state, but I would rather be standing here for the crime that, so help me God, I never remember committing, than to be sitting down there eagerly waiting to see a man die. Let the state of Illinois take shame upon itself. Goodbye.

EDWARD J. BRISLANE, convicted of murder, Illinois. Executed February 11, 1921

While robbing the Crawford Theater, Brislane shot its manager, William Mills. "I shot Mills," he said. "There was no reason. I was drunk and a damned fool." Sheriff Peters rejected Brislane's suggestion to have him hanged in Grant Park.

I have something to say, but not at this time.

GROVER CLEVELAND REDDING, convicted of murder, Illinois. Executed June 24, 1921

Redding had claimed that he was the prince of Abyssinia and was just trying to bring the people of his race back to their homeland. During a riot that was started by Redding and his followers, two were shot to death. Redding had built up a following with his anti-government and religiously motivated teachings.

Old gal, old pal,
You left me all alone—
Old gal, old pal,
I'm just a rolling stone—
Old pal, why don't you
Answer me . . .

CARL WANDERER, convicted of murder, Illinois. Executed September 30, 1921

Wanderer remained calm the day before his hanging, refusing playing cards and shunning gifts from fellow prisoners. Prison officials tried to get Wanderer to confess to the murder of his wife and unborn child, but he would not. On the way to the death cell, Wanderer explained that he was not afraid to die. He said that he had fought in France and has always been ready to go.

The day before his execution:

They won't hurt my feelings when they hang me. It is nothing to dread.

EUGENE WEEKS, convicted of robbery and murder, Iowa. Executed September 15, 1922

On the morning of Weeks's execution, he joked with the judge who sentenced him, and asked to be brought to the gallows early so he could address the crowd waiting to see him hang. Weeks spent that time telling the crowd that his accomplice in the murder was not guilty and should not also receive the death penalty. According to reports, Weeks was hung by the first ordained minister to carry out an execution.

Dope started me on my way. I've seen the time I'd give my life for the stuff. Now I'm giving it away any way.

GEORGE DONNELLY, convicted of murder, California. Executed February 23, 1923

A "cell tender" at Folsom Prison, Donnelly was serving fourteen years for a drugstore robbery. As the prisoners were lined up for supper, Donnelly overheard Earl Morse and another inmate fighting. He made his way toward the men and stabbed Morse in the back of the neck with a makeshift knife. Morse lived long enough to identify his attacker.

Beautiful world . . . I've forgiven everybody. . . . I haven't a thing to say. Turn 'er loose. . . . Goodbye, Doc. . . . You're a wonderful old boy. I haven't got a thing against any-

body in the world. I forgive everybody. I can do that because of this wonderful Jewish rabbi. That's all. Goodbye.

CHARLES BIRGER, convicted of murder, Illinois. Executed April 19, 1928

A gang leader in southern Illinois, Birger was convicted of hiring
two men to murder the mayor of West City. Birger scoffed and jeered
during his sanity trial while deputies were trying to testify, and at
one point he got up and remarked, "We'll take a smoke on that,
judge, as you can't do any more to me than you already have." When
asked where he wanted to be buried, Birger said, "A Catholic cemetery because that's the last place the devil would look for a Jew."

Written request to the governor:

. . . my heart be removed from my remains and that it
be sent to N. M. Wheatley. So that he may gaze upon the
heart of a man who, through his cowardice, caused the
ignoble death of a man better then himself.

EDGAR LAPIERRE (AKA EDGAR CARL DENMAN, GEORGE WARNER),
convicted of murder, California. Executed February 15, 1929

Hailing from Canada, LaPierre made his living in the United States
as a career criminal in cooperation with his wife and an accomplice.
After twenty-two burglaries, LaPierre's wife found the police at her
doorstep holding a warrant for their arrest. The situation quickly
degenerated, giving way to gunfire. LaPierre fired the shot that fatally wounded Officer William Davis. While on death row for murder, he and inmates Perry Coen, Louis Lazarus, and John Malone
nearly escaped by digging two tunnels through the prison wall, but
were caught by a guard. LaPierre believed that he landed on the gallows somehow through the efforts of N. M. Wheatley, his former
employer.

I have something of interest to tell—

PAUL ROWLAND, convicted of murder, California.
Executed September 27, 1929

Serving time for a robbery, Rowland approached Alger Morrison, a man whom he claimed as a good friend, and stabbed him with a five-inch homemade knife. Rumors circulated among the inmates that Rowland and Morrison had had a "degenerate" sexual relationship, rumors that Rowland found unendurable. His last words were cut short as the trap sprang from beneath his feet.

The world loves a good sport and hates a bad loser.

EVA DUGAN, convicted of murder, Arizona. Executed February 21, 1930

Convicted of murdering A. J. Mathis, Dugan first tried to tie the crime to a mysterious figure named Jack. She then later claimed insanity, saying, "Anybody can look at me and see I'm bughouse." Rejecting last-minute religious consolation, she said, "I'm going to die as I lived." The quote above comes from an interview, when she responded to a question about her "iron will."

What made her death most notable was its botched outcome: her head severed from her body as she plunged through the trapdoor.

A prayer—please, say a prayer for me.

GORDON STEWART NORTHCOTT, convicted of murder, California.
Executed October 2, 1930

In his book *88 Men and 2 Women,* prison warden Clinton T. Duffy wrote that Northcott admitted to molesting, torturing, and killing as many as twenty young men and boys in what became known as the Wineville Chicken Coop Murders. The woman Northcott knew as his mother, Sarah Louise Northcott, initially confessed to the crimes herself but ultimately could not protect him from the gallows. Northcott's story is central to Clint Eastwood's film *Changeling*.

Make it snappy.

CHARLES H. SIMPSON, convicted of murder, California.
Executed July 17, 1931

Known as "the Torch Slayer," Simpson was already a convicted car thief and burglar when he entered Albina Voorhies's grocery store. Simpson had known Voorhies because she rented the building from his father. Recognizing him, Voorhies turned her back to get him some cookies. That's when Simpson struck her in the back of the head with a police club. Simpson eventually tied her to a chair, hit her again, and poured coal oil on her clothes, which he then set on fire. Simpson's nerve faltered—he tried to take Voorhies to the bathroom to put the fire out—but by then the fire had spread. Panicking, Simpson left her in the store to bury the club and burn the clothes he wore. Simpson could give no reason for his actions other than robbery. He had taken three dollars from the cash register.

Written statement:

There's only one person on earth lower than me and that's the one who told this affair to my mother.

GEORGE HOFFMAN, convicted of murder and robbery, Montana.
Executed August 29, 1933

Hoffman did not want his eighty-two-year-old mother to know that her son was a murderer, so he told her that he was in California. An unidentified person told Mrs. Hoffman the truth in time for her to visit Hoffman twice before the execution, much to his displeasure. Hoffman made no final statement on the gallows and left only this note.

I want to warn others of my race. I wish some of them were here to see how we go. It's awful.

JOHNNY JONES, convicted of rape, Mississippi. Executed March 16, 1934

As part of a large spectacle, Jones, twenty-three, and two other young African American men were hung in front of a crowd that mocked and shouted at them while on the platform. Jones was buried in a plain coffin and dumped into a grave that would never be marked.

At least one source spelled Jones's first name "Johnnie."

Written statement:

Just a few lines to you as I depart of this world. I want you to know that I regret and I am sorry for what I have done. I am not sorry because I have to go, but for the wrong I have done to others. I am not afraid to die. Do not forget the Lord; to you all good-bye.

Spoken statement:

It is just this, I am sorry for what I have done. Although I am not sorry that I am leaving this world because I feel I am going to something better. I hope you will always pray through life because you don't know what way you will be called out. A few minutes before this happened if anyone had told me that I would be here, I would have said they were crazy. But remember, anything can happen to anybody. You can walk out on the street and die of heart trouble. Or you can go out on the street and get run over. I think that will be all.

GEORGE CRINER, convicted of murder, Montana. Executed October 16, 1935

Criner came home very drunk one night and tried to take his girl-friend's diamond ring. She refused to let him, and he beat her with an iron poker and cut her with a pocketknife, then shot the police officer who tried to intervene. At the preliminary hearing, Criner said that he very much wished he hadn't been there.

The ending of Bud Kimball's six-stanza poem "Bud Kimball's Philosophy":

I've been enmeshed and now I must pay
An unjust penalty in my ensnared despair
My eyes are blind but not my mind
Still my heart is kind

EARL BUD KIMBALL, convicted of murder, California. Executed May 22, 1936

Kimball, age twenty-one, shot business partner James Kennett twice in the head with a rifle and caved in his skull with a pick after Kennett flashed a knife at him. He was convicted of murder and later admitted to killing twenty-five other men. Kimball later re-tracted his statement, saying: "I told them all of that stuff out to devilment to get more bananas and cigarettes."

I have a right to choose the way I die!

DOUGLAS VAN VLACK, convicted of murder, Idaho.
Executed December 9, 1937

Van Vlack kidnapped his ex-wife and killed her, as well as two police officers. A few hours before his hanging was scheduled, Van Vlack broke away from his guards and scrambled over the cell block to cling to the ceiling rafters. He stayed in the ceiling for a half an hour as his lawyer and the prison chaplain begged for him to come down; he jumped thirty feet below just before the guards entered the cell block with a net. Van Vlack's hanging was unsuccessful; technically he died the next day, December 10, after a few hours in a coma.

I wish to see you all in heaven some day. I'm going to glory. Good-bye.

ORVILLE ADKINS, convicted of kidnapping, West Virginia.
Executed March 21, 1938

Adkins plummeted to the concrete through the trapdoor before a noose could be put around his neck. According to an Associated Press account, "He was put on a stretcher and handed back through the trap." Adkins was hanged with two accomplices in "West Virginia's first execution for kidnapping." Their victim was Dr. James I. Seder, described as an "anti-saloon crusader." Seder died four days after his eleven-day-long captivity with the men.

I want to praise God I am being taken out of this world of sin tonight and I feel confident that you people will meet us all up there. God bless you all. Pray for my loved ones. That is all. [As the sheriff adjusted the noose:] Don't choke me.

W. LEE SIMPSON, convicted of murder, Montana.
Executed December 30, 1939

Simpson had a list of sixteen people labeled "Rats" whom he intended to kill. He succeeded in killing three of them—including a sheriff—before he was arrested. After he confessed, Simpson slashed his wrists with broken glass. He survived, but before he passed out from blood loss he wrote a note in his own blood. It said, "The result of a frame-up through my wife and . . ."

I can't see why this is being done to me.

WALTER BEYER, convicted of murder, Kansas. Executed July 10, 1945

A member of German General Rommel's Afrika Korps during World War II, Beyer was hanged along with four others for murdering a fellow POW at Fort Leavenworth Military Prison. A headline in the *New York Times* called them "the first war captives executed in the U.S." The execution was witnessed by only seven reporters. Beyer, who was considered the ringleader of the group, had beaten the POW to death because, in his eyes, he was a traitor.

There was so much hate in me then and it keeps building up and there was no release for it and I did not care what happened. The Doctors said I felt justified when I killed those people and they are right. I did. It was revenge I was after. The love that I was denied because my parents spent too much time doing church work and they still do, and forcing me to stay home and lead the life they wanted me to live. I got my revenge and I am not sorry now and never will be. . . . I've had enough of it, I want to die. I'm fed up with it all. I did kill those people to hurt my parents and their good standing in the church. Who failed me? It was not only my parents but myself and a lot of others. My life is a real mess now and I will be glad when it is all over with.

BARTON KAY KIRKHAM, convicted of robbery and murder, Utah. Executed June 7, 1958

Kirkham was an air force deserter who walked into a small grocery store with the intention of robbing it. When he was given a lesser amount of money than he believed was in the store, he brought the store owner into the back room, where he found another woman, and he laid them both on the floor and shot them. After his murder conviction Kirkham said that he chose to hang because of the novelty and publicity, and to inconvenience the state. The *St. Petersburg Times* recorded his last words as "I've asked God to forgive me."

I don't have any hard feelings. You're sending me to a better place.

RICHARD EUGENE HICKOCK, convicted of murder, Kansas.
Executed April 14, 1965

Hickock met Perry Smith in prison, where the two concocted a plan to rob the Clutter family of ten thousand dollars that they supposedly kept in a safe at home. After finding no money, the convicts murdered all four family members. Smith and Hickock's lives, trial, and crimes were the subject of Truman Capote's book *In Cold Blood*.

Capote recorded Hickock's final words slightly differently from newspaper accounts: "I just want to say I hold no hard feelings. You people are sending me to a better world than this ever was."

Then, Capote wrote, Hickock greeted the witnesses to his execution with a smile, saying, "Nice to see you."

I think it's a hell of a thing that a life has to be taken in this manner. I think capital punishment is legally and morally wrong.

PERRY EDWARD SMITH, convicted of murder, Kansas.
Executed April 14, 1965

The product of a broken home, Smith spent most of his life in and out of detention homes and prisons. In November 1959, he and Richard Hickcock broke into the home of the Clutter family in Holcomb, Kansas. Their purpose was to rob the family, whom they had heard possessed a safe containing ten thousand dollars. The pair found no such safe and murdered of all four members of the family.

In his book *In Cold Blood*, Truman Capote records Perry's last words as the above plus "Maybe I had something to contribute—It would be meaningless to apologize for what I did. Even inappropriate. But I do. I apologize."

I was asked by somebody, I don't remember who, if there was any way sex offenders could be stopped. I said no. I was wrong. I said there was no hope, no peace. There is peace. There is hope. I found both in the Lord Jesus Christ.

WESTLEY DODD, convicted of rape and murder, Washington. Executed January 5, 1993

Shortly after Dodd was released from prison for having kidnapped a seven-year-old boy, he was arrested for raping and killing three other small boys. Dodd himself admitted guilt, and during his incarceration he claimed numerous times that child molesters could not be reformed. In court, Dodd was even quoted as saying: "I must be executed before I have an opportunity to escape or kill someone else. If I do escape, I promise you I will kill and rape again, and I will enjoy every minute of it."

The *San Francisco Chronicle* reported: "[Dodd] chose hanging over lethal injection because, he said, he had hanged his youngest victim's body in a closet after killing him."

CHAPTER TWO

THE FIRING SQUAD

John Doyle Lee sat on his coffin.

In 1877, from this spot in Mountain Meadows, Utah, Lee delivered his final statement—a long, eloquent speech about his belief in the Church of Jesus Christ of Latter-day Saints and its founder, Joseph Smith. "There are thousands of people in the church, honorable, good-hearted, that I cherish in my heart," he said. He was less kind to church leader Brigham Young, whom Lee blamed for making him a scapegoat in what became known as the Mountain Meadows Massacre. "I have been sacrificed in a cowardly and dastardly manner," he said. "I declare I did nothing wrong designedly in this unfortunate affair."

Twenty years earlier, Lee had had a leading role in the slaughter of an estimated 120 Arkansas and Missouri emigrants traveling through Utah territory to California. The Mormon militia, fearing more of the persecution that had met them in Illinois and Missouri, attacked the convoy after tensions mounted between the emigrants and Mormon settlers. After a five-day siege, Lee negotiated the group's surrender under a white flag. The defeated men, women, and children were marched out of the area, believing they had secured the safety of their families. But at a prearranged signal, the militiamen turned and executed their unarmed prisoners. Only seventeen children were spared.

Initially, efforts were made to blame the deaths on local Paiute Indians, who also participated in the attacks. Almost two decades later, however, a territorial grand jury indicted nine white men for the mass murder, though only Lee was prosecuted (twice) and executed. An article in the *Salt Lake Tribune* the day after Lee's execution was headlined, in part, "Poetic Justice on the Bloody Fields of Mountain Meadows." Lee was returned to the scene of the crime to be executed, a rare occurrence in capital cases—even high-profile ones.

Even at that time, the firing squad was used sparingly. According to most records, an estimated 149 men have been executed by firing squad in the American colonies or the United States since 1608. Eighteen states have employed the firing squad. Except in Utah, the vast majority of executions by shooting took place well before the turn of the twentieth century, during the Revolutionary and Civil wars.

During wartime, the firing squad was employed for crimes such as desertion, cowardice, murder of a superior officer, and, at times, rape. In military forums the firing squad was often considered an honorable way to die. Prisoners of war were hung, not shot; bullets were reserved for officers of higher rank. The last American serviceman to die by firing squad was Pvt. Eddie Slovik, in France. He was shot for desertion January 31, 1945, by his own unit, much to the distaste of his fellow soldiers. Pvt. Slovik's last words and history are addressed later in this chapter. Except for a few notable cases documented in this chapter, few military final statements survive. In those that do, the soldier often responded "No, sir" when asked if he had any last words.

Nonmilitary executions by firing squad did occur prior to 1900, mostly in Utah, California, and Oklahoma. Utah is the only state to have used this method of capital punishment recently, in 1996, and is most famous for the high-profile capital case of Gary Gilmore. In 1977, Gilmore was the first prisoner put to death after the U.S. Supreme Court's moratorium on capital punishment. Gilmore's last words, as documented by Norman Mailer in his novel *Executioner's Song*, were "Let's do it!"

Under state law, those condemned in Utah had the option of choosing their own method of execution. Possibly because of the state's strong roots in the Mormon religion, it has been written, most prisoners favored firing squad because it adhered to the doctrine of "blood for blood" favored by founder Joseph Smith. Smith took his inspiration directly from the Bible's book of Genesis, in which God tells Noah's sons, "Whoso sheddeth man's blood, by man shall his blood be shed" (Genesis 9:6, King James Version). In his *Doctrines of Salvation*, Smith wrote: "The founders of Utah incorporated in the laws of the territory provisions for the capital punishment of those who willfully shed the blood of their fellow men. This law, which is now the law of the state, granted unto the condemned murderer the privilege of choosing for himself whether to die by hanging or whether to be shot, and thus have his blood shed in harmony with the law of God: and thus atone, so far as it is in his power to atone, for the death of his victim."

His successor, Brigham Young, echoed this belief. Young wrote that men should willingly choose and endorse blood atonement because "there are sins that men commit for which they cannot receive forgiveness in this world, or in that which is to come, and if they had their eyes open to see their true condition, they would be perfectly willing to have their blood spilt upon the ground, that the smoke thereof might ascend to heaven as an offering for their sins; and the smoking incense would atone for their sin; whereas, if such is not the case, they will stick to them and remain upon them in the spirit world." Not many final words, however, reflect this sentiment, and historians have debated the historical record of such a practice. In 1978, the LDS Church repudiated blood atonement.

In early last words recorded in Utah Territory there's often a sense of atmosphere, of time and custom. The prisoners sometimes spoke directly to their executioners. A firing squad didn't always find the paper target over their charge's heart, and stories of painful death resonate in the final statements of those facing execution in this manner. At one point in his speech, the Mountain Meadows Massacre's Lee spoke to the men pointing rifles at him: "Center on my heart, boys. Don't mangle my body."

Utah did away with the firing squad in 2004 because lawmakers believed that it let death row inmates go out in a "blaze of bullets" and drew too much media attention. State Representative Sheryl Allen said: "We have a media blitz when we have the firing squad.

Utah is a grand and wonderful, joyful place to live. When we get international media it should be for the goodness of our people, the beauty of the state, and not the method of execution." She added that prisoners who chose firing squad were engineering "one last magnificent manipulation of the system to bring attention to themselves."

The firing squad ban does not, however, apply to those sentenced before its enactment. And there's another loophole in the Utah code. Provo's *Daily Herald* recently observed: "If the U.S. Supreme Court were to decide that lethal injection is 'cruel and unusual' under the Constitution, Utah would simply revert to firing squads, which were long approved by the high court."

With my comrades I fought! With them I die!

JEAN BAPTISTE NOYAN, convicted of treason, Louisiana. Executed October 25, 1769

Noyan was of one five leaders executed in the Rebellion of 1768, a revolt by local settlers to stop the handover of the French-controlled Louisiana territory to Spain. Noyan was sentenced to hang on the same day as four other French ex-patriots, but there was no public executioner to drop the gallows. Noyan was marched into New Orleans' Place d'Armes with the others but, while handcuffed, was offered clemency from the governor. Noyan, a nephew of the founder of New Orleans, refused.

Gentlemen, I ask your pardon for all my offenses, and expect yours in return.

CHIEF ANTONIO GARRA, convicted of murder, California. Executed January 16, 1852

A Native American educated at San Luis Rey mission near San Diego, Chief Garra of the Cupenos tribe attempted to unite Californian tribes to attack and drive out white settlers. Federal soldiers refused to preside over Garra's trial but provided the ammunition for a citizens' militia to carry out the execution. Garra was tried before a militia court-martial, found guilty, and shot. January 10 has alternately been reported as his execution date.

Written:

I'm about to suffer death, which punishment I am willing to bear for a warning to others which may be led astray by bad company. Fellow soldiers, you should take

warning by me and keep out of bad company, and shun everything that is bad. Keep good company, and you will be respected by your worst enemies.

Oh! may God bless the officers of the Forty-Seventh New York Regiment for the kindness they have shown me, a wicked sinner. They have done everything that was in their power, and they brought me tracts to read and religious papers that led me the right road to my Savior. Oh! may God help and sustain them through the perils of battles, that they may come out victorious in them all, and God speed the time when peace shall once more be, and the friends that is here at war will be going home to their families.

WILLIAM W. LUNT (AKA ALBERT W. LUNT), convicted of desertion, South Carolina. Executed December 1, 1862

Union Pvt. Lunt had a youthful disposition that "led him into every species of childish vice," according to one newspaper account. He was convicted of both highway robbery and desertion to Confederate forces. While in enemy hands, Lunt divulged information that led to the death of one and the capture of seven others on the Union side. A *New York Times* correspondent wrote: "But Lunt's conduct with the rebels was so bad that even they refused to have his company, and returned him to our lines, with the request that deserters from them might be treated in a similar manner."

Lunt continued to profess his innocence before facing the firing squad. "I am willing to die, and it is a great deal better to die innocent than guilty. For the sake of my family, I want it published that I am innocent. Tell my fellow soldiers that I have been a hard boy, and done a good many wicked things, and they must take my death as a warning not to be led astray by bad company."

Just moments before Lunt was shot, he said, "Fellow soldiers: I want you to take warning by me, and seek salvation from the Lord before it is too late. I am not guilty of the crime which I am condemned to death for."

No complete final statement exists, but Jason Luce talked about his evil associates *and railed against those who* had betrayed him, *indicating his* desire to brand them before the world. *He proclaimed his lawyer to have been his betrayer, confessed to his sins, and said good-bye.*

JASON LUCE, convicted of murder, Utah. Executed January 12, 1864

Luce was convicted of murdering a man whom he had invited to his house for dinner. According to Luce, the man beat him for admitting that he was a Mormon. Later, when Luce happened to encounter the man, he pulled a bowie knife and nearly severed the man's head in retaliation for the beating. On the day of Luce's execution he was described as being cool, calm, and collected. He asked his brother to take care of a woman carrying his child.

Comrades: I want to acknowledge that I am guilty and that my punishment is just. But I want also that you should know that I did not desert because I lost faith in our cause. I believe we are on the right side, and I think it will succeed. But take warning from my example, and whatever comes do not desert the old flag for which I am proud to die.

WILLIAM E. ORMSLEY, convicted of desertion, Massachusetts. Executed February 7, 1864

A private in Company E, Second Massachusetts Cavalry, Ormsley deserted from picket duty in Virginia. A returning scouting party recognized him in an enemy attack, where they captured him. On the day of his execution, Ormsley requested to speak to the troops when delivering his final words.

Judge, I hope to meet you in heaven.

WILLIAM CAREY, convicted of murder, Arkansas. Executed July 29, 1864

Carey was executed, along with three other "bushwhackers," for leading a force of twenty-plus men disguised in Union uniforms and killing eight federal cavalrymen. At age nineteen, Carey was the youngest of the condemned. Before his death, he confessed to killing more than twenty-one men and waging a private war against the North, which also made him an outlaw among Confederates. On the day of his execution, Carey and three other men were taken from the jail to stand in a line beside their coffins. While shaking the judge advocate's hand, Carey delivered his final words.

I have but little to say this morning. Of course I feel that I am upon the brink of eternity, and the solemnities of eternity should rest upon my mind at the present. I have made out, or endeavored to do so, a manuscript and an abridged history of my life. This is to be published, sir. I have given my views and feelings with regard to all these things. I feel resigned to my fate. I feel as calm as a summer morning. I have done nothing intentionally wrong.

My conscience is clear before God and man, and I am ready to meet my Redeemer. I am not an infidel. I have not denied God or His mercy. I am a strong believer in those things.

The most I regret is parting with my family. Many of them are unprotected and will be left fatherless. When I speak of those little ones, they touch a tender chord within me. I have done nothing designedly wrong in this affair. I used my utmost endeavors to save these people.

I would have given worlds, were it at my command, to have avoided that calamity. But I could not. I am sacrificed to satisfy my feelings, and I am used to gratify parties, but I am ready to die. I have no fear. Death has no terror. No particle of mercy have I asked of the court or officials to spare my life. I shall never go to a worse place than the one I am now in. I have said it to my family, and I will say it today, that the Government of the United States sacrificed its best friend, and that is saying a great deal, but it is true.

I am a true believer in the gospel of Jesus Christ. I do not believe everything that is now practiced and taught by Brigham Young. I do not agree with him. I believe he is leading the people astray; but I believe in the gospel as it was taught in its purity by Joseph Smith in former days. I have my reasons for saying this. I need to make this man's will my pleasure, and did so for thirty years. See how and what I have come to this day. I have been sacrificed in a cowardly and dastardly manner. There are thousands of people in the church, honorable, good-hearted, that I cherish in my heart. I regret to leave my family. They are near and dear to me. These are things to rouse my sympathy.

I declare I did nothing wrong designedly in this unfortunate affair. I did everything in my power to save all the emigrants, but I am the one that must suffer. Having said this I feel resigned. I ask the Lord my God to extend his mercy to me and receive my spirit. My labors are done.

To his executioners:
Center on my heart, boys. Don't mangle my body.

JOHN DOYLE LEE, AKA JOHN D. LEE, convicted of murder, Utah. Executed March 23, 1877

Lee's biography begins this chapter, but a few more details: Lee asked a photographer present to send each of his three wives a copy of the photograph taken just prior to his death. Though Lee was excommunicated from the Church of Jesus Christ of Latter-day Saints, the ruling was posthumously reversed. Several versions of this speech have been published, each of a different length. His last line has also been reported as "Let them shoot the balls through my heart! Don't let them mangle my body!"

I give you my word. I intend to die like a man, looking my executioners right in the eye.

After the initial volley of bullets failed to kill him:
Oh my God! Oh my God! They have missed!

WALLACE WILKERSON, convicted of murder, Utah. Executed May 16, 1879

Wilkerson, age forty-five, refused the traditional blindfold and restraints during his execution for killing a man over a disputed card game. A cigar remained in his hand during his final moments. Unfortunately for Wilkerson, the bullets missed his vital organs, and he struggled for breath for fifteen to twenty-seven minutes, depending on the account, before dying. A reporter from the *Ogden Junction* newspaper criticized the execution, writing: "The French guillotine never fails."

Gentleman, I have come to meet my fate. Had justice been done at my first trial, I would not be here today for this purpose. I have no ill-will toward any man living, and am prepared and ready to meet my God.

FREDERICK HOPT, convicted of murder, Utah. Executed August 11, 1887

Hopt was convicted of murdering the Provo city marshal. He claimed that he murdered him because the marshal had abused him while he was incarcerated in the Provo jail. Before Hopt was executed, he gave his few possessions to fellow inmates and requested that his body be buried outside the prison instead of being donated to science.

Boys, I am told that you want to see me die game. That's just the way I am going to die. I shall die like a man for I am a man amongst men.

After saying he didn't want to die hungry and being offered food:
No hot coffee? Then give me hot whiskey. I like that better anyway.

Just before the shots rang out:
[I do not want to] die like an Indian.

ENOCH DAVIS, convicted of murder, Utah. Executed September 14, 1894

No minister was present at the execution of Davis for the crime of murdering his wife. He refused any spiritual counsel, saying he did not believe in any religion. During his final moments, Davis asked the sharpshooters to come out from behind the tent that shielded them, as he preferred to face his executioners. The riflemen did not comply with his wishes.

You never killed a gamer man in all your life than you will today.

PATRICK COUGHLIN, convicted of murder, Utah.
Executed December 15, 1896

Coughlin moved from Massachusetts to Utah with the construction of the Union Pacific railroad. Described as an angry child, he had accumulated numerous charges by age twenty-one. Coughlin and an accomplice were convicted of killing two law officers. He was offered the choice between hanging and firing squad. Coughlin chose the latter.

To this world I want to say, and I swear by the heavens above, by the earth beneath and by all that I hold near and dear on earth, that I am not guilty of that cowardly murder of my dearest friend. I ask, therefore, no man's pardon for aught that I have done in life. I am confident that my life is an example to most people.

Seconds before being shot:
I have nothing to say except that I am innocent.

PETER MORTENSEN, convicted of murder, Utah.
Executed November 20, 1903

Because of his cocky attitude, Mortensen was so unpopular with other prisoners that during an escape his fellow prisoners opened every cell but his. On the day of his execution he praised guards, the warden, and other officers involved in his case, and he declined an opiate and a cigar. After Mortensen was executed, pieces of the bullets were given to officers as souvenirs.

So long, fellows.

FRANK ROSE, convicted of murder, Utah. Executed April 22, 1904

The bravado of Frank Rose was well documented in Utah publications during his trial. On the day of his execution Rose walked with "almost a swagger to the death chair." Rose had shot his wife on Christmas Day and left his two-year-old son in the room with the dead mother for two days without food or water. Rose refused to enter a plea to the court, and when a not-guilty plea was entered for him, he refused to offer any evidence on his behalf. In a statement released the day before his death, Rose confessed to many murders and burglaries throughout the West. Officials doubted whether he was speaking truthfully.

I have nothing to say, sheriff. All I ask is that you get it over with as quickly as possible and please don't blindfold me.

HARRY THORNE, convicted of robbery and murder, Utah.
Executed September 26, 1912

Called a "highwayman" in the papers, eighteen-year-old Thorne was executed for killing a grocery clerk. Thorne showed great interest in the executions preceding his. "Well, did he die like a man?" he would ask guards.

When asked if he was ready:
No, not yet. I want my breakfast first.

After being refused food and read his death warrant:
Everybody knows that and I don't want to hear it. Let's go now.

He continued to utter curses and threats at the presiding sheriff.

FRANK ROMEO, convicted of robbery and murder, Utah.
Executed February 20, 1913

An Italian coal miner, Romeo shot a manager of a gambling house who was carrying the day's take to his home. Romeo and an accomplice were chased nearly fifty miles before capture. During execution proceedings, Romeo appeared extremely agitated. Two guards had to support him into the death chair, and "desperately he tried to find an excuse to delay the execution," according to reports.

The *Washington Post* recorded his last words as "For God's sake, don't shoot me—not that way! I know I chose shooting when the judge asked me whether I preferred shooting or hanging, but I don't want to be shot—not now. Hang me, but don't shoot me!"

Gentlemen, I die with a clear conscience. I never did anything wrong in my life. I die fighting, not like a coward. Well, I'm going, good-bye.

Shouting as the prison officer started to give the command to shoot:

Fire!

JOE HILL (AKA JOSEPH HILLSTROM), convicted of murder, Utah. Executed November 19, 1915

Born Joel Emmanuel Hagglund in Sweden, he changed his name upon arriving in California. A convert to socialism, Hillstrom was a singer and songwriter whose songs, composed under the name Joe Hill, were published in union newspapers and sung on picket lines and demonstrations.

While in Utah, where he organized a successful strike against the United Construction Company, Hill was arrested and charged with the murders of J. G. Morrison, a grocery store owner, and his son. The Industrial Workers of the World (IWW) organization, or Wobblies, came to Hill's defense, contending that he had been framed due to his political activity. President Woodrow Wilson and author Helen Keller were among those who campaigned for clemency. Eventually Utah's governor refused.

On his last day, Hill fought off his jailers, wielding a broken broom handle as a weapon. Sheriff J. C. Corless had to be summoned to reason with Hill.

"Joe, this is all nonsense. . . . You promised to die like a man," Corless said.

Newspaper accounts said Hill "hesitated a moment, then yielded." He calmed and said: "Well, I'm through. But you can't blame a man for fighting for his life."

Before his execution, Hill wrote Bill Haywood, an IWW leader. "I die like a true blue rebel. Don't waste any time in mourning. Organize . . ." Mourners in Chicago wore sashes that echoed this sentiment: "Don't mourn—organize, Joe Hill."

Hill's case was included in the 1992 book *In Spite of Innocence* among almost two dozen cases in which the editors believed "an innocent person was executed."

Several folk songs were written about Hill, and his last will, written as a poem, was set to music. It read:

My Last Will

My will is easy to decide
For there is nothing to divide
My kin don't need to fuss and moan
"Moss does not cling to a rolling stone."
My body — Oh. — If I could choose
I would to ashes it reduce
And let the merry breezes blow
My dust to where some flowers grow

Perhaps some fading flower then
Would come to life and bloom again

This is my Last and Final Will
Good luck to all of you.

Joe Hill

Forgiveness. The most bitter of my friends are forgiven. I am ready to go, and the day of reckoning will come. That cannot be avoided. If only I could make them understand, but I can't. May the Almighty God protect all that I leave behind and see that even to my enemies no harm shall befall.

GEORGE GARDNER, convicted of murder, Utah. Executed August 31, 1923

When Gardner's former business partner, Joseph Irvine, and a police officer arrived to retrieve property that Irvine claimed was his, Gardner invited them into his home and then opened fire on them both. His examining psychologist called him "irresponsible and only 60 percent normal" because of a traumatic childhood. Three appeals were undertaken to further determine his psychological state, but he was found to be sane.

I have tried the best I could to give the exact truth to the pardon board in every particular. I believe—and it is my dying statement—that Vadney was the smaller of the two robbers. I am as innocent today as the day my mother gave me birth. I am prepared to meet my maker in peace.

My conscience is clear and undisturbed. I have never in my life harmed my wife or any other human being, to my knowledge.

I consider that the board of pardons held one idea—that I am guilty. They consider me a condemned man and would not believe me although I spoke as near the truth as I could. I call upon God as a witness to what I say. I forgive all. I shall soon see God and it shall be in perfect peace.

I will see my wife—she will meet me with outstretched arms. She knows I never harmed her but I was always kind and good, not only to her but to everyone.

My brothers have been loyal and done everything they could, but they apparently could not change the decree. I do not think the Supreme Court treated me right.

They had the one idea that I was guilty. I am not. In a few minutes I will be ushered into eternity where all secrets are known. Over there they will judge me and they will say I am innocent.

After the blindfold was placed on his head:
Say goodbye to my brother and daughter.

OMER R. WOODS, convicted of murder, Utah. Executed January 18, 1924

To the last moment, Woods staunchly denied his guilt in the killing of his sickly wife. He allegedly killed her in her bed and then attempted to set fire to the body to collect insurance. Woods maintained that robbers had killed her and even named one of them.

Written:
I shall not feel that I have died in vain if my passing will show to you that there is only one road that leads to happiness and that is the straight and narrow path of honesty, virtue, and truth. Please do not treat this as only the dying admonition of a fellow convict. Its observance by you will mean to me that my sacrifice may prove your salvation.

HENRY C. HETT (ALIAS GEORGE ALLEN), convicted of murder, Utah. Executed February 20, 1925

When Hett's verdict was read, he looked to his attorney and said, "Now what do we do?" Hett, a longtime criminal, was found guilty at trial and at two hearings by the state board of pardons, and he eventually refused to ask for a reprieve from the governor. Two years earlier, after being stopped and questioned by a police sergeant, Hett had pulled a revolver and shot him, paralyzing the sergeant. During his imprisonment, Hett reportedly said, "I'm sorry I shot you, Sergeant Pierce." The officer died four months later.

Ere this will have been handed to and read by you, my soul will have been wafted before its Maker. My last wish and desire on this earth will be realized when I am able to have published my closing words in the form of advice to the youth of the nation. To you I say obey your parents, seek the advice of your elders, and live an honest and clean life with thoughts of brighter and cleaner things, at all times seek the finer things in life, and by all means obey the teachings of God and be able through these teachings to receive ultimate celestial glory.

EDWARD MCGOWAN, convicted of murder and rape, Utah.
Executed February 5, 1926

The first black man to be executed in Utah, McGowan was convicted of raping a mother and her daughters, and killing the woman's husband at their home, where he had been a guest. McGowan's last request was to die wearing an old pair of rubber shoes and not his boots on. Inmates raised money so that McGowan could receive a proper burial.

My God! Have mercy on me.

DELBERT GREEN, convicted of murder, Utah. Executed July 10, 1936

Green had been convicted of murdering his wife because, he said, she was unfaithful. The same evening, he also killed his stepfather and mother-in-law. After he was convicted and sentenced to death, he tried to plead insanity on the grounds that his whole family had a history of mental illness—his father and aunt had been sent to asylums, and his grandfather committed suicide. In the days before his execution, Green's mother and fellow inmates wrote letters attempting to sway the governor to commute his sentence. Green's daughter, who was seven at the time of his execution, defended her father almost forty years later in an interview with the *Ogden Standard Examiner*, saying that he would have done anything for her mother, who was unfaithful.

When I was a kid raising hell everyone told me I'd end up on the gallows, so I thought I'd fool them. Also, there's an old saying I like: "Live by the sword and die by the sword."

JOHN DEERING, convicted of murder and robbery, Utah.
Executed October 31, 1938

Deering had spent seventeen years in jail after a robbery and shooting. Suspected of a second robbery, he was captured in Michigan and confessed to the murder of Oscar Meredith Jr. in a Salt Lake City robbery to avoid a fifteen-year Michigan jail sentence. Deering agreed to be hooked up to a machine that measured his heart rate during execution proceedings. When he was asked for a final statement, his heartbeat "fluttered wildly, then calmed after he spoke," according to a *Chicago Daily Tribune* article.

It's getting light. What's holding those fellows up?

ROBERT WALTER AVERY, convicted of murder, Utah.
Executed February 5, 1943

"When a man faces death like I am," said Avery in a prison interview, "life looks good under any circumstances." Convicted in the murder of Detective Hoyt L. Gates, Avery blamed his criminal ways on a life of drugs. In a ten-page autobiography written prior to his death, Avery wrote: "Death to me is simply the cashing in of a stack of chips all of us receive at birth and while I have lost heavily in the game of life, I intend to face the cashier as a good loser."

The condemned shoved Sheriff John R. Watson with his elbows when asked for a last statement. As his death warrant was read aloud, he stuck out his tongue.

AUSTIN COX, convicted of murder, Utah. Executed June 19, 1944

Little was written about Cox except that he "ran wild" in Ogden with a shotgun, killing five people, including a district judge.

A member of the firing squad: "Try to take it easy, Eddie. Try to make it easy on yourself—and on us."

Don't worry about me. I'm okay. They're not shooting me for deserting the United States Army—thousands of guys have done that. They're shooting me for bread I stole when I was 12 years old.

EDWARD DONALD "EDDIE" SLOVIK, convicted of desertion, northeastern France. Executed January 31, 1945

On the French front lines Pvt. Slovik's rifle unit suffered heavy shelling, and the young private attempted desertion twice. The second time he was recaptured in Belgium. In the final months of the war, Allied commander Dwight D. Eisenhower personally ordered Slovik's execution in order to discourage would-be deserters. It wasn't until 1987 that Slovik's remains were shipped home to Detroit.

So long.

JAMES JOSEPH ROEDL, convicted of robbery and murder, Utah.
Executed July 13, 1945

Roedl killed Abigail Williams with a hammer after she picked up him and an accomplice while they were hitchhiking. According to authorities, one of them sang the pop tune "Love Letters in the Sand" to signal the murder. Just before his execution, Roedl served cherry pie and coffee to the press, laughing and joking. According to the prison chaplain, however, Roedl "broke into sobs" when he was strapped to the "old wooden chair" used in previous executions.

I'm ready to go. No one will miss me. My life has been worthless.

RAY GARDNER, convicted of rape and murder, Utah.
Executed September 29, 1951

Gardner raped and killed seventeen-year-old Shirley Jean Gretzinger, who answered his call for a babysitter. He applied repeatedly for clemency but was denied. The location of his execution was improvised in an unfinished corridor of Utah's new state penitentiary.

As a black hood was fastened over his head:

Do I have to wear this thing? I have nothing to be ashamed of. I am innocent; I have no malice against anyone.

DON JESSE NEAL, convicted of murder, Utah. Executed July 1, 1955

As Neal was shopping with a female companion, police waited for the couple to come out of a store to arrest them for possession of a stolen car. Not long after their arrest, an officer escorting them to the station was fatally shot in the stomach. Though Neal was convicted of shooting, some believed he was innocent. At trial, it had been asserted that his female accomplice's purse was never searched for the pistol.

His last words have also been recorded as "Wilma, confess your crime or I will die."

Neal also took an ad out in local newspapers before he was executed. It read: "Wilma Tulley, for God's Sake write Governor, confess your crime or I will die July 1. Hurry don't let me die."

In a joint statement issued hours before their execution:

May our tragic lives and ending serve as a warning to all—young and old. [We blame our crimes on] coming from broken homes, growing up in neglect and not having a fair chance in life.

MELVIN SULLIVAN AND VERNE BRAASCH, convicted of robbery and murder, Utah. Executed May 11, 1956

Sullivan was shot side by side with his partner in crime, Braasch. The men were convicted together of the murder of a service station attendant during a twenty-dollar robbery in Beaver, Utah. Their executions had been moved back four times.

When asked if he had any last request:
Why yes, a bulletproof vest!

JAMES RODGERS, convicted of murder, Utah. Executed March 30, 1960

Under Utah's "double choice" law, Rodgers could be either hanged or shot for killing a coworker at a uranium mining camp. He chose the firing squad, the thirty-seventh man to do so in Utah. When the sentence was carried out, four of the five riflemen fired into his heart, with one using a blank cartridge. This ceremonial practice was to ensure that each of the riflemen could believe he might have not delivered a fatal shot.

Let's do it!

GARY GILMORE, convicted of murder, Utah. Executed January 17, 1977

With a hood over his head and a paper target attached to his chest, Gilmore became the first man executed in nearly ten years since the U.S. Supreme Court's reinstatement of the death penalty. Gilmore confessed to shooting motel clerk Bennie Bushnell, age twenty-five, twice in the head while he lay on the floor during a robbery. Gilmore's troubled life was chronicled by Norman Mailer in his book *Executioner's Song*, and he was portrayed by actor Tommy Lee Jones in the TV adaptation of the book.

I would like to say for my family and my friends, as the poem was written, "Remember me, but let me go."

JOHN ALBERT TAYLOR, convicted of rape and murder, Utah. Executed January 26, 1996

Taylor's was the first Utah firing-squad execution since 1977. Convicted of raping and strangling an eleven-year-old girl, Taylor lifted his chin for the prison warden to secure a strap around his neck before his execution was carried out. Sherron King, the mother of Taylor's victim, sat alone in a hotel the night of the execution. "I felt something pass through my heart around midnight and felt he was dead," she told the Associated Press.

"Part of me wanted him to die and the other part of me felt bad for him," she said. "My heart goes out to his mom."

CHAPTER THREE

THE ELECTRIC CHAIR

The Age of Science brought new ideas, new technologies, and with them, a new humanity to capital punishment. Gone would be the barbarism of the noose and hangman, or so went conventional wisdom just before the dawn of the twentieth century. New York State's newly elected governor, David B. Hill, campaigned to retire the gallows altogether. "The present mode of executing prisoners by hanging has come down to us from the Dark Ages," he said in 1885. Hill commissioned a study of more than forty methods of execution, including one promoted by inventor Thomas Alva Edison: the electric chair. "This is a step forward in the cause of humanity," wrote the *New York Times* in 1888 as New York legislators passed an act abolishing hanging and replaced it with electrocution.

Edison, the visionary "Wizard of Menlo Park," had already brought the world the phonograph and electric light. Edison's staff had been electrocuting dogs and cats publicly via Nikola Tesla's alternative current, or AC, which Edison had previously criticized as dangerous compared to his own direct current, or DC. Yet no human being had ever been subject to electrocution as a form of capital punishment.

Once Gov. Hill cleared the legal pathway, convicted murderer William Kemmler became the first to face the electric chair on August 6, 1890. Kemmler was cautious, almost curious, about the process. As a deputy sheriff cut his hair to make room for electrodes, Kemmler told his jailers, "I'll promise that I won't make any trouble. . . . Don't let them experiment on me more than they ought to." In his final statement, Kemmler said: "Gentlemen, I wish you all good luck. I believe I'm going to a good place, and I'm ready to go. A great deal has been written about me that's untrue. I'm bad enough. It's cruel to make me out worse."

Though officially these were his last words, Kemmler had more to say. As in many later cases of electrocution, the prisoner participated in the process. After a pair of doctors attached electrodes to his head and the base of his spine, Kemmler remained circumspect and cooperative. "Take your time, warden, and do it right," he said, now strapped to the chair. "There's no rush. I don't want to take any chances on this thing, you know."

"It won't hurt you, Bill," the warden replied. "I'll be with you all the time." After the electrodes were moistened with a watering can, leather straps were applied to Kemmler's chin and forehead. But it wasn't tight enough. "Warden," Kemmler requested, "make that a little tighter. We want everything all right, you know." After a few more adjustments, one of the attending physicians, Dr. Edward Charles Spitzka, said, "God bless you, Kemmler," to which Kemmler replied, "Thank you."

A moment later, on the warden's cue, the dynamo clicked—causing every muscle in Kemmler's body to strain. A fingernail cut into his hand so deeply that blood ran down the arm of the chair. Kemmler's hands and face burned red. Seventeen seconds later, the current was shut off. The body sagged. Spitzka pronounced Kemmler dead. Another physician, Dr. Alfred Southwick, remarked, "There is the culmination of ten years work and study. We live in a higher civilization from this day."

But as the straps were loosened, the corpse heaved to life. Kemmler's mouth foamed, his throat gurgled. Witnesses jolted backward. The crowd panicked. "For God's sake," one voice cried out, "kill him and be done with it!"

"Quick, turn on the current!" Spitzka said. As the electricity hit Kemmler again, he sat bolt upright. A cloud of gray smoke rose from the top of his head. Doctors pronounced him dead, for the second time.

Reaction to this first "scientific" execution brought both declarations of the triumph of modern science and passionate pleas for its suspension. Edison, for his part, said he only "glanced" at the report of Kemmler's execution. "It wasn't pleasant reading," he told one newspaper. "One mistake was in leaving everything to the doctors." One of those physicians, Dr. Spitzka, was criticized roundly for pronouncing Kemmler dead prematurely and then panicking. For his part, Spitzka declared electrocution cruel and barbarous. "I have seen hangings that were immeasurably more brutal than this execution, but I've never seen anything so awful. . . . All this goes to show that the new method will not take from capital punishment the barbarous features of execution," Spitzka told the *New York Tribune*. The *New York Times* printed a complete reversal of its position the day after Kemmler's death. "Far Worse Than Hanging," read a page-one article.

Dr. Southwick continued to proclaim electrocution's promising future. "There will be hundreds more executions by electricity, for the experiment of yesterday morning was a success. I don't care what anybody says, science has proved that Kemmler died an absolutely painless death."

It should be noted the term *electrocution* was seldom used in the latter half of the nineteenth century. A proper name for this method of execution was hotly debated. Edison suggested scientific-sounding words such as *ampermort*, *electromort*, and *dynamort*. Others advocated *Browned*, *Gerrycide*, and *Westinghoused* after the developers of the electric chair. Even *judicial lightning* had supporters. Eventually, *electrocution* entered prominent use, along with morbid nicknames for the chair itself, among them "Old Sparky," "The Hot Seat," and, in Louisiana, "Gruesome Gertie."

From the early 1900s to the late 1980s, the electric chair was the dominant method of execution in the United States. Some of the most famous figures to die during this period were convicted spies Julius and Ethel Rosenberg, anarchists Nicola Sacco and Bartolomeo Vanzetti, and notorious serial killer Ted Bundy.

Between 1925 and 1960, the height of electrocutions in the United States, last words continued to run the gamut of human experience and emotion, but they grew more political. The press became more involved, and more preexecution interviews were granted. The words of condemned persons became part of the national dialogue.

Few cases were more politically charged than that of two Italian immigrant anarchists, Nicola Sacco and his partner Bartolomeo Vanzetti. In 1921, the pair was convicted of killing two people while robbing a shoe factory. Despite international attention—and support from anarchist, communist, socialist, and labor organizations—both men died in the electric chair in 1927. "If it had not been for these things I might live out my life talking at street corners to scorning men. I might have died unmarked, a failure, unknown," Vanzetti told a reporter before his execution. "Now we are not a failure. This is our career and our triumph. Never in our full life could we hope to do such work for tolerance, for justice and for man's understanding of man as we do now by accident. Our words—our lives—our pains—nothing! The taking of our lives— the lives of a good shoemaker and a poor fish peddler—all!"

Some of the last words from this era directly reference the electric chair itself. Walter Dittman, convicted of murder in Illinois in 1934, wrote a poem to serve as his final words and incorporated the method of his death in the title:

The Chair of Death

I see it grimly waiting patiently for me,
To send me as its victim into eternity.
Not a whit or bit of mercy does it show for man or beast.
Its only song is, "Die, you dog, for your slide to hell is greased."

It's not the thought that I'm to die that makes me want to pray.
It's because I'll not be there, my own, to wipe your tears away.
God knows, and so do you, that I never slew nor stole,
And though the whole world's turned against me,
He'll have mercy on my soul.

The tenor of last words also changed during this period. Executions had not been public for some time, but compared to hangings—which required a large amount of open space—the electric chair and its witness chamber offered more privacy, more proximity to victims' families and scribbling journalists. Accordingly, last words shifted from blanket messages of caution, regret, and apologies to more intimate, direct statements. In 1940, Herbert Goddard addressed the parents of his victim outside the Florida execution chamber: "I very humbly ask their forgiveness and the forgiveness of my God. I want to say I am morally responsible. I killed Francis Dunn . . ."

By early in the twenty-first century, however, only a few states listed electrocution as an alternate form of execution, among them Alabama, Florida, South Carolina, and Virginia. To date, more than forty-three hundred prisoners have been executed by the electric chair.

Warden, these are probably my last words, and I want you to be in a position to speak with certainty concerning any confession which in the future you may hear I have made. I want to say to you now that I am entirely innocent of the crime for which I am about to be executed. There was no more morphine in that woman as administered by me than there is in you at this moment. I suppose I am not the first innocent man to be executed.

ROBERT BUCHANAN, convicted of murder, New York. Executed July 1, 1895

Buchanan was put to death for the murder of his second wife, Annie Sutherland, a woman nearly twenty years his senior who he told friends was his housekeeper. When she threatened to leave and no longer support him, prosecutors contended, Buchanan killed her with a dose of morphine and arsenic. After her death, Buchanan remarried his first wife, but rumors of a poisoned spouse still dogged him. When Sutherland's body was exhumed, traces of arsenic were found and Buchanan was arrested.

Written:

On the verge of death I desire to say that I do not think I had a fair trial. Extraordinary means were taken to convict me, and testimony given by Mr. Lansing was absolutely untrue. I am sorry for Ross' family, and for the gloom it has cast over them, but I did not go to the polls on election day to shoot Robert Ross, and had no intention of injuring him. I die for a crime I did not commit. I am an innocent man. I bid you all farewell.

Spoken:
I am innocent, Father, innocent.

BARTHOLOMEW SHEA (ALIAS BAT SHEA), convicted of murder, New York.
Executed February 11, 1896

In Troy's much-contested mayoral election of 1894, "fighting was general all over the city," but there was only one instance of bloodshed. Shea, a "notorious character," was charged with gunning down Robert Ross, a "fair play" election reformer.

God help me.

MARTHA PLACE, convicted of murder, New York. Executed March 20, 1899

The first woman to be executed in the electric chair by the state of New York, Place had been savagely jealous, according to newspaper accounts. While her husband was away, Place threw sulfuric acid at her seventeen-year-old stepdaughter Ida during a quarrel, then smothered her with a pillow. That day Mr. Place came home to find his wife wielding an ax, with which she struck him twice in the head but failed to kill him.

I killed the president because he was an enemy of the good people—of the working people. I am not sorry for my crime. I'm awfully sorry I could not see my father.

LEON FRANK CZOLGOSZ (AKA LEON FRANS CZOLGOSZ), convicted of murder, New York. Executed October 29, 1901

Czolgosz assassinated President William McKinley after waiting in line to shake his hand in Buffalo. Czolgosz's reasons for doing so were not entirely clear, though he did express grievances against the United States and claim that the American dream was a lie. Eight weeks after the murder, he was electrocuted; his body was dissolved in acid as it was buried.

I deserve to die, and the sooner they put an end to my troubles the better. I've got an uncontrollable temper, and if released would only commit more violent crimes. I'd kill a man for 5 cents as quick as for anything else.

FRANK HENRY BURNESS, convicted of murder, New York.
Executed June 27, 1904

Burness smiled in the execution chamber while awaiting electrocution for killing the captain of a schooner. He boasted that he had killed no fewer than nine people and vowed he'd do it again if given the chance. "Burness" was assumed to be just another alias; his true name was never discovered.

How many minutes will you give me?

Just before the current flowed:
Wait now.

WILLIAM MORSE, convicted of murder, New York. Executed January 3, 1910

Morse had tried to rob a woman and then shot policeman Edward J. Kavanaugh after the officer chased and cornered him.

While Morse, age twenty-five, was strapped into the electric chair, his chaplain recited "Rock of Ages." No one claimed his body, which was buried in the prison's cemetery.

I am innocent of this crime. Let us hope and pray they will never do this thing to another man, innocent or guilty.

RICHARD "RICKEY" HARRISON, convicted of murder, New York. Executed May 13, 1920

As Harrison and four other gunmen robbed a private Manhattan social club, police arrived, and the ensuing gun battle left one patron dead. Prosecutors contended, in a reconstruction of the incident, that Harrison fired the fatal shot. His fellow accomplices received jail sentences, but Harrison, age twenty-six, faced capital punishment.

As he left death row, fellow condemned inmates shouted, "Goodbye Rickey, we know you are innocent!" He replied: "It is the best thing that ever happened to me."

You see an innocent man dying tonight. Thank you, warden. You have been a kind man.

JOSEPH USEFOF, convicted of murder, New York. Executed December 9, 1920

Usefof was executed along with three other men (discussed in the entries following this one) for the 1918 murder of subway ticket agent Otto Fialo in the Bronx. Joseph Milano, one of Usefof's codefendants, exonerated Usefof in a written confession, which he later retracted. Usefof maintained his innocence; he was the first of his group to be executed because he was considered the most likely to suffer a breakdown.

Usefof did not take part in this crime.

JOSEPH MILANO, convicted of murder, New York.
Executed December 9, 1920

As Milano walked to the death chamber, condemned accomplice James Cassidy began to sing, "Oh, What a Pal Was Mary."

Entering the death chamber:
I know I've done wrong. I know I'm paying for it. Hello warden, I see you back there, Old Timer.

Sitting down in the chair:
Give her the gas, kid. I'm taking it with a smile.

JAMES CASSIDY, convicted of murder, New York. Executed December 9, 1920

Cassidy, too, was part of Milano and Usefof's gang. Though a doctor said he had "the mind of a nine-year-old child," the diagnosis didn't keep Cassidy from facing the electric chair. Just before his execution, he presented Warden Lewis E. Lawes with a brief from his appeal and asked him to keep it as a "remembrance." Cassidy was illiterate but had been learning to read. He pointed to the word "remembrance," which he'd written on his cell wall.

He said, "Isn't it hell, warden, when you get so you can write words like that to have to be bumped off?"

God bless you, boys. I got the old smile on my face.

CHARLES MCLAUGHLIN, convicted of murder, New York.
Executed December 9, 1920

While the warden made his last rounds, McLaughlin reached through the bars, extended his hand, and said, laughing, "Shake, put it there, shake."

If I've got to leave this good old Earth, I want to make a statement before I go. I'm feeling all right, but it's over others I'm worrying.

HOWARD BAKER, convicted of murder and robbery, New York. Executed December 9, 1920

Baker left his wife and three children to join a gang headed by his own forty-five-year-old mother and her twenty-three-year-old lover. The gang robbed the Buckminster and Graves clothing store, and Baker shot a night watchman during the getaway attempt.

"Goodbye, boys," he said to his fellow death-row inmates as he left the cellblock. He told Dr. Squire, the head prison physician, "I appreciate everything you have done."

Baker was executed on the same night as the Milano gang (see four previous entries).

To the prison physician:
Good-bye, Doc.

LUTHER BODDY, convicted of murder, New York. Executed August 31, 1922

Infamous "cop fighter" Boddy was sought for questioning in connection with the shooting injury of a patrolman. Within two hundred feet of the police station, he fired on and killed two detectives who had apprehended him. After a manhunt involving forty thousand law-enforcement personnel, Boddy was apprehended outside Philadelphia, after disguising himself as a woman and forcing a taxi driver to take him there. When asked why he killed the detectives, he claimed the pair had previously abused him and he thought they were taking him to the station house to beat him. Boddy, twenty-three, grinned at the verdict and in the electric chair.

To executioner:

Don't be afraid of me. I would as soon have you do it as anyone.

BEN RICHARDSON, convicted of murder, Arkansas.
Executed February 2, 1923

Little was written about Richardson except that he arrived in the death chamber before it was ready for him. After bidding the attendants good morning, he inspected the electric chair and moved toward the switchboard, causing his executioner to "quickly move away." In response, Richardson tried to put the man at ease with his final words.

Viva l'anarchia! [*Italian:* Long live anarchy!]

A moment later, in English:

Farewell, my wife and child and all my friends.

After the death mask had been fitted:

Farewell, mia madre! [Farewell, my mother!]

FERDINANDO NICOLA SACCO, convicted of murder, Massachusetts.
Executed August 23, 1927

Sacco and friend Bartolomeo Vanzetti, both Italian immigrants, stood trial for killing Alessandro Berardelli, a security guard, and Frederick Parmenter, a pay clerk, during an armed robbery in 1920. The controversial case gripped the nation, as both men were Galleanists, members of an Italian anarchist group suspected in a string of bombings.

Numerous books have since been written questioning the guilt or innocence of the men. Their case was included in the 1992 book *In Spite of Innocence* among almost two dozen cases in which the editors believed "an innocent person was executed."

I wish to say to you that I am innocent. I have never done a crime, some sins, but never any crime. I thank you for everything you have done for me. I am innocent of all crime, not only this one, but of all, all. I am an innocent man.

Just before execution:
I wish to forgive some people for what they are doing to me.

BARTOLOMEO VANZETTI, convicted of murder, Massachusetts. Executed August 23, 1927

Vanzetti immigrated to the United States when he was twenty years old. He sold fish and washed dishes before becoming involved in left-wing politics and protesting World War I. He had been in America for a decade before meeting Nicola Sacco at an anarchists' meeting.

In 1977, Massachusetts governor Michael Dukakis stopped short of exonerating the pair but declared: "Any stigma and disgrace should be forever removed from the names of Nicola Sacco and Bartolomeo Vanzetti. We are not here to say whether these men are guilty or innocent. We are here to say that the high standards of justice, which we in Massachusetts take such pride in, failed Sacco and Vanzetti."

An interesting postscript: A letter from famed novelist and muckraker Upton Sinclair (*The Jungle*) surfaced in 2005. While doing research for *Boston*, his two-volume "documentary novel" of the Sacco and Vanzetti case, he consulted with Fred Moore, one of their attorneys. "Alone in a hotel room with Fred, I begged him to tell me the full truth," Lewis wrote. "He then told me that the men were guilty, and he told me in every detail how he had framed a set of alibis for them."

I am innocent of the killing of that cop. I committed other crimes and I lay that to evil companions. But I didn't kill the cop. I wouldn't kill one. Didn't I try to save the life of one? Graham was one, wasn't he, and didn't I try to prove him innocent?

GEORGE APPEL, convicted of murder, New York. Executed August 9, 1928

Police Lieutenant Charles J. Kemmer walked into a Brooklyn restaurant just as Appel and an accomplice finished robbing it. In the ensuing scuffle, prosecutors said, Appel shot Kemmer three times. Though mortally wounded, Kemmer jotted down the plate number of their getaway car. The clue was crucial and landed the partners in jail.

The Graham in Appel's last statement was Daniel J. Graham Jr., a former patrolman convicted of killing a paymaster. Appel, age forty-one, confessed to the murder in prison, but "the evidence was found to be so flimsy, no new trial was ordered," according to a newspaper account. Graham was executed the same evening as Appel.

Appel's last words have been erroneously reported as "Gentlemen, you are about to see a baked Appel."

I am innocent. I was arrested for grand larceny and for assault on a previous occasion, but I was found innocent of those charges. I went into the army during the World War when I was only 15. This is the reward.

DANIEL J. GRAHAM JR., convicted of murder, New York. Executed August 9, 1928

The third uniformed member of the New York Police Department to die in the electric chair since 1915, Graham was accompanying Midtown paymaster Judson Pratt to a construction site when, prosecutors said, he shot the man in the head and stole the forty-seven-hundred-dollar payroll. Graham then moved Pratt's body into the passenger seat and drove from Fifty-third Street all the way to the Bronx with the dead man. Because of a downpour, nobody noticed.

Pratt's body was found propped up in the driver's seat under a viaduct. Another Sing Sing prisoner (see above entry) claimed responsibility for the crime, but a judge threw out the confession for lack of evidence. Graham was twenty-six years old.

To the warden, two hours before execution:

I don't want to die with a lie on my lips. I lied when I said this killing was a result of gin and anger. I deliberately planned a robbery. I was watching for anybody worth robbing. I had a revolver and an automobile. I know how to handle revolvers, but this was the first time I had ever handled an automatic. As I pressed it against the man and told him to put his hands up, the gun went off, although, so help me God, I didn't mean to shoot.

AUGUST VOGEL, convicted of murder, Illinois. Executed May 9, 1930

Vogel was known as "the Whim Slayer" for shooting a man who bumped into his car, according to newspapers. Vogel led a gang of Chicago thieves that included his brother George, who confessed to the murder in a last-ditch effort to save Vogel. Vogel, age twenty-seven, had previously attempted to pin the murder on George. But neither was able to shift the blame, and Vogel was electrocuted as planned.

Father Mac is the greatest man who ever lived.

JOSEPH CALABRESE, convicted of murder and robbery, New Jersey. Executed December 29, 1930

"Father Mac" was Rev. Cornelius McInerney, chaplain of the Essex County penitentiary. Calabrese, age twenty-one, also gave the chaplain a rose and "asked him to wear it in his memory," according to the *New York Times*. Along with accomplice Arthur Cort—executed minutes later—Calabrese had been convicted of murdering druggist Morris Grossman in a holdup.

O my God, I am sorry for having offended thee.

WILLIE GREEN, convicted of murder, Illinois. Executed December 11, 1931

The *Chicago Daily Tribune* recorded little about Green, age thirty-one, who faced the electric chair for killing grocer Max Newman. He was executed the same day as three other convicted murderers at the Southern Illinois Penitentiary in Menard. He delivered his last words while shaking hands with a priest.

Written statement given to the press:

Frank Bell, having been baptized, made confession and received communion. He felt resigned to God's holy will and stated that he was perfectly sure that Leo Brothers is innocent of the crime he is charged with. The reason I make this statement is because I would have appeared at Brothers' trial if the Supreme Court should have given him a new one. I regret that the Supreme Court did not grant a decision before [it was] too late for me to act. I made a statement contradicting my testimony given to officials denying I had anything to do with the Lingle murder. My first statement which I made was the true facts pertaining to the Lingle case.

FRANK BELL, convicted of robbery and murder, Illinois.
Executed January 8, 1932

Bell faced the electric chair for his part in the murder of restaurant manager Chris Patras, who allegedly had promised Bell and his gang (which included Leo Brothers) ten thousand dollars for the killing of *Chicago Daily Tribune* crime reporter Alfred Lingle. Lingle was shot in the middle of the day in a crowded subway in downtown Chicago; Brothers was convicted of his murder. Bell fingered fellow gang member Richard Sullivan as the triggerman in Patras's slaying.

I don't mind it.
My love to mother and tell Mrs. Lawes I appreciate all she did for me.

Waving to a guard:
How is it, Sarge?

FRANCIS "TWO-GUN" CROWLEY, convicted of murder, NewYork. Executed January 21, 1932

Crowley killed patrolman Frederick Hirsch after the officer asked for his driver's license. Characterized by the press as a "petty city thug," Crowley had been wanted for questioning in another murder case. After fleeing, Crowley, his girlfriend, and an accomplice were cornered two days later and staged a two-hour standoff with police, during which he wrote the following: "Underneath my coat will lay a weary kind of heart what wouldn't hurt anything. I hadn't anything else do to. That's why I went around bumping off cops."

Crowley's last words previously had been reported as "You sons of bitches. Give my love to Mother," but no original record of this account could be found.

I no want minister. There no God. It's all below.
I'll go myself, I no scared of lectric chair . . . See, I no fraid of lectric chair.
No cameraman? No movie to take a picture of Zangara? Lousy capitalists—no picture—capitalists, no one

here take my picture, all capitalists lousy bunch of crooks.

Good-bye, adios to all the world.

Push the button!

GIUSEPPE ZANGARA, convicted of murder, Florida. Executed March 20, 1933

After President-elect Franklin D. Roosevelt finished a speech in Miami, Zangara attempted to assassinate him with a pawn shop revolver. Instead of hitting Roosevelt, Zangara wounded four others, including Chicago mayor Anton J. Cermak, who later died of his wounds. Zangara, an Italian immigrant, claimed that "pains in his stomach" caused him to hate people in power, according to a newspaper report.

It looks pretty dark, but if I have to, I guess I can take my medicine.

MORRIS COHEN, convicted of murder, Illinois. Executed October 13, 1933

A thirty-eight-year-old barber, Cohen got the electric chair for the murder of Officer Joseph Hastings during a robbery attempt at Chicago's Navy Pier. A secondary headline in the *Chicago Daily Tribune* read "Record for Speedy Justice Is Set." He had been executed less than two months after the crime.

While waiting in his cell, on efforts for clemency:

I won't get a break.

ROSS KING, convicted of murder, Illinois. Executed October 16, 1933

In a jailhouse interview, convicted cop killer King said, "Swift death in the 'hot seat' is better than life in prison. I know: I've been to prison. To go there for life would be a lifetime in hell."

As his execution time moved closer, King changed his tune. "If you can pull anything to get me out of this, I'd appreciate it."

King, age thirty-four, lost his composure in the end, according to one report. He repeated, "God have mercy on my soul!" as he "half walked, half dragged" himself the final few paces to the electric chair.

I don't hold it against all you folks because you have condemned me without a fair trial. I don't even hold it against the jury. Ignorance is not the fault of the ignorant. I don't even have any malice for the courts, although they defied all laws in affirming my case. I forgive all of you. You loved the girls. You let your desire for revenge overshadow your sense of justice.

EARL QUINN, convicted of murder, Oklahoma. Executed November 24, 1933

Quinn was described as a "one-time alcohol runner" by the Associated Press, but few other details survive except the names of his victims: schoolteacher sisters Jessie and Zexia Griffith.

I want to die this way. I can't stand the thought of going to the chair. Don't—please don't—try to save me for that.

HARVEY EDWARDS, convicted of murder, Indiana. Executed March 2, 1934

When his request for a commutation to life in prison was denied, convicted wife-killer Edwards, thirty-nine, broke his glasses and slit his wrists with the shards. It appears that his last words were taken at this time. The war veteran was given a blood transfusion so he could face execution. In the end, he regained strength and walked himself to the electric chair.

In a letter to his family:

Please smile and laugh, for that's all you now can do. If you'll be happy I'll be happy, too. I have only myself to blame . . . The thought never occurred to anyone during the trial to show the circumstances of John Scheck as a mere boy who was lured and tempted into the life of crime because of his intense devotion to his parents and to his home that they were about to be deprived of as victims of a nationwide economic depression . . . So John Scheck plotted the escape which resulted in failure and the unfortunate death of a policeman.

. . . As a boy, John Scheck is fighting a battle to live in grief and sorrow for a mistake that is very close to him.

JOHN SCHECK, convicted of murder, Illinois. Executed April 20, 1934

Bank robber Scheck, twenty-one, held on a murder charge, killed policeman John G. Sevick in an escape attempt from a courtroom. The shocking crime led to "the court's war on crime, and he was among the first hit by the reaction," wrote the *Chicago Daily Tribune*.

I want to thank you, gentlemen. I go to die, but I am innocent. That is all I can say. I wish you good luck—all of you—all your life.

SAMUEL FERACI, convicted of murder, New York. Executed August 9, 1934

Samuel Feraci was one of Anna Antonio's two accomplices in murder and attempted insurance fraud (see next entry). The trio attacked, shot, and stabbed her husband on Easter Sunday. Antonio promised Feraci eight hundred of the expected five-thousand-dollar settlement. Instead, he followed her to the electric chair.

I don't care what you do to me. I am not afraid to die. I have nothing on my conscience. I never killed any one.

ANNA ANTONIO, convicted of conspiracy to murder, New York. Executed August 9, 1934

Antonio, age twenty-eight, claimed it was fear rather than money that motivated her. A diminutive woman, weighing approximately one hundred pounds, Antonio had been married to a large, violent drug dealer who she claimed had abused her and caused the early death of one of their four children. Her apparent lack of grief did not help her case. When the governor refused to commute her sentence, she said, "It looks as if they've all turned me down. God alone can help me. I'm not thinking of myself so much. I'm thinking what it will mean to the future of my children. Nobody can know how terrible it is to be here except someone who has been through it."

Antonio was the fourth woman in the state of New York to go to the electric chair. She wore a blue gingham dress to her execution and approached the chair without assistance, ignoring the witnesses present.

I wish I had Corrick and Wynn on my lap.

FRED BLINK, convicted of murder, Illinois. Executed April 23, 1935

The men Blink addressed in his final statement were Tim Corrick, the husband of one of his victims, and L. L. Wynn, the prosecutor in the case. Blink claimed that Corrick gave him poisoned whiskey, which caused his murder spree. The World War I veteran was convicted in the shooting deaths of his former business partner and four other people. After the verdict was pronounced, Blink had to be lifted from his chair and forced from the courtroom.

I want to give out a message to the people of Albany. They double-crossed me, but I'm a better man than they are. I thank you, warden.

LEONARD SCARNICI, convicted of murder, New York. Executed June 27, 1935

Scarnici and five of his gang held up a Rensselaer County Bank with a machine gun and a slew of pistols. Unbeknownst to the robbers, they had tripped the silent alarm, which brought two police detectives running to the scene. Detective James A. Stevens was gunned down the instant he passed through the bank doors, and a deafening exchange of fire ensued. Two of Scarnici's men were shot dead and the rest escaped with two thousand dollars.

To the warden:

If I have to die, I will die innocent. I never killed Harry Wright or anyone else.

EVA COO, convicted of murder, New York. Executed June 27, 1935

Coo, proprietor of a "speakeasy brothel," was sent to the electric chair for the murder of Harry Wright, a handicapped man she had employed as a handyman. News reports from the era painted Coo as a ghoulish figure who mistreated Wright, burned down his dead mother's house for insurance money, and then tried to collect an insurance policy on Wright. She became the fifth woman to die in New York's electric chair.

Written:

I am glad that my life in a world which has not understood me has ended. Soon I will be at home with my Lord, so I am dying an innocent man. Should, however,

my death serve for the purpose of abolishing capital punishment—such a punishment being arrived at only by
circumstantial evidence—I feel that my death has not
been in vain. I am at peace with God. I repeat, I protest
my innocence of the crime for which I was convicted.
However, I die with no malice or hatred in my heart. The
love of Christ has filled my soul and I am happy in Him.

BRUNO RICHARD HAUPTMANN, convicted of kidnapping and murder, New
Jersey. Executed April 3, 1936

Hauptmann was executed for "the Crime of the Century," the abduction and kidnapping of Charles Augustus Lindbergh Jr., the
toddler son of famed pilot Charles Lindbergh. It was hypothesized
that the Lindbergh baby actually died during the abduction, when
he was dropped from the ladder used to climb into his nursery. Decades later Hauptmann's widow maintained her husband's innocence, calling him "framed from beginning to end."

Hauptmann's case was included in the 1992 book *In Spite of Innocence* among almost two dozen cases in which the editors believed
"an innocent person was executed."

To a guard:

The chair will be a good enough [Christmas] present
for me.

HARRY SINGER, convicted of murder, Indiana. Executed December 26, 1936

The twenty-five-year-old former farmhand kept mostly to himself
Christmas Day, playing checkers and eating "heartily," according to
the Associated Press. Few details of the crime have survived, except
the names of his victims: Mr. and Mrs. John Wesley Kaufman and
their daughter, age twelve. In prison, Singer also confessed to the
murder of Joseph Bryant, age twenty, of Detroit.

This is where injustice triumphs.

THEODORE DI DONNE (ALSO RECORDED AS "DI DIONNE"), convicted of robbery and murder. Executed New York, January 7, 1937

Di Donne, age thirty-one, faced execution along with six members of his gang for slaying Brooklyn Transit Authority employee Edwin Esposito in a heist gone sour. At the eleventh hour, however, the governor of New York commuted the sentences of all, save the two directly responsible for the killing, di Donne and accomplice Joseph Bolognia. Di Donne denied firing the fatal shot and hoped his family would believe him.

I want to speak to reporters. Newspaper men have made a fine mess of things calling me "Tough Tony." I have always been a good kid.

After sitting down:
I am innocent.

JOSEPH BOLOGNIA, convicted of robbery and murder.
Executed New York, January 7, 1937

Bolognia and accomplice Theodore di Donne robbed and killed a transit authority worker, then escaped with $250 in change. Police and press alerted city residents to be aware of any men trying to pay with large numbers of coins. A bar waitress noticed this very thing, and the pair was soon arrested.

Well, I hope you are satisfied.

GEORGE CHEW WING, convicted of murder, New York.
Executed June 10, 1937

"The first Chinese to be electrocuted in New York state in more than 20 years" is all one press service recorded. According to authorities, Wing murdered another Chinese man, Yip Chow, while robbing his Manhattan apartment. He sneered his last words at his executioners.

Wing's case was included in the 1992 book *In Spite of Innocence* among almost two dozen cases in which the editors believed "an innocent person was executed."

I did not merit the electric chair.

LESTER BROCKELHURST, convicted of murder, Arkansas. Executed March 18, 1938

Brockelhurst, a former Sunday school teacher, confessed to killing three men across eighteen states after he and a female companion embarked on a robbery spree.

Good-bye all of you and God bless you . . . Mr. Woodard [the warden], don't do this to me. Think of my boy. Can't you think of my baby? Isn't there anybody who will help me? Is nobody going to help me?

ANNA MARIE HAHN, convicted of murder, Ohio. Executed December 7, 1938

Hahn was convicted of poisoning four elderly people, prosecutors claimed, with the motive of stealing their money after a series of losses at the horse track. She had been found with crystallized poison in her possession, the same substance that crime scientists found in the stomach lining of all the victims. Authorities described Hahn as calm throughout her trial and incarceration, but she began to break down when led to the death chamber, collapsing and crying frantically for her life.

In a letter enclosing playing cards—four aces and a joker, with the ace of spades underlined:

You never know when. Life is like a deck of cards and we are all the jokers. First it's hearts, then it's diamonds. Next it's clubs, and now it's spades.

EDWARD "PADDY RYAN" RILEY, convicted of murder, Illinois. Executed June 20, 1941

Riley, who had had prior convictions and had served time twice in Michigan, held up a tavern in Chicago with two accomplices. In the process, they shot and killed an undertaker and wounded two police officers, one of whom also died. The trio fled to Detroit and were captured. Riley wrote ten letters in his last few hours, seven of them to women. He went to the death chamber quietly.

In a letter to a victim's widow:

Dear Mother Speaker, that is, if I may call you that? I would like to express my gratitude for the way you took my message from Father Connolly, and I would also like to thank you for saying the Stations of the Cross for me. I know I'm no good and I hope you forgive me for what I've done to your husband. If I knew then what I know now, this tragedy would never have happened. I know that Mr. Speaker is up there praying for me; I will probably meet him there tonight if God wills it. Please say a prayer for me. I need it. May I always be your friend.

In the electric chair:

I got it coming.

BERNARD SAWICKI, convicted of murder, Illinois. Executed January 17, 1942

Sawicki shot a seventy-two-year-old farmer who he claimed had him put in a St. Charles juvenile correctional facility. He then went on a robbery and murder spree which claimed three more victims, including a policeman, Charles Speaker.

In a letter to his wife and daughter:

These are the last lines I can write to you. I should like to tell you that I have always loved you and that I came here to make a better life for you, my dear ones. But unfortunately, God willed it otherwise. . . . Tell Kappe or one of his people that George Dasch and Peter Burger betrayed us. Begin a new life and think of me often.

RICHARD QUIRIN, convicted of espionage and conspiracy to commit sabotage, Washington. Executed DC, August 8, 1942

Quirin, a machinist working for Volkswagen, was recruited to take part in Operation Pastorius, a Nazi plot to sabotage various economic targets in the United States. Quirin was a member of the first group of men involved in the plan, who were under the command of George Dasch. Their mission was foiled and all eight men were arrested when Dasch turned himself in and exposed the plot.

Written, to his parents:

I have only a few hours left in this life. I and my comrades are dying for you and for Germany. I know that our Führer will bring Germany to victory. . . . When I heard my sentence I could not grasp it at first. But my nerves are strong enough. I am quite at ease now. Just as thousands of German men lay down their lives every day at the front, so also shall I die courageously as a German soldier.

To his American wife:

Never thought they would take our life away. But as I write these lines I have control of my nerves again. If it only would not hurt so much, it would not be so hard. But I shall try to be brave, and take it as a soldier. . . . A priest is with me, and he will be with me to the last minute. So my Alma, chin up, because I want you to be good and goodbye, until we may meet in a better world, may God bless you! I love you, Your Hermann.

HERMANN NEUBAUER, convicted of espionage and conspiracy to commit sabotage. Executed Washington, DC, August 8, 1942

Neubauer was a Nazi saboteur in the failed Operation Pastorius. His part of the assignment took him to Chicago. He was the last of the group to be captured when comrade George Dasch turned himself in. Though he had not actually committed an act of sabotage, he and the others were tried by a military tribunal and executed.

Written, to his wife:

Marie, my wife—I am with you to the last minute! This will help me to take it as a German! Even the heaven out there is dark. It's raining. Our graves are far from home, but not forgotten. Marie, until we meet in a better world! May God be with you. My love to you, my heart to my country. Heil Hitler! Your Ed, always.

EDDIE KERLING, convicted of espionage and conspiracy to commit sabotage, Washington. Executed DC, August 8, 1942

Kerling was among the eight men who were part of Operation Pastorius, a Nazi sabotage mission. The plan: a series of attacks on American economic targets, such as the hydroelectric plant at Niagara Falls.

O Heavenly Father, they have crucified an innocent girl
and now they are going to crucify an innocent man.

ELI SHONBRUN (ALIAS TED LEOPOLD), convicted of robbery and murder,
New York. Executed April 29, 1943

The "innocent girl" in Shonbrun's last statement was Madeline
Webb, his accomplice, who was convicted but not sentenced to
death with him in the murder of Susan Flora Reich. Webb had
asked permission from the state to marry Shonbrun while incarcerated but was denied.

Spoken, after his last meal:
Tell my mother I'm sorry, especially as far as she is concerned. Nothing in my past bothers me as much as the
thought of how she will take this. It will be harder on her
than it is on me.

Written in a note to the warden:
By my death, the state will gain nothing, while I will
gain eternal life.

ERNEST WISHON, convicted of murder, Illinois. Executed November 26, 1943

After the army rejected him and he separated from his wife, Wishon
turned to drink. When funds ran out, he "decided to pull a job to
get more money for booze." During the hold-up of a jewelry store,
Wishon killed seventy-nine-year-old owner Joseph Schulte.

I am anxious to have it clearly understood that I did not offer to talk and give information in exchange for any promise of commutation of my death sentence.

LOUIS BUCHALTER (ALIAS LOUIS LEPKE), convicted of conspiracy to commit murder, New York. Executed March 4, 1944

The New York press referred to Buchalter as "the former overlord of the crime syndicate Murder, Inc." The reputed gangster's last words worked to preserve his reputation.

Buchalter was linked to more than twenty homicides, and his influence was said to have permeated all of Manhattan's major manufacturing unions. By the 1930s, Buchalter was executive director over hundreds of union workers and more than 250 professional bounty hunters. Eventually, the operation began to fray, as factions opposing Buchalter congealed within the gang, and law enforcement officials put a twenty-five-thousand-dollar prize on his head. His paranoia grew until he finally broke down and turned himself in to federal authorities. Originally given thirty years to life for conspiracy, drug trafficking, and obstruction of commerce, Buchalter was eventually sentenced to death when an investigation linked Murder, Inc. to the slaying of Joseph Rosen, who had worked for an affiliate trucking business.

Buchalter faced Sing Sing's electric chair with two of his lieutenants, Mendy Weiss and Louis Capone (no relation to Al Capone).

Criminal justice writer Scott Christian said, "Buchalter's statement is noteworthy because it was widely believed that had he 'squealed,' he could have implicated several prominent politicians and law enforcement officials. He had the goods on a lot of corrupt people."

I'm here on a framed-up case. And Governor Dewey knows it. I want to thank Judge Lehman . . . He knows

me because I am a Jew. Give my love to my family . . .
and everything.

EMANUEL (MENDY) WEISS, convicted of murder, New York.
Executed March 4, 1944

Small-time criminal Weiss became entangled in one of the largest
and most powerful gangs in American history when he joined two
other Murder, Inc. henchmen in the killing of potential witness and
informant Joseph Rosen.

In a note to the warden:

I am write [sic] you this letter to let you know how much
I appreciate what you have did for me tell all the Boys
in here and on the outside that Crimes don't pay no one
but the lawyers.

En route to the death chamber:

I'm going to sit in the chair and go to sleep.

ERNEST GAITHER JR., convicted of murder, Illinois.
Executed October 24, 1947

Gaither went to the electric chair for the shooting death of Max
Baran during a three-hundred-dollar bar robbery. He spent his final
day reading the Bible and writing letters, and requested a bowl of
cornflakes for his last meal. Waiting for midnight to arrive, he sang
gospel songs including "Just a Little Talk with Jesus" and "I Know
the Lord Has Laid His Hand on Me." Witnesses to his execution included his two sons.

To his friend and attorney Emanuel Bloch, from Julius Rosenberg:

Be strong for us, beloved friend, and we wish you long life to continue your fruitful work in health and happiness. . . . NEVER LET THEM CHANGE THE TRUTH OF OUR INNOCENCE.

JULIUS AND ETHEL ROSENBERG, convicted of espionage, New York. Executed June 19, 1953

Julius and Ethel Rosenberg were American Communists accused of passing atomic secrets to the Russians. Ethel's brother David Greenglass confessed to selling nuclear secrets and accused Julius of doing the same. Greenglass also accused his sister of typing up notes of a secret meeting, but decades later he recanted the story.

Both Rosenbergs declined to make official final statements before their executions.

Philosopher and novelist Jean-Paul Sartre called the execution a "legal lynching which smears with blood a whole nation. By killing the Rosenbergs, you have quite simply tried to halt the progress of science by human sacrifice."

In 2008, however, Rosenberg codefendant Morton Sobell admitted that he and Julius were spies for the Soviets. Julius even had two code names, first "Antenna," then "Liberal," according to recently released KGB documents. The papers do not reveal whether Ethel had a covert identity. The extent of her involvement in the case remains in question.

To a guard, after tearing the heel off one of his shoes:

I don't want anybody else to stand in my shoes.

RICHARD CARPENTER, convicted of murder, Illinois. Executed December 19, 1958

Carpenter, age twenty-seven, went to the electric chair for murdering a policeman on a subway platform. According to one newspaper, prior to being led to the death chamber he said, "I don't be-

THE ELECTRIC CHAIR 157

lieve in God. I'm going to the electric chair, and there's nothing I can do about it." Although the *Chicago Daily Tribune* reported that Carpenter went silently to the chair, another publication quoted him as saying, "Get it over with quick"—words that were muffled by the black hood over his head.

I have one consolation . . . when I do take that walk . . . I know that the Lord knows that I'm speaking the truth.

A moment later:

The ones who conspired with their underhanded tactics to obtain their conviction will have to live with it for the rest of their lives.

VINCENT CIUCCI, convicted of murder, Illinois. Executed March 23, 1962

When Ciucci's wife discovered he had a mistress, prosecutors said, the thirty-five-year-old grocer killed their three small children, then his wife, with a rifle. Before his execution, Ciucci himself offered several versions of events, including one in which his wife killed their children.

A circled passage in the section "He Is Sentenced to Death," in Plato's Apology:

"The hour of departure has arrived and we go our ways, I to die and you to live. Which is better God only knows."

JAMES DUKES, convicted of murder, Illinois. Executed August 24, 1962

Dukes was executed for killing Detective John Blyth Sr., who had pursued him after he had beaten his girlfriend in church and shot two other men who tried to stop him. On Dukes's execution day, Detective Daniel Rolewicz, who took part in the final gun battle, told a newspaperman, "I've been waiting a long time for this night." Dukes made no oral statement but left behind a copy of the *Apology* for the press.

Gents, this is an educational project. You are about to witness the damaging effect electricity has on Wood.

FREDERICK WOOD, convicted of murder, New York. Executed March 21, 1963

After he killed five people, Frederick Wood's last desire in life was to die, specifically by the electric chair. He made no appeal for a stay of execution, saying he wanted to "ride the lightning" to oblivion. According to newspaper accounts, people around Wood had described him as a derelict.

Man is what he chooses to be; he chooses that for himself.
If this comes down, I hope that some good will come of it.

JOHN SPENKELINK, convicted of murder, Florida. Executed May 25, 1979

Though prison officials reported that Spenkelink wished to leave no final statement, these quotations were passed on by an Episcopal priest, the last person to talk to the prisoner.

After Spenkelink escaped from a California jail, he killed an ex-convict named Joseph Syzmankiewicz, whom Spenkelink claimed had robbed him, held him prisoner, and forced him into homosexual acts. Spenkelink's last words have previously been reported as "Capital punishment: them without the capital get the punishment," but newspaper accounts do not confirm this.

I don't hold no grudges. I'm sorry it happened. I know what I'm doing.

STEVEN T. JUDY, convicted of rape and murder, Indiana.
Executed March 9, 1981

A serial rapist, Judy openly courted capital punishment. At his trial for killing a woman and her three children (ages five, four, and two), Judy told a jury to condemn him or else he might kill them, their children, and the judge. He showed no remorse for the murders, telling reporters, "I don't lose sleep over it." Judy asked for death. "I've lived my hell," he said. "So [what waits for me] has to be better." Slightly different accounts of his final words have been recorded as well.

To his fellow inmates on death row:

In spite of what is about to happen, do not quit. . . . I hold no malice to none. May God bless us all.

ROBERT SULLIVAN, convicted of murder, Florida.
Executed November 30, 1983

Sullivan was sentenced to the electric chair for killing Donald Schmidt, an assistant manager of a Howard Johnson's Motor Lodge where he had once worked. An accomplice testified against him, though Sullivan claimed innocence. Before his death, Sullivan read from a two-page statement, the full text of which is now unavailable. In the end, he thanked Pope John Paul II for requesting that his life be spared.

Is it necessary to have the hood?

ROBERT W. WILLIAMS, convicted of murder, Louisiana.
Executed December 14, 1983

Williams maintained that when he walked into the A&P supermarket to rob it, he never intended to shoot the on-duty security guard; he said that his sawed-off shotgun went off accidentally. Williams was the tenth prisoner executed since the federal government had reinstated the death penalty seven years earlier.

To the father of one of his victims:

Mr. LeBlanc, I can understand the way you feel. I have no hatred in my heart, and as I leave this world, I ask God to forgive what . . . I have done. I ask you to have forgiveness.

ELMO PATRICK SONNIER, convicted of murder, Louisiana. Executed April 5, 1984

To the stepfather and mother of his victim:

I would just like to say, Mr. and Mrs. Harvey, that I hope you get some relief from my death. Killing people is wrong. That's why you've put me to death. It makes no difference whether it's citizens, countries or governments. Killing is wrong. [He then asked the warden to remove his hood and winked at Sister Helen Prejean, his spiritual adviser.]

ROBERT LEE WILLIE, convicted of murder, Louisiana. Executed December 28, 1984

Sister Helen Prejean wrote her book *Dead Man Walking* about Sonnier and Willie, and they were the basis for a composite character played by Sean Penn in the film adaptation of the book. Prejean became spiritual adviser to both men when they were imprisoned for their crimes: Willie was convicted of raping and murdering an eighteen-year-old woman; Sonnier was convicted of murdering a teenage couple in a sugarcane field in New Iberia.

Many of my friends have mentioned to me to look for the light, but I already saw the light when I accepted Christ as Lord many years ago. Only now I get to go stand in it and enjoy it with the Lord.

CARL SHRINER, convicted of murder, Florida. Executed June 20, 1984

Described by the Associated Press as a "boyish-faced drifter," Shriner faced the electric chair for the shooting death of store clerk Judith Ann Carter. In an earlier prison interview, the thirty-year-old Shriner said, "Police, prosecutors . . . are powerful. They can make anybody look guilty if they want to."

I'd like to say to the families of all my victims, I'm sorry for all the grief and heartache I brought to them. If my death brings them any satisfaction, so be it.

DAVID WASHINGTON, convicted of murder, Florida. Executed July 13, 1984

Even by his own account, former choirboy Washington "had the best breaks in life, all the best opportunities." But, he told reporters, "I think my life was just one big mistake. . . . Seemed like everything I touched, I destroyed. Family, wife, friends, everything. I just destroyed." Washington was sentenced to the electric chair for the stabbing deaths of three people. On the day of his execution, he held his daughter on his knee and said, "I want you to do better."

To those who oppose the death penalty in South Carolina, I say continue the fight against the hatred, violence, and revenge of this punitive form of punishment.

Addressing Gov. Richard W. Wiley directly:
Killing is wrong when I did it. It is wrong when you do it. I hope you have the courage and the moral strength to stop the killing. I have no bitterness toward anyone. May God bless and forgive you all.

JOSEPH CARL SHAW, convicted of murder, South Carolina. Executed January 11, 1985

Shaw's pending execution reignited capital punishment politics in the state, leading the South Carolina Coalition Against the Death Penalty to place a large ad in the state's largest newspaper. The opposition distributed more than a thousand bumper stickers with a picture of the electric chair and the caption "Use it!"

Shaw pleaded guilty in the shooting deaths of a teenage couple, after which he had mutilated the young girl's body. The *New York Times* reported, "Mr. Shaw was also sentenced to life in prison for murdering Betty Swank about a week before the other killings." The newspaper noted that Shaw had accomplices in both crimes.

In his cell:

Yes, sir. I wish to make the following statements prior to my death. First, to the family of Roger Tackett, I send to you my remorse for the death of your loved one from the bottom of my heart. I did not kill Roger Tackett, and I remorse deeply for his death. To my supporters I send my—all my deepest respect. Thank you. It was—it has been due to your effort that I have received the degree of justice in my case. To the world, I suggest that people need to reach out more and help the needy and the homeless. To my family and children, I send you all my love, and I want you to know that I love you very much. And do not be bitter. Work hard, be honest in all life, and you will be successful in America. Van Roosevelt Solomon.

A moment later:

This is Van Solomon again, and I'd like to say to America: how long will America limp between two opinions? How can you counsel someone and don't even keep your own counsel about killing people. Thank you.

In the death chamber:

Yes, I'd like to say I'd like to give my blessing to all the people that seeked to save my life, and I'd like to curse everyone that seeked to take my life. Farewell.

VAN ROOSEVELT SOLOMON, convicted of murder, Georgia. Executed February 20, 1985

A former Baptist assistant pastor, Solomon sat in the electric chair for the murder of Roger Tackett, a Georgetown University honors graduate and convenience store manager. Outside the prison, the Associated Press reported, fifty opponents and eight proponents of the death penalty stood in the rain. One held a sign reading "Let he who is without sin cast the first stone." Another placard read "Let me pull the switch."

Newspapers reported Solomon's last words as "I would like to give my blessings to all the people who tried to save my life." A longer recording of his final statements was part of a collection of subpoenaed Georgia execution tapes, later made into the audio documentary *The Execution Tapes.*

I am as a grain of sand on the beach of the black race. The black race has lost its pride and dignity and is slowly dying from within and without. My death ends my tears, and the fortune of watching my race slowly die. If there is such a thing as an Antichrist, it ain't one man, but the whole white race.

MARVIN FRANCOIS, convicted of murder, Florida. Executed May 29, 1985

When Francois's mask fell off during the robbery of a drug house, according to witnesses, he said all eight people who saw his face had to die. He shot six victims in the head with a shotgun. Two others were wounded but survived to help convict Francois.

In his cell:

I would like to thank the Lord for giving me the opportunity to make this statement. And I thank the Lord for the chaplain. And for all the people of this administration that He has placed in to work here. And if my execution is carried out, I know that it will be done—did by the Lord's will. And I just want the people to know that I am not the same person that I was once upon a time because I was baptized here in 1980, and the old creature was destroyed and I became a new creature. And I would just like to just ask that people remember me as the Christian and not as the old Jerome Bowden because the old Jerome Bowden is no more. The new Jerome Bowden is here, and when he has paved the way, he will be remembered as the Christian Jerome Bowden.

And I would just like to thank all the people out in the world that have fought so hard to preserve my life. And I'm not giving up. I might give out, but I cannot give up because I know that the Lord is still here with me no matter what may happen. And I would just like to thank the whole entire world and the people that's in the world. And also the fine people of this administration that I have had the opportunity to come in contact with the time that I have been here—including Chaplain [name].

And I would just say that I'm thankful that Mr. [name] and all his administration have done whatever they could do to make this thing much more easier for me to deal with because it is a very hard thing to deal with, and I know it and they know it. That's why they are still standing close by: to make sure that everything goes according to plan. And I would like to thank Correction Officer [name] that has stayed with me from the time that things started until now. And for what this man did to me, I would just like to close out and say God bless Mr. [name] and all the administration.

In the death chamber:
I am Jerome Bowden, and I would just like to state that my execution is about to be carried out. And I would like to thank the people at this institution for taking such good care of me in the way that they did. And I hope that by my execution being carried out that it may bring some light to this thing that is wrong. And I would like to have a final prayer with Chaplain [name] if that is possible. Thank you very much.

JEROME BOWDEN, convicted of murder, Georgia. Executed June 24, 1986

Bowden, who had an IQ of 65, was convicted of murdering fifty-five-year-old Kathryn Striker during a robbery in her home. His case drew protests from groups concerned about mental retardation and from rock stars such as Lou Reed, Sting, and the band U2. Two years later, the state of Georgia banned executions of murderers found "guilty but mentally retarded."

It has taken me some time, but I have learned that I'm a part of everyone, and everyone is a part of me. And that no matter where I go or how I go, everyone goes with me.

RICHARD TUCKER, convicted of murder, Georgia. Executed May 22, 1987

Tucker's statement was the briefest captured in a collection of subpoenaed Georgia execution tapes, later made into the audio documentary *The Execution Tapes*. He was convicted in the kidnapping, rape, and murder of retired nurse Edna Sandefur.

Yeah, I think I'd rather be fishing.

JIMMY GLASS, convicted of murder, Louisiana. Executed June 12, 1987

Jimmy Glass was a twenty-five-year-old high school dropout who received the death penalty for murdering Newt and Erlene Brown on Christmas Eve in their home. Glass claimed that cellmate Jimmy Wingo, with whom he had escaped from jail on the same evening, held a gun to his head and forced him to perform the murders after he called Wingo by name. Wingo was executed a few days later for the same crimes.

I am an innocent man. You are murdering me this day. I do still love you all in Christ. God bless you all.

JIMMY WINGO, convicted of murder, Louisiana. Executed June 16, 1987

A former Boy Scout and park ranger, Wingo claimed he had never entered the house where the Browns were killed (see previous entry). Outside the prison, on the night of his execution, a sixteen-year-old boy whose sister had been killed by another inmate held a sign that read "Tell them about Jesus, then put them in the chair."

I'd just like to tell the Richard family that I'm very, very sorry. I hope in their hearts they can forgive.

WILLIE CELESTINE, convicted of rape and murder, Louisiana. Executed July 20, 1987

Serial rapist Celestine faced the electric chair for the rape, beating, and strangulation of eighty-one-year-old Marceliane Richard. Witnesses to the execution included his attorney Millard Farmer and death-penalty opponent Sister Helen Prejean, who served as his spiritual adviser.

I was not guilty for the charge for which I was arrested and this morning I tell you I am not guilty of the charge for which I am about to be executed. I go this morning with a clear conscience. I bear no guilt. I'm at peace with myself, with the world, with each of you. God bless you.

WILLIE JASPER DARDEN, convicted of murder, Florida.
Executed March 15, 1988

Despite intervention from Amnesty International, Rev. Jesse Jackson, and *Superman* actress Margot Kidder, Darden died for the shooting death of James Turman, a furniture store owner. Turman's wife identified Darden as the man who robbed her of fifteen dollars and forced her to perform oral sex on him as her husband lay dying from a gunshot "between the eyes." Darden maintained his innocence for fourteen years on death row and claimed to have an alibi to prove it.

I hope with all my heart I will be the last sacrificial lamb of a system that is not just, and all these people know it is not just. Let's hope there are not many more that have to be sacrificed. The executions serve no purpose. . . . Some of you look at this as an execution. I look at this as freedom. I've been in prison for 15 years. Now I'm free.

JEFFREY DAUGHERTY, convicted of murder, Florida.
Executed November 7, 1988

Though Daugherty delivered a six-minute statement prior to his execution, little survives. Prosecutors claimed he killed four women in a three-week period while traveling with his girlfriend, Bonnie Jean Heath, and an uncle. Daugherty received life terms for three of the murders but was sentenced to death for the shooting of hitchhiker Lavonne Sailer. Heath testified against him in exchange for a twenty-five-year sentence for second-degree murder.

I'd like you to give my love to my family and friends.

TED BUNDY, AKA THEODORE ROBERT BUNDY, BORN THEODORE ROBERT
COWELL, convicted of murder, Florida. Executed January 24, 1989

Serial killer Bundy confessed to thirty murders, and the actual
number of victims may have been even higher. He preyed mostly on
white women aged fifteen to twenty-five, whom he often lured into
his vehicle.

In a final jailhouse interview, Bundy blamed pornography for
playing a role in his sex crimes and defended his family. He told in-
terviewer James Dobson, "I grew up in a wonderful home with two
dedicated and loving parents, as one of five brothers and sisters.
We, as children, were the focus of my parents' lives. We regularly
attended church. My parents did not drink or smoke or gamble.
There was no physical abuse or fighting in the home. I'm not saying
it was 'Leave It to Beaver,' but it was a fine, solid Christian home. I
hope no one will try to take the easy way out of this and accuse my
family of contributing to this . . ."

I hope and pray that all the new and reopened wounds will be healed quickly after my passing. My death is the Lord's will and I am now with my Lord and Savior Jesus Christ in Heaven.

AUBREY ADAMS JR., convicted of murder, Florida. Executed May 4, 1989

Adams, a prison guard at the time of his arrest, was sentenced to
death for smothering eight-year-old Trisa Gail Thornley. He had
made an obscene phone call to the child's home and then took her
from the residence. Naked and mutilated, her body was found two
months later in a plastic bag.

Outside the prison, Thornley's mother told reporters: "It's a decade too late, but we finally got justice today. I wish my husband
were here today. This killed him."

One mistake . . . 13 years ago, and that's a long time. Nothing is going to be accomplished. I have peace with myself . . . To the Cleveland family, they say it wasn't for the revenge, but it's hard for me to see, to understand. I hope they're happy.

DALTON PREJEAN, convicted of murder, Louisiana. Executed May 18, 1990

At age fourteen, Prejean shot and killed a taxi driver, a crime for which he was sent to reform school for two and half years. Just six months after his release, he shot Louisiana state trooper Donald Cleveland in the face after the officer pulled him over for a broken tail light. Amnesty International claimed that Prejean, an African American, had not received a fair trial from an all-white jury. Supporters said that he had suffered brain damage from an abusive aunt and had an IQ of 71.

Let my death serve as an instigator that will awaken a nation to fight and adopt the philosophy of the late, great Dr. Martin Luther King Jr., who said, "Injustice anywhere is a threat to justice everywhere."

WALLACE THOMAS, convicted of murder, Alabama. Executed July 13, 1990

Fourteen years after the abduction and fatal shooting of Quenette Shehane, age twenty-one, and several appeals later, Thomas was executed. Both of Thomas's accomplices had implicated him in the shooting. Thomas, a black man, vehemently protested the death penalty, calling it racist. He even wore a purple ribbon and a sticker that said "Execute justice, not people," to his own execution.

I want it to be over with, not for me, but for the victims' families. I'm ready to go to a better place. I want it to be put to rest. I've asked for forgiveness from a lot of people and I was able to forgive myself. . . . Let me be the last person. There is a better way to deal with crimes than taking peoples' lives.

BUDDY EARL JUSTUS, convicted of murder, Virginia.
Executed December 13, 1990

Justus delivered his final words in a radio interview with Roanoke's WFIR on the morning of his execution. He had received multiple death sentences for slaying three women, including a pregnant nurse he raped before killing.

I'm disappointed with the almost total lack of fairness in the American criminal justice system. This is truly a sad time in our country's history, when political concerns take on more importance than the fundamental rights of the individual.

ROY ALLEN HARICH, convicted of rape and murder, Florida.
Executed April 24, 1991

Harich was the first prisoner executed after the Supreme Court limited inmates to one federal appeal, a fact reflected in his last words. In 1981, according to court documents, Harich had offered a lift to Carlene Gayle Kelly, age eighteen, and her friend Deborah Miller, seventeen, then drove them to a remote area to smoke marijuana. He slashed their throats and shot both in the head, but Miller survived to testify against him.

I cannot change what I have done in the past, no matter how much I wish that I could. Nothing I can say or do will stop the pain that I have caused. I do not expect people to forgive me for what I have done in my life. For I am and have paid for my ways.

ALBERT CLOZZA, convicted of rape and murder, Virginia.
Executed July 24, 1991

Clozza confessed to having raped and murdered of Patricia Beth Bolton, age thirteen, after abducting her as she walked home. Clozza did not ask for clemency. He was the 150th inmate executed since the Supreme Court reinstated capital punishment in 1976.

An innocent man is going to be murdered tonight. When my innocence is proven I hope Americans will recognize the injustice of the death penalty as all other civilized nations have.

ROGER K. COLEMAN, convicted of rape and murder, Virginia.
Executed May 20, 1992

A media flurry, including an appearance on the TV talk show *Donahue*, fueled speculation that Coleman was innocent of killing his sister-in-law Wanda McCoy, despite evidence to the contrary and his failure of a polygraph test. Coleman's supporters claimed that another man boasted of the killing and that he did not receive adequate counsel. His last meal included a pepperoni pizza, fudge cookies, and a 7-Up. Posthumous DNA evidence did not exonerate him.

Again, I am sorry for what I have done. I do not know if my death will change anything or if it will bring anyone peace. I want to ask the families . . . to forgive me.

JOHN JOUBERT, convicted of murder, Nebraska. Executed July 17, 1996

Joubert was found guilty of murdering three boys. He was denied a last-minute request to have his brain scanned to search for abnormalities.

I bear witness that there is no God but Allah and I bear witness that the prophet Mohammed is the messenger of God.

JOHN MILLS JR., convicted of murder, Florida. Executed December 6, 1996

Mills and another man robbed Lester Lawhon, then took him to an abandoned airstrip and beat him with a tire iron. When Lawhon tried to escape, Mills shot him twice. While in prison, Mills converted to Islam and asked that the name Yuhanna Abdullah Muhammed be added to his file. Lawhon's mother did not attend the execution, saying, "Another family is suffering." Mills's accomplice, Michael Frederick, pleaded no contest to second-degree murder and received 347 years in prison.

I am still innocent.

PEDRO MEDINA, convicted of murder, Florida. Executed March 25, 1997

As Medina was being electrocuted, blue and orange flames burst from his head, igniting the death mask. The event overshadowed details of the Cuban native's conviction for shooting a teacher in 1982. After the execution, Attorney General Bob Butterworth said, "People who wish to commit murder, they better not do it in the state of Florida because we may have a problem with our electric chair."

CHAPTER
FOUR

THE GAS CHAMBER

The first words—the first *last* words—uttered from the gas chamber are lost. On February 7, 1924, in Carson City's Nevada State Prison, Gee Jon, a Chinese immigrant, was the first person to die in the gas chamber. Officials had built the three-room chamber outside the prison to placate concerns about gas leaking from the cell. Gee died in six minutes, according to newspaper accounts. "When the gas was turned on," reads a *Boston Globe* story, "he raised his head and looked around at the hissing sound of the liquid hydrocyanic acid being blown in. . . . Then his head fell forward. His expression remained placid during the six minutes he continued to breathe. His head rolled back and fell forward periodically." His last words, if he had any, do not survive.

But the gas chamber would mark a turning point in the last-words ritual. In some cases history has recorded not only a last formal statement but also a final exclamation. For the first time, inmates could now talk during the execution, as the cyanide pellets mixed with sulfuric acid and the gas overwhelmed them. Famously, in 1943, convicted murderer Warren Cramer said, "I can't smell anything yet," as his execution began. Then, a moment later: "It smells like rotten eggs."

Until the 1920s, the United States relied on two methods to execute most condemned inmates: hanging and electrocution. Both

175

the gallows and the electric chair were touted as deterrents to future criminals. But during the latter half of the nineteenth century, a movement arose advocating what seemed to be a quicker, less painful form of execution: the gas chamber. In 1896, a group of Pennsylvania doctors declared death by inhaling lethal gas to be more humane than electrocution or hanging. "No doubt the gas chamber will be at once more effective, cheaper, and less repugnant to the gentler sentiments than the electric chair," read a *New York Times* article from December 1896.

The gas chamber procedure was developed in the 1920s by U.S. Army Medical Corps's Major D. A. Turner after he witnessed the effects of poison gas on the battlefield during World War I. The first to adopt this method of execution, Nevada's legislature unanimously passed a bill opting to use the gas chamber in 1921, just one week after the state's deputy attorney general declared lethal gas executions to be more humane than electrocution. Nevada's original plan was to place condemned inmates in an airtight cell the week they were scheduled to die. Without telling the inmate the specific day, jailers could pump hydrocyanic acid, a pesticide for orange trees, into the cell at night while he or she was sleeping. Given the often gruesome outcomes of hanging and electrocution, the idea of killing prisoners in their sleep with lethal gas was attractive.

In fact, critics of using lethal gas said it would be too nice to the condemned. "It is said to be a painless death, and on that account is recommended to the tender-hearted," read a June 1901 opinion piece in the *Los Angeles Times*. "At the same time, perhaps it isn't well to have it understood that capital punishment is to be made a luxurious proposition."

A Carson City reporter stated that Nevada had moved "one step further from the savage state" after the execution of Gee Jon. His quick and seemingly painless death led others to believe that the gas chamber was a more efficient and humane means of execution, but this proved not to be always the case. Death took twelve minutes for Albert Kessel and fifteen and a half minutes for Robert Lee Cannon on December 2, 1938. Both had received death sentences for participating in a Sacramento prison riot in which the warden, a guard, and two inmates died. Kessel and Cannon were the first two inmates to test California's new gas chamber at San Quentin State

Prison. When the gas was turned on, Cannon smiled and mouthed, "There's nothing to it!" before he lost consciousness. Meanwhile, witnesses heard Kessel say, "It's bad!" as the gas hit him. Both convulsed repeatedly and bobbed their heads until they died. Many in the audience had seen a number of hangings, but they said watching a gas chamber execution was much more painful. "That was the most terrible thing I've ever seen," said the prison chaplain in the *Los Angeles Times.* "I've witnessed 52 hangings, I could find nothing humane about it, and I never want to watch anything like that ever again."

A total of 592 people have died in gas chambers in the United States since 1924, but only a relatively small percentage of their final words were recorded. As of this writing, just eleven people have been executed by lethal gas since capital punishment was reinstated in 1976.

The lime-green gas chamber at San Quentin, as California's primary site of lethal gas execution until 1992, executed 195 men and women. The site became a final platform for a variety of political statements, many of them against the death penalty.

"Perhaps my execution will help to do away with capital punishment," said prisoner Robert Harmon in 1960.

But perhaps the most famous gas-chamber death was that of Caryl Chessman. In 1948, the state of California sentenced Chessman to death for kidnapping and raping two women, in addition to several other charges. Before Chessman's arrest, the perpetrator of the crimes was called "the Red Light Bandit" for using a cellophane-covered spotlight on his car for spotting potential victims. Chessman, who had a long record of petty crimes, continued to claim his innocence. He filed appeals as his own attorney throughout the 1950s and later sold the rights to his autobiography, *Cell 2455, Death Row,* which was adapted into a feature film.

Chessman's case triggered significant uproar in the United States and abroad because he had never been convicted of murder. (The statute used to sentence Chessman to death on kidnapping charges was repealed in 1955.) He won eight reprieves of his execution but lost his appeal to the California Supreme Court in 1960. Ten minutes after notification of the ruling was received, he was strapped into the chamber and, taking the advice of doctors, inhaled the gases deeply to speed up the cyanide's effects. Meanwhile, federal judge Louis E. Goodman tried to reach San Quentin to order a one-hour stay, but his secretary had miscopied the prison's phone number. By the time she had dialed the correct number, prison workers had already dropped the cyanide pellets into Chessman's chamber. His final words were recorded two ways: "So long, Father . . . So long, Reverend." "Tell Rosalie [Asher, his lawyer] I said goodbye. It's all right."

Don't strap me to the chair too tightly. It might keep the gas from my lungs.

JOSEPH BEHITER, convicted of murder, Nevada. Executed July 13, 1934

Behiter whistled a tune as he walked to the gas chamber, but few other details of his execution survive. Behiter received the death penalty for murdering Maxine Armstrong, a Las Vegas dancehall girl; he was the seventh man executed by lethal gas in the state of Nevada. The entire account of his execution measured five paragraphs in the *Los Angeles Times*.

All set, warden, I'm ready to go. Lead me to it. I've had a swell time here and I'm not anxious to get rid of any of these swell fellows. The warden has treated me wonderfully.

LEONARD BELONGIA, convicted of murder, Colorado. Executed June 21, 1935

Working as a sheep rancher for room and board, Belongia lived with the family of Albert E. Oesterick. Needing more money to get married and feeling that he was underpaid, Belongia murdered Oesterick, wounded his wife, and beat their son with a rifle. During his trial he admitted his crime, and a physician testified that Belongia had "the mentality of a ten-year-old." Making no attempt to appeal, Belongia donated his body to a Denver medical school, which later rejected him because no one wanted to pay ten dollars to ship the body.

On his way into the chamber:

I feel fine. I'm going right ahead.

Asked if he wanted anything else:

You might get me a gas mask.

JACK SULLIVAN, convicted of murder, Arizona. Executed May 15, 1936

In his final moments Sullivan, age twenty-three, smoked a cigar, drank a glass of whiskey, and mugged for the camera. He grinned and waved at witnesses during his execution for the slaying of a railroad officer.

There's nothing to it.

ROBERT LEE CANNON

So long.

ALBERT KESSELL

KESSELL (SOMETIMES RECORDED AS KESSEL) AND CANNON, convicted of murder, California. Executed Dec. 2, 1938

Having taken part in the Folsom Prison riot dubbed "Bloody Sunday," Kessell, Cannon, and two others were sentenced to death after Warden C. A. Larkin died from stab wounds.

The pair spent the night of their execution shouting to one another in adjoining cells, singing, and listening to records. Ten minutes before the execution, they smoked a cigar and took a shot of whiskey. They were executed together.

While in the death chamber, Cannon looked to spectators, mouthed his last words, and began to say something else when his face contorted, eyes rolled, and head dropped.

I am a young man still. To me, life is life whether inside a penitentiary or out. I stand convicted of murder, but in my heart, I am no murderer. Here, surely, is the contingency for which the alternative penalty was planned.

DEWITT COOK, convicted of rape and murder, California.
Executed January 31, 1941

Cook, age twenty-one, listened to the radio on the last night of his life, which he spent sleepless, and come morning he refused breakfast. He had been convicted two years prior for bludgeoning to death Anya Sosoyeva, a twenty-four-year-old dancer and art student. His appeal for clemency was rejected. During his last night, he spoke with a guard. "I made up my mind," he said. "I have to go."

As the execution began:
I can't smell anything yet.

A moment later:
It smells like rotten eggs.

WARREN CRAMER, convicted of murder, California. Executed May 14, 1943

A career pyromaniac and car thief, Cramer had turned to violent assault during the robbery of a drugstore. He pleaded guilty and openly stated that he preferred capital punishment. San Quentin Warden Clinton Duffy described Cramer as a "brilliant" man who thought he had a "rotten streak in his system which he couldn't control."

I have nothing to say except that I am innocent. It's easier to convict a Negro than a white person. So long everybody

ROBERT E. FOLKES, convicted of murder, Oregon. Executed January 5, 1945

Folkes, age twenty-three, was convicted of slashing a woman's throat on a Southern Pacific train while working as a cook. The Associated Press described him as "the first condemned man to see the chamber," as Folkes was the first prisoner to ever walk into the Oregon gas chamber without a blindfold on.

To reporters:

I came from cultured, educated people. I have a background of culture. My parents were not delinquents and they did not rear delinquent children.

Also to reporters:

The Governor is a gentleman—and no gentleman could send a lady to her death.

To the warden:

I'm ready. I've been ready for a long time.

To a guard, who suggested she wear a blindfold:

I don't want to wear a mask.

LOUISE PEETE (AKA LOUISE PEETE JUDSON OR LOFIE LOUISE PRESLAR), convicted of murder, California. Executed April 11, 1947

Facing the gas chamber for the murder of an elderly woman, Peete had already spent eighteen years in prison for the shooting death of a man. Between those murders, at least two husbands from her three marriages had committed suicide. One reporter observed that she "kept a roomful of newsmen guffawing. . . . It was a most amazing interview with a woman about to die."

To the warden, having spat at a priest:

I hate your guts.

He then said he looked forward to joining his friends in hell.

ROBERT BATTALINO, convicted of murder, Colorado. Executed January 7, 1949

Restaurant cook Battalino received the death sentence for shooting his boss, Michael Randolph, a Denver restaurant owner, after he fired Battalino and accused him of taking money from the register.

As guards strapped Battalino into the gas chamber chair, he "spurned religious overtures from two prison chaplains." The *Rocky Mountain News* headline read "Battalino Dies Smiling."

Thanks for a million things. Thanks for a million things. I've got a son, six foot three inches, one hundred and seventy pounds. He's married, got two kids. He's in the service overseas right now. . . . So I've left something good—one decent thing out of a dirty life . . .

LLOYD EDISON SAMPSELL (AKA "THE YACHT BANDIT"), convicted of robbery and murder, California. Executed April 25, 1952

Sampsell and an accomplice plundered Pacific Coast banks before stealing away in his yacht. He pilfered a total of $200,000 in his career but died with only $5.27 to his name. Sampsell, age fifty-two, was convicted of killing Arthur W. Smith in a San Diego finance company robbery.

Before the gas took its effect, he turned to the nearly one hundred witnesses gathered and winked.

I've lived a rough life, but I wonder if God has a place for people like me?

JOHNSON WILLIAM CALDWELL, convicted of murder, California. Executed May 6, 1955

After serving time in the Texas State Prison for embezzlement, Caldwell found his way to California, where he met Lilly Pearl Storts. Three days and one drunken party later, they were married. When Caldwell asked for an informal loan one night, Storts refused. The next morning he returned home, hit her with an iron pipe, and strangled her to death with two belts. When stopped by an officer in Arkansas, he surprised the lawman by saying: "I'm the man you want for the murder of my wife."

Don't you fellows do anything I wouldn't do.

JOHN (JACK) SANTO, convicted of murder, California. Executed June 3, 1955

Santo was one of two men with whom Barbara Graham shared the murder conviction for having killed Mabel Monohan. Santo's execution would immediately follow Graham's. A reporter and witness described Santo as a "swaggering dandy." As his execution neared, Santo sat with fellow inmate Emmett Perkins talking about cars, eating fried chicken and a tomato and avocado salad, and watching *You Bet Your Life*.

After two last-minute stays:
Why do they torture me? I was ready to go at 10.

After requesting a blindfold:
I don't want to have to look at people.

BARBARA GRAHAM, convicted of robbery and murder, California. Executed June 3, 1955

Graham was convicted for her role in the murder of Mabel Mono-han, an elderly Burbank widow (see previous entry). A mother of three when she was convicted at age thirty-two, Graham had a history with police dating back to age thirteen. The night before her execution, she told her attorney, "Good people are always so sure they're doing justice," a statement that was later reported as "Good people are always so sure they are right"—and mistaken for her last words. After Graham's execution, she was portrayed by Susan Hayward in the 1958 film *I Want to Live.* Hayward won an Oscar for Best Actress in the role.

I'm innocent! I'm innocent! I'm innocent!

As guards dragged him into the gas chamber:
Don't let me go like this, God!

While being strapped into the chair:
I did wrong but I didn't kill anybody!

To witnesses and reporters:
You're the ones that put me here. God, you're a dirty son of a bitch because I'm innocent!

ROBERT OTIS PIERCE, convicted of murder, California.
Executed April 6, 1956

With an accomplice Smith Edward Jordan, Pierce killed an Oakland cabdriver in a seven-dollar robbery turned murder. The man, Charles Rose, died after being struck several times by the butt of Pierce's gun.

After his conviction, Pierce spent his time in prison writing "All of God's Children Got Rhythm," but the manuscript was confiscated by prison officials and was lost.

The previous day, Pierce vowed to put on a show for the other death row inmates, saying, "It will take two guys to get me in that chair, 'cause I'm going to go out fighting, kicking and screaming."

On his execution day, Pierce slashed his throat with a broken shard of mirror. After wrapping his neck with a prison shirt, he fought guards all the way to the chamber. It took the combined strength of four guards to strap him into the chair, where he continued to struggle and curse.

Witnesses looked on in horror as he bled, wept, and cursed in the gas chamber.

In the death chair, after Warden Tinsley patted him on the shoulder:

Thanks, Warden.

JOHN "JACK" GILBERT GRAHAM, convicted of murder, Colorado. Executed January 11, 1957

Once a petty criminal and drifter, Graham would eventually force drastic changes in airport security measures on one of the darkest days in Colorado's history. A twenty-three-year-old husband and father whose family lived with his mother, Daisie King, Graham owed more than four thousand dollars in bad checks. In an attempt to cash in on his mother's life insurance policy, Graham placed a bomb made of twenty-five sticks of dynamite in her suitcase. Eleven minutes after takeoff, the bomb went off in the cargo hold, killing forty-four people on the plane. *Time* magazine quoted Graham saying, "As far as feeling remorse for those people, I don't. I can't help it. Everybody pays their way and takes their chances. That's just the way it goes."

We might as well have gone in there six years ago.

LOUIS SMITH (AKA GENE E. GARLAND), convicted of murder, California. Executed February 8, 1957

Smith, along with accomplice John Allen, was convicted of killing inmate/barber Willard Burton while all three were serving life sentences in Folsom Prison. The evening before their execution, Allen and Smith played pinochle for hours with a guard.

Perhaps my execution will help to do away with capital punishment.

ROBERT HARMON, assault with a deadly weapon while under a life sentence, California. Executed August 9, 1960

Despite the efforts of the American Civil Liberties Union, Harmon saw himself as too violent and bloodthirsty to go on living. A four-time convict serving ten years to life for armed robbery, Harmon was convicted of knifing a fellow inmate, a crime punishable by death. Harmon stated that if not put to death he would continue his attacks. He demanded that no one interfere with his sentence.

To his chaplain:

I've been an ugly sinner.

Later:

[I'm] truly sorry for the heartaches I've caused.

ROBERT LEE GOLDSBY, convicted of murder, Mississippi. Executed May 31, 1961

After nineteen appeals, two trials, and several rescheduled execution dates over seven years, Goldsby faced the gas chamber for the murder of Mozelle McCorkle Nelms. Goldsby shot Nelms at the café service station run by her husband, after a fight broke out. The night before his execution, he told a reporter: "I know I am going to a better place. I'm positive I've been saved by Jesus Christ."

I am Jesus Christ—look what they have done to me.

AARON C. MITCHELL, convicted of murder, California. Executed April 12, 1967

Having left school and his drunken, abusive father behind in Tennessee, Mitchell spent considerable spans of time in Missouri and Colorado prisons. After attempting to rob a tavern, he killed Officer Arnold Gamble in a gunfight outside the establishment. Many campaigned to save Mitchell from the chamber, and he did an interview for *Ebony* magazine in which he said, "Every Negro ever convicted of killing a police officer has died in that gas chamber, so what chance did I have? . . . I'm not bitter, I don't think. But I know that my being a Negro has been a big factor in everything that's happened to me."

I guess nobody is going to call, I guess nobody is going to call. . . . Let's go with it, let's go with it.

EDWARD EARL JOHNSON, convicted of murder, Mississippi.
Executed May 20, 1987

Thirty feet from the gas chamber, Johnson sat in his cell and read the Bible, sang hymns, and played chess with family. Although he had no prior criminal record, Johnson had been convicted of shooting town marshal Jake Trest five times. A key witness initially said Johnson was not the killer, then changed her story. Johnson claimed to have been intimidated into a false confession when, he contended, officers threatened him and his grandparents with violence. Johnson and his family maintained his innocence to the end. Until the last moment, he believed a telephone call would halt his execution.

Johnson's execution and case were the basis of the documentary *Fourteen Days in May*.

You can be a king or a street sweeper, but everyone dances with the Grim Reaper.

ROBERT ALTON HARRIS, convicted of murder, California. Executed April 21, 1992

Harris was the first person to receive the death penalty after the state of California reinstated it in 1976. He went to the gas chamber for two 1978 murders: he and his brother abducted two sixteen-year-old boys from a fast food establishment, drove them to a remote location, and shot and killed them. Harris's brother testified against him, received a six-year sentence, and was discharged in 1983. Harris's last words are paraphrased from the comedic portrayal of the character Death in the 1991 film *Bill & Ted's Bogus Journey*.

To all my loved ones, I hope they find peace. To all of you here today, I forgive you and I hope I can be forgiven in my next life.

WALTER LAGRAND, convicted of murder, Arizona. Executed March 3, 1999

German citizen LaGrand protested his death sentence by choosing the gas chamber over lethal injection with the hope that his punishment would end up being ruled cruel and unusual punishment. The Supreme Court overruled that logic, but not without protest from the German government and other countries worldwide. The World Court held a thirty-minute hearing in which a Sri Lankan judge urged the U.S. government to prevent the execution, but Arizona governor Jane Hull proceeded with it. LaGrand's brother Karl had been executed for his role in the crime a week prior.

CHAPTER FIVE

LETHAL INJECTION

Though lethal injection was first administered in 1982, the needle had been considered as a method of execution almost one hundred years earlier. Circa 1885, lethal injection was favored by El-bridge T. Gerry, founder of the Society for the Prevention of Cruelty to Children. This philanthropist and politician headed New York state's famed "Death Commission," which eventually recommended the abolition of the gallows in favor of the electric chair. Gerry thought an overdose of morphine administered by a hypodermic needle would be the least invasive, most humane method of delivering death. But only a small minority of experts polled favored this method at the time. Lethal injection featured some logistical problems. What if the condemned had a history of intravenous drug addiction? This, combined with the concern that doctors used morphine as a painkiller and therefore did not want to create a public fear of the drug dissuaded the legal community from adopting lethal injection.

Yet after nearly a hundred years, the debate came full circle. Oklahoma became the first state to adopt lethal injection, but Texas became the first to use it. On December 7, 1982, Charles Brooks Jr.—who was convicted of murdering a mechanic after a test drive—prayed to Allah with his spoken last words. As the first inmate to die by lethal injection, he released this statement to the media: "I, at this very moment, have absolutely no fear of what may happen to this body. My fear is for Allah, God only, who has at this moment the only power to determine if I should live or die. . . . As a devout Muslim, I am taught and believe that this material life is only for the express purpose of preparing oneself for the real life that is to come. . . . Since becoming Muslim, I have tried to live as Allah wanted me to live." Since Brooks was executed, Texas has outpaced the rest of the country in its rate of execution, which accounts for the state's prominence in this sample collection.

While last words collected in past era were often political, few have been as consistently, vehemently anti–capital punishment as those from the current age of lethal injection.

While the same statements of innocence, rage, forgiveness, and peace remain, the increased number of capital punishment challenges has led a great number of prisoners to use their final words to protest the death penalty. For example, Henry Dunn confessed to kidnapping, torturing, and murdering a gay man. He was convicted of a hate crime and strapped to a Texas gurney in 2003. "The death penalty in Texas is broke," he said.

When an attorney can be forced to represent you who is not qualified to represent you under Texas laws, the system does not work. When an attorney can dismiss your appeal process, by missing a filing deadline or for failing to file documents on behalf of a client, that's not due process of law as guaranteed under the United States Constitution; the system does not work.

When officials of any state, such as the state of Texas, have so much confidence in their justice system, mistakes will be made, and innocent people will be executed. Texas has executed innocent people, and tonight, Texas has shown just how broke and unfair its system is. There is no clemency in Texas, a process that needs to be reviewed, and fixed. Most importantly, the Texas justice system needs to be fixed. I hope the politicians such as Elliot Naishtat, Harold Dutton, Rodney Ellis, and others, continue to do their part in trying to fix the Texas justice system, and until so is done, continue to work for a moratorium on the death penalty in Texas.

To my family and friends . . . who have always been there for me and done everything in their will and power to help me and stand by my side, I love you dearly, and you will always be in my heart forever. Please continue to struggle and fight against the death penalty, as its only use has been for revenge, and it does not deter crime. It's time for a moratorium in the state of Texas.

The word *moratorium* became politically viable again. In 2000, for the first time in any state since 1972, when the U.S. Supreme Court suspended capital punishment in forty states, Illinois governor George Ryan called a moratorium on the death penalty. "We have now freed more people than we have put to death under our system—13 people have been exonerated and 12 have been put to death. There is a flaw in the system, without question, and it needs to be studied," he said.

In 2003, Gov. Ryan went further, commuting the sentences of all 167 inmates on death row and saying: "Our capital system is haunted by the demon of error: error in determining guilt and error in determining who among the guilty deserves to die. What effect was race having? What effect was poverty having? Because of all these reasons, today I am commuting the sentences of all death row inmates."

Ryan's actions would become part of what anti–capital punishment forces called "the Innocence Revolution." Since 1973, according to the Death Penalty Information Center, more than 130 death row inmates have been exonerated through DNA evidence and other means.

Starting in 2006, California, Maryland, Florida, and other states likewise suspended capital executions. In Florida, after convicted murderer Angel Diaz took thirty-four minutes and two injections to die, Gov. Jeb Bush and a U.S. district court judge halted the practice, fearing that lethal injection might risk violating "the constitutional ban on cruel and unusual punishment." Diaz proclaimed his innocence to the end, saying: "The state of Florida is killing an innocent person. The state of Florida is committing a crime, because I am innocent. The death penalty is not only a form of vengeance, but also a cowardly act by humans. I'm sorry for what is happening to me and my family who have been put through this."

On April 16, 2008, the Supreme Court rejected *Base v. Rees*, a Kentucky challenge to lethal injection's constitutionality. Executions resumed in capital punishment states, as did litigation against the death penalty.

I want to say that I am sorry for all the hurt that I have caused. I know that everybody has gone through a lot of pain—all the families connected—and I am sorry, and I want to thank everybody who has been supporting me all these six years.

I want to thank my family for standing with me through all this and my attorneys and all the support to me, everybody, the people with this prison department. I appreciated everything—their kindness and everything that they have shown me during these six years.

VELMA BARFIELD (AKA MARGIE VELMA BARFIELD), convicted of murder, North Carolina. Executed November 2, 1984

The first woman to die by lethal injection, Barfield confessed to the lethal poisoning of four people, including her fiancé. She refused a last meal and instead opted for Coca-Cola and Cheez Doodles. Barfield was the subject of Jerry Bledsoe's book *Death Sentence*.

Translation from Spanish:

God, forgive my brothers and my sisters for the sins I have committed. God, forgive me. God, I give my life for my brothers and sisters.

JESSE DE LA ROSA, convicted of murder, Texas. Executed May 15, 1985

De La Rosa was convicted of slaying a man during a convenience store robbery. Because the store's cash register wouldn't open, the take from the robbery was only a six-pack of beer.

I want to thank Father Walsh for his spiritual help. I want to thank Bob Ray [Sanders] and Steve Blow for their friendship. What I want people to know is that they call me a cold-blooded killer when I shot a man that shot me first. The only thing that convicted me was that I am a Mexican and that he was a police officer. People hollered for my life, and they are to have my life tonight. The people never hollered for the life of the policeman that killed a thirteen-year-old boy who was handcuffed in the back seat of a police car. The people never hollered for the life of a Houston police officer who beat up and drowned Jose Campo Torres and threw his body in the river. You call that equal justice. This is your equal justice. This is America's equal justice. A Mexican's life is worth nothing. When a policeman kills someone he gets a suspended sentence or probation. When a Mexican kills a police officer this is what you get. From there you call me a cold-blooded murderer. I didn't tie anyone to a stretcher. I didn't pump any poison into anybody's veins from behind a locked door. You call this justice. I call this and your society a bunch of cold-blooded murderers. I don't say this with any bitterness or anger. I just say this with truthfulness. I hope God forgives me for all my sins. I hope that God will be as merciful to society as he has been to me. I'm ready, Warden.

HENRY M. PORTER, convicted of murder, Texas. Executed July 9, 1985

Porter, a former painter's assistant, was convicted of shooting and killing Fort Worth police officer Henry P. Mailloux. The officer stopped Porter in the investigation of three armed robberies.

I deserve this. Tell everyone I said goodbye.

CHARLES WILLIAM BASS, convicted of murder, Texas.
Executed April 12, 1986

After robbing a lounge at gunpoint, Bass was coincidentally stopped
by two city marshals on a traffic warrant. When the officers noticed
that Bass's pockets were stuffed with rolls of coins and dollar bills,
he pulled a pistol, shot at both men, and killed one.

Goodbye to my family; I love all of you, I'm sorry for the
victim's family. I wish I could make it up to them. I want
those out there to keep fighting the death penalty.

RANDY WOOLLS, convicted of murder, Texas. Executed August 20, 1986

Woolls struck, stabbed, and set fire to ticket-taker Betty Stotts during the robbery of a drive-in theater. He said he was under the influence of Valium and beer at the time. During his execution, he
helped technicians find a vein they could use for the injection.

Mother, I am sorry for all the pain I've caused you.
Please forgive me. Take good care of yourself. Ernest
and Otis, watch out for the family. Thank all of you who
have helped me.

ANTHONY WILLIAMS, convicted of murder, Texas. Executed May 28, 1987

Williams had no prior arrest record when he abducted a thirteen-
year-old girl from a bowling alley. The girl was sexually assaulted
and then beaten to death with a board.

I did pretty good until about five minutes ago. Now my nerves are gone.

ARTHUR GARY BISHOP, convicted of murder, Utah. Executed June 10, 1988

A former Eagle Scout, honor student, and Mormon missionary, Bishop was arrested for molesting and murdering five young boys over a five-year span. Bishop had lived with so much guilt for committing the crimes that after he was convicted he dismissed his lawyers to expedite his death sentence.

Spoken to the prosecutor:
I love you.

SEAN FLANNAGAN, convicted of murder, Nevada. Executed June 23, 1989

Flannagan killed two men in Las Vegas because, he said, they were homosexuals.

I want to say I hold no grudges. I hate no one. I love my family. Tell everyone on death row to keep the faith and don't give up.

CARLOS DE LUNA, convicted of murder, Texas. Executed December 7, 1989

Although De Luna maintained his innocence in the murder of Wanda Lopez, a filling-station clerk in Corpus Christi, he did not use his final words to protest it. But De Luna maintained that the true murderer was actually Carlos Hernandez, a man who resembled him. Hernandez died in prison on another charge, and De Luna's story was covered by Steve Mills and Maurice Possley in the *Chicago Tribune*.

De Luna's execution became central in Steve James and Peter Gilbert's documentary *At the Death House Door*, wherein longtime prison chaplain—and former capital-punishment proponent—Reverend Carroll Pickett maintains his belief that De Luna was wrongfully executed.

I've already spoken the truth, but because it was spoken by someone accused, the truth was not respected. It must come from the man who spoke the lie. I am not the killer. I myself did not kill anyone. I go to my death without begging for my life. I will not humiliate myself. I will let no man break me. It just can't be done. There is a price to be paid. I want people to wake up to the reality of executions. The price to be paid will be a dear one.

JAMES SMITH, convicted of murder, Texas. Executed June 26, 1990

A former retail merchant, Smith saw his execution as a "point of honor" and requested a "lump of dirt" as his last meal, a request that was denied. Smith was found guilty of shooting insurance company employee Larry Don Rohus during a robbery in an office building. Smith had been arrested in a nearby apartment complex after being chased by Rohus's coworker, a man on the street, and workers inside the complex. He would later escape the courthouse during the jury selection for his trial, only to be apprehended again by an officer several blocks away.

Let's do it, man. Lock and load. Ain't life a [expletive deleted]?

G. W. GREEN, convicted of murder, Texas. Executed November 12, 1991

Green was convicted in the murder of a juvenile probation officer, John Denson, during a burglary. Green and two accomplices entered the man's home to steal his gun collection. Denson fought back until Joseph Starvaggi, one of Green's accomplices, shot and killed him. Green allegedly urged Starvaggi to kill Denson's family as well, but Starvaggi refused. Green's final words were redacted by the prison's press office.

I'm still awake.

ROBYN PARKS, convicted of murder, Oklahoma. Executed March 10, 1992

Parks's last words were spoken after his execution injection had been administered. He was reinjected and died shortly after.

I would like to tell young kids who might read this that drinking and hanging with the wrong people will get you where I am sitting right here.

ROBERT SAWYER, convicted of murder, Louisiana. Executed March 6, 1993

Sawyer was the first person executed by injection in Louisiana, after he and an accomplice were convicted in the murder of a babysitter. She died a couple of months after Sawyer and another man beat, raped, and poured scalding water on her before lighting her on fire. His lawyers claimed he had an IQ of 68.

Some sources that he also said, "I'm sorry for any hurt and pain they say I caused. I have no hard feelings toward anyone. I just want my sister, my brother-in-law, my son, all of my family to know that I love them and I'll be waiting on them in heaven."

I am innocent, innocent, innocent. Make no mistake about this; I owe society nothing. Continue the struggle for human rights, helping those who are innocent, especially Mr. Graham. I am an innocent man, and something very wrong is taking place tonight. May God bless you all. I am ready.

LEONEL TORRES HERRERA, convicted of murder, Texas. Executed May 12, 1993

Herrera was convicted in 1981 for the shooting death of a Los Fresnos police officer. Before he died, the officer, Enrique Carrisalez, identified Herrera from a police mug shot. At the time, authorities argued, Herrera was fleeing the scene of the murder of another public safety officer—a crime Herrera later pleaded guilty to.

Years later, attorneys argued that it was actually Leonel's brother Raul (murdered in 1984) who had committed—and confessed to—both killings and supplied sworn affidavits from witnesses who claimed to hear the confessions. The case, *Herrera v. Collins*, made it all the way to the Supreme Court, where Chief Justice William Rehnquist ruled that Herrera's "actual innocence" claim did not warrant federal habeas corpus relief.

In the 6–3 majority opinion, Justice Rehnquist wrote, "Once a defendant has been afforded a fair trial and convicted of the offense for which he was charged, the presumption of innocence disappears." After reviewing the evidence of the case, Sandra Day O'Connor wrote in a concurring opinion that Herrera was not innocent "in any sense of the word."

However, in dissent, Justice Harry Blackmun wrote: "The execution of a person who can show that he is innocent comes perilously close to simple murder."

One year later, after Herrera had been executed, Blackmun argued that capital punishment was inconsistent with the U.S. Constitution and "the death penalty experiment has failed.

"From this day forward, I no longer shall tinker with the machinery of death," he wrote.

Herrera is named on the Center on Wrongful Convictions' list of thirty-nine executions that took place "in face of compelling evidence of innocence or serious doubt about guilt."

I'm an African warrior, born to breathe and born to die. [After a pause:] I feel the poison running now.

CARL KELLY, convicted of murder, Texas. Executed August 20, 1993

Kelly, initially sentenced to prison for robbery, was released before the end of his term but couldn't maintain his good behavior on the outside. Within the year, he was wanted for robbery and multiple murders. Kelly was convicted of capital murder for shooting a convenience store clerk and another man, then throwing their bodies off a cliff. His accomplice received a life sentence for murder with a deadly weapon.

This execution is not justice. This execution is an act
    of revenge! If this is justice, then justice is blind.
Take a borderline retarded young male
who for the 1st time ever in his life committed a
    felony
then contaminate his TRUE tell all confession
add a judge who discriminates
plus an ALL-WHITE JURY
pile on an ineffective assistance of counsel
and execute the option of rehabilitation
persecute the witnesses
and you have created a death sentence for a family
    lasting over 10 years.

I will say once again. . . . This execution isn't justice—but an act of revenge. Killing R. J. will not bring Anil back, it only justifies "an eye for an eye and a tooth for a tooth." It's too late to help R. J., but maybe this poem will help someone else out there.

Seeing Through the Eyes of a Death Row Inmate

Sometime I wonder why, why he? Why did he go out into the world to see? To be out there and see what really did exist, now his name is written down on the Death Row list. I can only imagine how lonesome he was all by himself. We both knew he had no future left! His hopes and dreams became a fantasy. He often said, "There's nothing left of me." I have asked myself, why did he get involved with drugs? He could never explain why he hung around with thugs. Did it really make him feel like a king—Did he actually think he was capable of getting away with anything? He knew the thought of life wasn't ticking in his head. There's nothing left but the memory of those who lay dead. What was did, cannot be undone. He was confessed, he was one of the guilty ones. What would he say to the victim's family?—I'm sorry and my head wasn't on straight. I hope you will accept my apology, even though it's too late. I never knew I would take a life and commit a crime. I regret it because now I have to face the lethal injection while doing death row time. I knew I would pay with struggle and strife, but I never thought the cost would be me losing my life.

Richard J. Wilkerson
Written through his sister
Michelle Winn

I'd just like to say I don't hate nobody. What I did was wrong. I hope everybody is satisfied with what is about to happen.

RICHARD J. WILKERSON, convicted of murder, Texas.
Executed August 31, 1993

Two weeks before Wilkerson and two associates murdered four employees at a Houston amusement center, Wilkerson had been fired as a pit attendant from the establishment. For a time Wilkerson laughed about the murders, but before he was put to death by the state he expressed deep regret.

To a prison guard on the way to his execution:
Kiss my ass.

JOHN WAYNE GACY, convicted of rape and murder, Illinois.
Executed May 10, 1994

Gacy became one of the most notorious serial killers in U.S. history after his conviction for the murder of thirty-three boys, many of whom he sexually molested and strangled. He hid most of his victims under his house, and others were found nearby. To friends Gacy was "Pogo the Clown," because he liked to entertain neighborhood children. The press labeled him "the Killer Clown."

I have news for you—there is not going to be an execution. This is premeditated murder by the state of Texas. I hope in my death I'm that little bitty snowball that starts to bury the death penalty.

I have committed lots of sin in my life but I am not guilty of this crime. I would like to tell my son, daughter and wife that I love them—Eden, if they want proof, give it to them. Thanks for being my friend.

JESSE DEWAYNE JACOBS, convicted of murder, Texas. Executed January 4, 1995

Jacobs and his sister, Bobbie Jean Hogan, were convicted of the shooting death of Etta Ann Urdiales, ex-wife of Hogan's boyfriend. Jacobs confessed that his sister offered him five hundred dollars and a room if he would kill Urdiales, who allegedly was pestering Hogan's boyfriend about child support and custody. Jacobs later recanted and said Hogan actually pulled the trigger. Hogan was convicted of manslaughter and then released.

There's love and peace in Islam.

WILLIE RAY WILLIAMS, convicted of murder, Texas. Executed January 31, 1995

Williams shot Claude Schaffer Jr. during an armed robbery of a delicatessen.

I love you, Mom. Goodbye.

JEFFREY MOTLEY, convicted of kidnapping, convicted of robbery and murder, Texas. Executed February 7, 1995

A former Wisconsinite and air-conditioning repairman, Motley had spent five years in jail for burglary. Motley abducted a woman and forced her to withdraw three hundred dollars from a bank, then shot her with a 12-gauge shotgun.

Written:
Mario Cuomo is wright [sic]. Life without parole is much worse than the death penalty. All jurors should remember this. Attica and Oklahoma State Penitentiary are living hells. . . . I give my life because it is the most precious act of remorse I can make. I hope everyone will treat each other so this act need not be repeated. Words break under this burden. Farewell.

Spoken:
Please tell the media I did not get my SpaghettiOs, I got spaghetti. I want the press to know this.

THOMAS GRASSO, convicted of murder, Oklahoma. Executed March 20, 1995

Grasso did not receive his SpaghettiOs, but it was reported that his last meal did include steamed mussels, a cheeseburger, spaghetti, a strawberry milkshake, and pumpkin pie. Grasso had been convicted for the murder of two elderly women—one in New York and one in Oklahoma.

His convictions were highly publicized, as the two states fought over how and where he should be punished. Grasso himself asked for the death penalty. His case heated up the 1994 New York gubernatorial race between pro–death penalty George Pataki and Mario Cuomo, who opposed capital punishment.

The *New York Times* wrote: "Mr. Pataki campaigned strongly on the issue of restoring the death penalty, and one of his first acts on taking office was to send Mr. Grasso back to Oklahoma to be executed."

Governor Tucker, look over your shoulder; justice is coming. I wouldn't trade places with you or any of your cronies. Hell has victories; I am at peace.

RICHARD SNELL, convicted of murder, Arkansas. Executed April 19, 1995

A white supremacist, Snell expressed no regret for killing a Jewish businessman during a robbery and a black police officer during a traffic stop. Snell quoted Hitler's deputy Rudolf Hess and told the clemency board that he would "probably" shoot the officer again "under the same circumstances."

I would like to say that I have no animosity toward anyone. I made a mistake 18 years ago—I lost control of my mind but I didn't mean to hurt anyone. I have no hate toward humanity. I hope He will forgive me for what I done. I didn't mean to.

JOHN FEARANCE, convicted of murder, Texas. Executed June 20, 1995

Fearance's criminal record included time served for theft and rape. In 1977 he stabbed a neighbor, Larry Faircloth, while burglarizing his home. Earlier that night Fearance, an auto-body repairman, had fought with his wife after she cooked him a meat casserole, which he disliked.

He would later say, "I just lost control of my mind. I just snapped."

Fearance was apprehended three hours after the crime, and the victim's wife identified him.

I just want to say that I know it's so hard for people to lose someone they love so much. I think it's best for me to just say nothing at all.

KARL HAMMOND, convicted of murder, Texas. Executed June 21, 1995

Hammond had been released from prison but was under supervision due to a rape and burglary charge prior to the murder that put him on death row. During his release, he raped and stabbed to death an FBI secretary, Donna Lynn Vetter, in San Antonio. On March 30, in Bexar County Jail for capital murder, Hammond escaped when a jailer left open a door to a visitation area; however, police recaptured him. The negligence that allowed Hammond to escape led to the firings of two jailers and two sergeants.

I am the happiest man in the world. I'm not afraid to die. I'm not crazy. Jesus, your baby is coming home. I love you. I love you, Lord.

SYLVESTER ADAMS, convicted of murder, South Carolina.
Executed August 18, 1995

Despite numerous appeals and a plea by his mother and death penalty opponents to commute his sentence, thirty-nine-year-old Adams was executed for the 1979 strangling death of his sixteen-year-old mildly retarded neighbor Bryan Chambers. Upon breaking into the neighbor's home and finding no money there, he took Chambers into the woods to kill him. Adams's jury never learned that IQ screenings indicated that he himself was mildly mentally retarded, nor did they hear that his mental condition involved sudden and unpredictable bursts of rage.

That I feel the death penalty is not an answer to the problems at hand. That I feel it sends the wrong message to the youth of the country. Young people act as they see other people acting instead of as people tell them to act. And I would suggest that when a person has thought of doing anything against the law, that before they did, they should go to a quiet place and think about it seriously.

WILLIAM GEORGE BONIN, convicted of murder, California. Executed February 23, 1996

Bonin, dubbed "the Freeway Killer," received California's first lethal injection. He was convicted of killing fourteen young boys and men—ranging in age from twelve to nineteen—from 1979 to 1980. Bonin and his accomplice may have claimed as many as thirty-six victims. Their tortured and sexually abused bodies were found along southern California highways, and the wave of killings created a panic in the region. Earle Robitaille, a police chief in the area during the string of murders, later told the *New York Times*: "It was no longer 'Is it going to happen again?' but 'Who's going to be the next victim, and where will he be abducted and where will he be picked up?'"

There are people all over the world who face things worse than death on a daily basis, and in that sense I consider myself lucky. I cannot find the words to express the sadness I feel for bringing this hurt and pain on my loved ones. I will not ask forgiveness for the decisions I have made in this judicial process, only acceptance. God bless you all.

JOE GONZALES, convicted of murder, Texas. Executed September 18, 1996

Gonzales shot and killed fifty-year-old William J. Veader and then made off with cash and other items. The single gunshot was orchestrated to look like a self-inflicted wound, so authorities at first assumed Veader's death to be a suicide.

Merry Christmas.

LEM TUGGLE, convicted of rape and murder, Virginia.
Executed December 12, 1996

Sporting an arm tattoo saying "Born to Die," Tuggle was the final man to be executed out of the six who pulled off the largest death-row escape in U.S. history. Already on death row for the rape and murder of a fifty-two-year-old woman, Tuggle, along with five other inmates, used stolen uniforms to escape in a prison van. Within three weeks all six were apprehended, and by 1993 all but Tuggle had been executed.

Not from me but I have a message to you from God. Save the children. Find one who needs help and make a small sacrifice of your own wealth and save the innocent ones. They are the key for making the world a better place.

RICHARD BRIMAGE JR., convicted of rape and murder, Texas.
Executed February 10, 1997

Brimage, an electrician and Washington State native, received the death penalty for abducting and murdering a woman in October 1987. Brimage lured the woman into his residence before sexually assaulting her, then strangling and suffocating her with a sock.

It was horrible and inexcusable for me to take the life of your loved one and to hurt so many mentally and physically. I am here because I took a life and killing is wrong by an individual and by the state, and I am sorry we are here but if my death gives you peace and closure then this is all worthwhile. To all of my friends and family, I love you and I am going home.

DAVID HERMAN, convicted of robbery and murder, Texas. Executed April 2, 1997

A stockbroker, Herman was convicted of shooting and killing twenty-one-year-old Jennifer E. Burns during the robbery of a topless nightclub that he had previously managed. When Herman attempted to sexually assault Burns, she tried to defend herself and he shot her three times. He shot two other club employees as well, but both survived.

Thank the Lord for the past 14 years that have allowed me to grow as a man. To J.D.'s family, I am sorry for the suffering you have gone through the past 14 years. I hope you can get some peace tonight. To my family, I am happy to be going home to Jesus. Sweet Jesus, here I come. Take me home. I am going your way.

KENNETH GENTRY, convicted of murder, Texas. Executed April 16, 1997

Gentry, an escapee from a Georgia prison, shot hitchhiker Jimmy Don Ham in an attempt to steal and assume his identity. During his stay in Denton County Jail, he made another escape attempt, having convinced his mother to smuggle him a pistol. A year later, Gentry tried yet again to escape, this time combining his efforts with those of another death row inmate. They were restrained and recaptured at the front gate.

First and foremost I would like to tell the victims' families that I am sorry because I don't feel like I am guilty. I am sorry for the pain all of them have gone through during holidays and birthdays. They are without their loved ones. I have said from the beginning and I will say it again that I am innocent. I did not kill no one. I feel like this is the Lord's will that will be done. I love you all. You know it. Don't cry. Tell my brothers I love them. You all be strong.

KENNETH RANSOM, convicted of murder, Texas. Executed October 28, 1997

Ransom was one of the three men who stabbed employees at a Houston amusement center, in what was considered one of the worst mass slayings in the city's history. Ransom was the second of the group to receive the death penalty. Before him was Richard J. Wilkerson, a former pit attendant at the facility.

You all brought me here to be executed, not to make a speech. That's it.

CHARLES LIVINGSTON, convicted of robbery and murder, Texas. Executed November 21, 1997

Outside a Houston grocery store, Livingston waited under the van of Janet Caldwell until she returned, whereupon he attempted to take her purse. During the ensuing struggle Livingston shot Caldwell twice in the throat, and then fled. He was caught and identified shortly later.

A lot of people view what is happening here as evil, but I want you to know that I found love and compassion here. The people who work here, I thank them for the kindness they have shown me and I deeply appreciate all that has been done for me by the people who work here. That's all, warden, I'm ready.

MICHAEL LOCKHART, convicted of murder, Texas. Executed December 9, 1997

Ohio native Michael Lockhart had ties to robberies and thefts nationwide but faced capital murder charges in Florida and Indiana. He had served one year of a robbery sentence in a Wyoming state prison before the governor commuted it. Three years later, he was convicted of murder and sentenced to death for the fatal shooting of Paul Douglas Hulsey Jr., a Texas police officer who had attempted to arrest him for driving a stolen vehicle.

Yes sir, I would like to say to all of you—the Thornton family and Jerry Dean's family that I am so sorry. I hope God will give you peace with this. Baby, I love you. Ron, give Peggy a hug for me. Everybody has been so good to me. I love all of you very much. I am going to be face to face with Jesus now. Warden Baggett, thank all of you so much. You have been so good to me. I love all of you very much. I will see you all when you get there. I will wait for you.

KARLA FAYE TUCKER, convicted of murder, Texas. Executed February 3, 1998

Gaining worldwide attention from the media, Tucker became the first woman executed by the state of Texas since the Civil War. In a robbery for motorcycle parts with an accomplice, Tucker had attacked Jerry Lynn Dean and Deborah Thornton with a hammer and a pickax. Police reported finding the ax still embedded in Thornton's chest. Tucker became a born-again Christian in prison and was the subject of a folk song by the Indigo Girls titled simply "Faye Tucker."

I am sorry for what I did to your mom. It isn't because I'm going to die. All my life I have been locked up. I could never forgive what I done. I am sorry for all of you. I love you all. Thank you for supporting me. I thank you for being kind to me when I was small. Thank you, God. All right.

JOSEPH CANNON, convicted of murder, Texas. Executed April 22, 1998

During his teenage years, Cannon faced burglary charges but found kindness in the legal system. Out of concern for his well-being following the burglary conviction, Anne Walsh, sister of his court-appointed attorney, took him in. During his stay, Cannon shot Walsh seven times with a .22-caliber pistol. He was convicted of capital murder at age nineteen and was executed nineteen years later.

I owe no apologies for a crime I did not commit. Those who lied and fabricated evidence against me will have to answer for what they have done. I know in my heart what I did and I call upon the spirit of my ancestors and all of my people, the land and the sea and the skies and I swear to them and now I am coming home. *Loch sloy.*

FRANK MCFARLAND, convicted of sexual assault and murder, Texas. Executed April 29, 1998

McFarland was executed for the stabbing death of Terri Lynn Ho-kanson in a suburb of Fort Worth. He was to meet the victim the night of the murder after she was done with work, but he said he got too drunk to keep the engagement. Fibers, hair, and a scarf of hers were found in his car, connecting him to the crime. McFarland ended his last statement by saying "Loch sloy," the battle cry of the Scottish McFarland clan.

McFarland is named on the Center on Wrongful Convictions' list of thirty-nine executions that took place "in face of compelling evidence of innocence or serious doubt about guilt."

I know you can't hear me now but I know that it won't matter what I have to say. I want you to know that I did not kill your sister. If you want to know the truth, and you deserve to know the truth, hire your own investigators. That's all I have to say.

PEDRO MUNIZ, convicted of rape and murder, Texas. Executed May 19, 1998

Muniz was twenty when he arrested for the 1976 rape and murder of nineteen-year-old Janis Carol Bickham, a Southwestern University student. He confessed but later said police had threatened him. Muniz spent twenty-one years on death row for the crime, and before his execution he gave the prison guards a prepared statement written half in English, half in Spanish. He told his friends, "Keep walking forward, because Chicanos like us do not have another alternative."

I'd like to say that for the murders of Ray Hazelwood and Frank Collier, I'm sorry for that pain it has caused you. To my friends, I'd like to say that I love you and I'm glad you've been a part of my life. Thank you. I'll miss

you. Remember that today I'll be with Jesus in paradise. I'll see you again.

Lord Jesus Christ, son of Almighty God, [have] mercy on me as a sinner, forgive me of my sins. I would like to offer up my death for the conversion of sinners on Death Row. Lord Jesus, into your hands I commend my spirit.

CLIFFORD BOGGESS, convicted of murder, Texas. Executed June 11, 1998

Boggess, an artist and pianist, was also a clinical psychopath and a two-time murderer. His story, final days, and execution were covered extensively by *Frontline* reporter Alan Austin in the documentary *The Execution*.

Before his death, Boggess wrote about his final moments and last words in a diary entry: "When the time of my execution is finally here, will I face death with strength and dignity, unwavering in my faith in God and in Jesus Christ as my savior? Will God strengthen me in that hour of need? Will the Spirit give me the words to say which will make the end of my earthly life a powerful witness for God's son?"

For seventeen years the attorney general has been pursuing the wrong man. In time he will come to know this. I don't want anyone to avenge my death. Instead I want you to stop killing people. God bless.

THOMAS MARTIN THOMPSON, convicted of murder, California. Executed July 14, 1998

Farmworkers found the body of Ginger Lorraine Fleischli, who had been stabbed and raped. Genetic material implicated Thompson, who had escaped to Mexico. Authorities located him there, made the arrest, and brought him back to the United States. He claimed innocence at the trial, but inmates claimed he had made a full confession. An accomplice, David Leitch, received fifteen years to life on a conviction of second-degree murder.

Keep it brief here. Just want to say, uh, family, take care of yourselves. Uh, look at this as a learning experience. Everything happens for a reason. We all know what really happened, but there are some things you just can't fight. Little people always seem to get squashed. It happens.

Even so, just got to take the good with the bad. There is no man that is free from all evil, nor any man that is so evil to be worth nothing. But it's all part of life, and my family, take care of yourselves. Tell my wife I love her. I'll keep an eye on everybody, especially my nieces and nephews. I'm pretty good. I love y'all. Take care. I'm ready.

DAVID CASTILLO, convicted of murder, Texas. Executed August 23, 1998

Castillo, an Illinoisan, served time in prison for aggravated robbery and was released on a bench warrant before being convicted for stabbing a liquor store cashier, fifty-nine-year-old Clarencio Champion, during a robbery. After Castillo demanded cash, the clerk resisted, and Castillo stabbed him in the chest and abdomen and slashed him across the face. The victim died a week later.

As the ocean always returns to itself, love always returns to itself. So does consciousness, always returns to itself. And I do so with love on my lips. May God bless all mankind.

JAMES RONALD MEANES, convicted of murder, Texas. Executed December 15, 1998

Ohio welder Meanes and his accomplice Sandoval "Carlos" Santana shot the driver of an armored car as it stopped at a Houston department store. They stole $1.1 million and fled only to be caught an hour later. The Associated Press reported that "judicial oversight resulted in an additional seven years on death row for Meanes after prosecutors lost track of his case once a federal judge rejected an appeal in 1988."

I really don't have much to say. All I want to say is that when the state introduced my sister and my niece as state witnesses, it's not that they testified against me. The thing is, my lawyers would not subpoena anyone, so they allowed the state to subpoena them to paint a picture to the jury that my own sister and niece was testifying against me.

Linda is innocent of this. I am innocent of this. Now all you all are seeing in the process a perfect example of ol' freaky deaky Bill Clinton when he signed that anti-terrorism law to shorten the appeals. This is a conspiracy. They used false testimony of a woman that said I had raped her, when the test showed that the foreign pubic hair that was found on her body belonged to no one in that room. They found a drop of sposmosa [sic] in the crotch of her pants that was tied to blood type B. My blood type is A. Now the same woman there they brought to testify against this murder case. That woman was under indictment for possession of methamphetamine, delivery of methamphetamine. She could have gotten out of both of those cases. Yet, she swore under oath that she had never been in trouble with the law and none of that mattered. So what does that make this great state? A very high-priced prostitute that sells itself, called justice, to the highest bidder.

I am being charged under article 19.83 of the Texas Penal Code of murder with the promise of remuneration. That means they got to have three people, the one that paid, the one that killed, and the deceased. And the alleged remunerator is out on the streets, so how come I'm being executed today, without a remunerator? This is a great American justice. So if you don't think they won't, believe me they will. Ain't no telling who gonna be next. That's all I have to say. Especially for the people of the deceased, Mims is innocent and so am I. So the murder is still not there. Today you are a witness, the state [cough]. Bye.

MARTIN SAUCEDA VEGA, convicted of murder, Texas.
Executed January 26, 1999

Martin Vega confessed to a "murder-for-hire" in 1988, three years after the body of James Mims was found shot. Mims's wife, Linda, had offered to marry Vega and share the $250,000 life insurance policy if he killed her husband.

I forgive all of you.

MANUEL PINA BABBITT, convicted of rape and murder, California.
Executed May 4, 1999

Leah Schendel, age seventy-eight, did not die of the beating Babbitt gave her. What killed her was the heart attack she suffered from the ordeal. Babbitt, a paranoid schizophrenic and Vietnam War veteran, denied any recollection of what he had done. During his appeal, his lawyers said the post-traumatic stress syndrome he suffered in the wake of his two tours of duty in Vietnam caused him to black out during the murder. Babbitt was awarded the Purple Heart while on death row.

Yes, to my family, I love you. Please do not mourn my death or my life. Continue to live as I want you to live. I hold no bitterness toward no one. Just remember the light. I'm gonna let this light shine. Let it shine. Let the light shine.

TYRONE FULLER, convicted of murder, Texas. Executed July 7, 1999

Fuller was the first Texas death-row inmate to be convicted of capital murder based on DNA evidence. Fuller, who nicknamed himself "Evil," was on parole when he attacked Andrea Duke during a burglary of her home. She was found on the lawn of her apartment complex, raped, tortured, and stabbed. Prosecutors originally thought Fuller might not be responsible for Duke's murder, but bodily fluid and hairs found on her body helped convict him.

. . . Oh, I would like to say in closing, "What about those Cowboys?"

WILLIAM PRINCE DAVIS, convicted of robbery and murder, Texas. Executed September 14, 1999

When Davis was twenty-one years old, he shot and killed Richard Lang, an employee of the Red Wing Ice Cream Company. Davis fled with a shotgun and $712. A week later, he returned to burglarize the business. He was convicted in a one-day capital murder trial. From childhood Davis had been in and out of reformatory institutions, and by the time he was executed at age forty-two, he had spent half of his life on death row.

In English:

I love you. I will be waiting for you on the other side. Son be strong no matter what happens, know that God is looking over you. Jesus mercy, Jesus mercy, Jesus mercy!

In Spanish:

Brother-in-law, take care of the family and let it be united. Yoli.

In German:

My beautiful princess. You are all my heart and soul and I love you so much.

DOMINGO CANTU JR., convicted of murder and sexual assault, Texas. Executed October 28, 1999

In 1988, at the age of twenty, Cantu sexually assaulted his ninety-four-year-old victim before beating her head on a concrete sidewalk, killing her. He fled the scene but later confessed to the crime. Cantu received the death penalty eleven years after committing the murder. The Texas native had previously served time for burglary.

Ah, just, ah, sorry y'all. I . . . tried everything I could to get in touch with y'all to express how sorry I am. I, I never was right after that incident happened. I sent a letter to somebody, you know a letter outlining what I feel about everything. But anyway I just wanted, right after that to apologize to you. I'm real sorry for it. I was raised by the California Youth Authority. I can't really pinpoint where it started, what happened, but really believe that's just the bottom line: what happened to me was in California. I was in their reformatory schools and

penitentiary, but they create monsters in there. That's
it, I have nothing else to say. Thanks for coming, Jack.

DAVID LONG, convicted of murder, Texas. Executed December 8, 1999

Long was convicted of the 1986 murders of three Texas women, an
act he later described as "satanic." Two days before he was to be executed, Long attempted suicide and was admitted to intensive care.
His public defenders claimed they were not granted adequate fund-
ing to fully assess Long's mental condition during his trial, yet then-
governor George W. Bush funded a full medical team to fly with
Long to his execution. Immediately before he received lethal injection, Long vomited the charcoal solution used to detoxify his body
of drugs.

I want to start out by acknowledging the love that I've
had in my family. No man in this world has had a better family than me. I had the best parents in the world.
I had the best brothers and sisters in the world. I've had
the most wonderful life any man could have ever had.
I've never been more proud of anybody than I have of
my daughter and my son. I've got no complaints and
no regrets about that. I love every one of them and
have always been loved all of my life. I've never had any
doubts about that. Couple of matters that I want to talk
about since this is one of the few times people will listen
to what I have to say. The United States has gotten to . . .
where they [have] zero respect for human life. My death
is just a symptom of a bigger illness.

At some point the government has got to wake up and
stop doing things to destroy other countries and killing innocent children. The ongoing embargo and sanc-

tions against places like Iran and Iraq, Cuba and other places. They are not doing anything to change the world, but they are harming innocent children. That's got to stop at some point.

Perhaps more important in a lot of ways is what we are doing to the environment is even more devastating because as long as we keep going the direction we're going the end result is it won't matter how we treat other people because everybody on the planet will be on their way out. We have got to wake up and stop doing that. Ah, one of the few ways in the world the truth is ever going to get out, or people are ever going to know what's happening as long as we support a free press out there. I see the press struggling to stay existent as a free institution.

One of the few truly free institutions is the press in Texas. People like the Texas Observer and I want to thank them for the job they've done in keeping me and everybody else informed. I hope people out there will support them, listen to them and be there for them. Without it, things like this are going to happen and nobody will even know. I love all of you. I always have I always will. I would like to address the State of Texas and especially Joe Price, the District Attorney who put me here. I want to remind Mr. Price of the mistake he made at Gene Hathorn's trial when he said that Gene Hathorn was telling the truth at my trial. Mr. Price is a one-eyed hunting dog.

He in fact is not a one-eyed hunting dog, and in fact Gene Hathorn lied at my trial. Everybody knew it. I'm dying tonight based on testimony, that all parties, me, the man who gave the testimony, the prosecutor he used knew it was a lie. I am hoping somebody will call him to the floor for recent comments he's made in the newspaper. It's bad enough that a prosecutor can take truth and spin on it and try to re-doctor it. But when they actually make facts up and present to the public as trial's evidence. That goes beyond fail, that's completely unforgivable and I hope somebody makes Mr. Price account for or explain the tennis shoes he is talking about that put me here. I'm still completely lost on that and I'm hoping that somebody will go back and verify the trial record and make him accountable for lying to the public and the press that way.

That's really all I have to say except that I love my family. And nobody, nobody has got a better family than me. I love you booger bear. I love doodle bug, too. Don't let them ever forget me. I'll never forget them. I'll see you on the other side, okay. Bye bye, Debbie. Bye bro, bye booger bear. Father Mike, Father Walsh, love you all. That's all, sir.

JAMES BEATHARD, convicted of murder, Texas. Executed December 9, 1999

Beathard assisted Gene Hathorn Jr. in the murder of Gene Hathorn Sr., Linda Sue Hathorn, and the couple's fourteen-year-old son. Hathorn promised Beathard he'd pay him $12,500 from his father's estate. The men tore apart the Hathorn home, stealing several items and a van to make it appear that the murders had been committed in the course of a robbery. Hathorn, who later learned his father had cut him from his will just weeks before the crimes, also received the death penalty.

Well, first, my people, you guys have heard everything I needed to say today. I hope I said the right things. I hope you heard me. And I hope you go beyond here and do what you need to do. Do the right thing. Strength in numbers. Look out for each other. You still got a chance with Shawn. Edwin you know what you gotta do. You have my love. It's the right thing. And for everybody else, those people who have malice in their heart, allow ambitions to override what they know. Be right. Even though they just gotta do their job . . . You've done nothing. I did this; I chose this. You've done nothing. Remember this, if all you know is hatred, if all you know is blood love, you'll never be satisfied. For everybody out there that is like that and knows nothing but negative, kiss my proud white Irish ass. I'm ready warden, send me home.

ROBERT ATWORTH, convicted of robbery and murder, Texas. Executed December 14, 1999

Atworth shot, stabbed, and robbed Thomas Carlson, then severed the victim's right-hand little finger, where he'd worn a ring. Upon being apprehended, Atworth blamed the crime on an alternate personality of his by the name of Nino. Later he asked that no appeals be made on his behalf.

Yes, I do. I want to tell you all how much I love you all, how much I appreciate everything. I love you all and my family. I treasure every moment that I have had. I want the guys to know out there not to give up, not to give in, that I hope someday the madness in the system, something will come about, something will be resolved.

I would gladly trade the last 24 years if it would bring back Mark Frederick. Give him back his life, give back my father his life, and my mother her health. All I ask is that I have one day and all the memories of you and my family and all the things that have happened. They are executing an innocent man because things did not happen as they say they happen . . . The truth will come out someday. I am not the same person as I was 24 years ago. Who would have thought it would have taken 24 years to get to this moment? Don't give up, don't give in. If I am paying my debt to society, I am due a rebate and a refund, but I love you all and you all watch out for Mom and you all keep up, keep going.

Thank you, Warden.

BILLY HUGHES, convicted of murder, Texas. Executed January 24, 2000

Hughes became the focal point of a massive manhunt after he shot and killed Mark Frederick, age twenty-six, when the state trooper stopped Hughes on suspicion of a stolen credit card. When Hughes was apprehended, he had a small collection of firearms, ranging from small to heavy, and one Halloween mask. During his twenty-four years on death row, Hughes earned two degrees in religious education, registered as a death penalty lobbyist, became a cartoonist, and wrote one book and one screenplay. Foes of the death penalty called Hughes "a model of rehabilitation." Victims' rights groups said he was an example of how convicts abuse the system with multiple appeals.

Dad, I love you both. You've been the best. All of you, all of you have truly been the best. And ah, I believe I'm going home. I'm sorry, and I really mean that, it's not just words. My life is all I can give. I stole two lives and I know it was precious to y'all. That's the story of my whole, that's what alcohol will do for you. Oh Jesus, Lord God, take me home. Precious Lord. Take me home Lord. Take me home. Yes, sir. Take me home oh Lord.

JAMES MORELAND, convicted of murder, Texas. Executed January 27, 2000

In October 1982, Moreland hitched a ride with Clinton Abbott and John Cravey, and the pair took him to Cravey's trailer home. The three men had been drinking heavily, and Moreland said when Cravey made sexual advances to him, he panicked and stabbed both men to death. Moreland never denied the crimes; as soon as police questioned him he confessed.

I'd like to send great love to all my family members, my supporters, my attorneys. They have all supported me throughout this. I thank you for proving my innocence, although it has not been acknowledged by the courts. May you continue in the struggle and may you change all that's being done here today and in the past. Life has not been that good to me, but I believe that now, after meeting so many people who support me in this, that all things will come to an end, and may this be fruit of better judgments for the future. That's all I have to say.

ODELL BARNES JR., convicted of murder and robbery, Texas. Executed March 1, 2000

Barnes was sentenced to death for the robbery and murder of Helen Bass in her home: she had been sexually assaulted, stabbed in the neck, shot in the head, and beaten with a lamp and rifle. Barnes took a .32-caliber pistol and some money when he fled. The twenty-one-year-old construction worker was later seen trying to sell the stolen pistol.

Oral statement:
Okay, thank you. To the Weis family, and ah I just want you to know from the bottom of may heart that I am

truly sorry. I mean it, I'm not just saying it. Through the years of being in prison I come to hear and respect our life. It was wrong what I did. I know you had to go through a lot of pain and I'm sorry. To the Jones family, the same is true, I am truly, truly sorry. I wanted to prepare a longer statement but time ran out. I had the chaplain write down a few words for my friends and for you, my family. I would like him to read them for me, and ah, just please find peace.

Written statement read by Chaplain Brazzil:
To the Jones Family: Please accept my sincerest apology and requests for what happened to your loved one. It was truly a horrible thing that I did and I regret it deeply. I do not know if this will ease your pain but I truly pray that this will help you find peace. I am sincerely truly sorry.

For the Weis Family: The same is true. I regret what happened. I have lived with the guilt and the pain in my heart for taking Donna away from you. There is no way that I can know your pain and sorrow for losing someone so close to you. I truly hope that you will find peace. Please know that I am sorry.

I feel that I have to speak out against the practice of the death penalty, although I have no regrets in my case. The death penalty is an unnecessary punishment for society who has other means to protect itself. You cannot rectify death with another death. Whenever the state chooses to take a life and take the power of God into their own hands, whenever our leaders kill in the name of justice, we are all diminished.

To my family and friends, father, sister and brother, those that have traveled so far to be here today, please just know that I am at peace. You have all been so good to me through this whole ordeal. I can never find the words to express my love for all of you. Just know that I go with God. Oum—Nama Shiveya I go with God.

Last oral statement:

No sir, I just want to pray a chant; do what you have to do.

TIMOTHY LANE GRIBBLE, convicted of rape and murder. Executed Texas, March 15, 2000

Gribble, a roofer with a history of mental illness and drug abuse, confessed to the 1987 rape and murder of NASA employee Elizabeth Jones. He was also charged but never tried for killing Donna Weis. Although Gribble did not take issue with his own death sentence, he spoke out against the death penalty itself.

There is no way no words can express how sorry I am for taking the lives of my babies. Now I can be with my babies, as I always intended. I love you my babies.

CHRISTINA RIGGS, convicted of murder, Arkansas. Executed May 2, 2000

Christina Riggs wanted to die. Convicted of murdering her two children, Riggs asked the jury for a death sentence, refused to appeal, and refused clemency. "I still believe in the death penalty," she said, "even though I'm sitting here on death row. In my case, I'm glad I have the option."

Yes sir, I would like to address the Robinson family. There is nothing I can say here or anything I could probably do. Now you are all probably mad at me and I would probably be in the same situation you all in if anybody I thought killed anybody in my family ahh. If I knew who killed Rosalyn I would let you know, but, I am going to say this: I am going to heaven with God as my witness. Ros was a personal friend of mine. She was a beautiful person, very educated, her. I'm very tight with the Robinson family. She was proud that she had a father that was a doctor.

My family is not here present and that is by my wish and my wish only. Now the tables is turned. You are all here, the Robinson family is here to see me executed. That is something that I would not want for my family. In no form or fashion would I have ever want to see Rosalyn dead. I left the scene of where the incident happened. I guarantee you if I would have been there you would not be standing where you are if I would have been there. You all have some very serious look on your face and something very serious fixin' to happen now. I will say this on my own behalf but then again I know it is not going to make any difference but what you fixing to witness is not a nice thing. It's not nice. It's not nice.

The media. I would just like to address to the media with everybody's permission. I would like to say before I go that it has been said that I have shown no remorse, but if you look at my record and my background, ask anybody that know me that in order for me to show any kind of remorse for killing that ever been done, this one time I can't show no remorse for something that I did not do and if I did I would be faking. I would totally be faking and believe me there is nothing fake about me. Nothing fake. I've done wrong, sure, I've paid the time.

This is one time that I know I cannot show no remorse for something that I did not do.

I am at peace, please believe me. Wherefore, I figure that what I am dying for now is what I have done in my past. This is what I am dying for. Not for killing Rosalind. I don't know what y'all call her but I call her Ros. I call her Ros. That's it.

TOMMY RAY JACKSON, convicted of murder, Texas. Executed May 4, 2000

In a halfway house where Jackson was paroled after a burglary charge, he met with an accomplice and they discussed how to steal a car to commit more robberies. Later they waited in a University of Texas–Austin parking lot to steal the car of Rosalind Robinson. Driving out of town, they took turns raping her and finally shot her in the back of the head. Jackson kept her car until police arrested him.

Written:

The Beatitudes:

Jesus lifted up his eyes on His disciples, and said, Blessed be the poor: for yours is the kingdom of God. Blessed are ye that hunger now: for ye shall be filled. Blessed are ye that weep now: for ye shall laugh. Blessed are ye, when men shall hate you, and they shall separate you from their company, and shall reproach you, and cast out your name as evil for the Son of Man's sake. Rejoice ye in that day, and leap for joy: for behold, your reward is great in Heaven: for in the like manner did their fathers unto the prophets. But woe unto you that are rich! for ye have received your consolation. Woe unto you that are full! for ye shall hunger. Woe unto you that laugh now! for ye shall moan and weep. Woe unto you, when all men shall speak well of you! for so did their fathers to the false prophets.

The supremacy of love over gifts: I Corinthians,
  Chapter 13: 4–8:

Love is patient, love is kind, and is not jealous, love does not brag and is not arrogant, does not act unbecoming; it does not seek its own, is not provoked, does not take into account a wrong suffered, does not rejoice in unrighteousness, but rejoices with the truth; bears all things, believes all things, hopes all things, endures all things. Love never fails; but if there are gifts of prophecy, they will be done away; if there are tongues, they will cease. Now abide faith, hope, love, these three: but the greatest of these is love.

Poem [attributed to Mary Elizabeth Frye]:

Do not stand at my grave and weep,
I am not there I do not sleep.
I am the diamond glints in the snow,
I am the sunlight on the ripened grain.
I am the gentle autumn rain.
When you awaken in the morning's hush,
I am the swift uplifting rush
of quiet birds in circled flight,
I am the soft stars that shine at night.
Do not stand at my grave and cry,
I am not there. I did not die.

Signed
Michael L. McBride #903
May 11, 2000
Huntsville, Texas

Spoken:

Thank you, um, I anticipated that I would try to memorize and recite beatitudes New Testament, more or less, Luke's beatitudes, I should say, and a, a chapter on love in 1st Corinthians chapter 13, ah, I pretty much knew that I would not be able to memorize so much. There was also a poem that went along with it and in anticipation of not being able to, um, fulfill that desire, I provided a written statement that will be made available to anybody that wants it, I believe. Isn't that correct? So, uh, I wanted you to hear me say that and I apologize and for any other grief I have caused you know, including the, ah, what you're about to witness now. It won't be very long. As soon as you realize that [it will] appear I am falling asleep. I would leave because I won't be here after that point. I will be dead at that point. It's irreversible. God bless all of you. Thank you.

MICHAEL LEE MCBRIDE, convicted of murder, Texas. Executed May 11, 2000

After a tumultuous eleven-month relationship, during which McBride, a bartender, moved closer to Texas Tech University to be with Christian Fisher, his ex-girlfriend, he shot Fisher and a friend to death outside his apartment. He proceeded to shoot himself in the head but survived to tell a male nurse, "If you ever need any pointers of information on how to handle your women, just let me know."

I would like to say that I did not kill Bobby Lambert. That I'm an innocent black man that is being murdered. This is a lynching that is happening in America tonight. There's overwhelming and compelling evidence of my defense that has never been heard in any court of America. What is happening here is an outrage for any civilized country to anybody anywhere to look at what's happening here is wrong.

I thank all of the people that have rallied to my cause. They've been standing in support of me. Who have finished with me.

I say to Mr. Lambert's family, I did not kill Bobby Lambert. You are pursuing the execution of an innocent man.

I want to express my sincere thanks to all of y'all. We must continue to move forward and do everything we can to outlaw legal lynching in America. We must continue to stay strong all around the world, and people must come together to stop the systematic killing of poor and innocent black people. We must continue to stand together in unity and to demand a moratorium on all executions. We must not let this murder/lynching be forgotten tonight, my brothers. We must take it to the nation. We must keep our faith. We must go forward. We recognize that many leaders have died. Malcom X, Martin Luther King, and others who stood up for what was right. They stood up for what was just. We must, you must brothers, that's why I have called you today. You must carry on that condition. What is here is just a lynching that is taking place. But they're going to keep on lynching us for the next 100 years, if you do not carry on that tradition, and that period of resistance. We will prevail. We may lose this battle, but we will win the war. This death, this lynching will be avenged. It will be avenged, it must be avenged. The people must avenge this murder. So my brothers, all of y'all stay strong, continue to move forward.

Know that I love all of you. I love the people, I love all of you for your blessing, strength, for your courage, for your dignity, the way you have come here tonight, and the way you have protested and kept this nation together. Keep moving forward, my brothers. Slavery couldn't stop us. The lynching couldn't stop us in the south. This lynching will not stop us tonight. We will go forward. Our destiny in this country is freedom and liberation. We will gain our freedom and liberation by any means necessary. By any means necessary, we keep marching forward.

I love you, Mr. Jackson. Bianca, make sure that the state does not get my body. Make sure that we get my name as Shaka Sankofa. My name is not Gary Graham. Make sure that it is properly presented on my grave. Shaka Sankofa.

I died fighting for what I believe in. I died fighting for what was just and what was right. I did not kill Bobby Lambert, and the truth is going to come out. It will be brought out.

I want you to take this thing off into international court, Mr. Robert Mohammed and all y'all. I want you, I want to get my family and take this down to international court and file a law suit. Get all the video tapes of all the beatings. They have beat me up in the back. They have beat me up at the unit over there. Get all the video tapes supporting that law suit. And make the public exposed to the genocide and this brutality world, and let the world see what is really happening here behind closed doors. Let the world see the barbarity and injustice of what is really happening here. You must get those video tapes. You must make it exposed, this injustice, to the world. You must continue to demand a moratorium on all executions. We must move forward Minister Robert Mohammed.

Ashanti Chimurenga, I love you for standing with me, my sister. You are a strong warrior queen. You will continue to be strong in everything that you do. Believe in yourself, you must hold your head up, in the spirit of Winnie Mandela, in the spirit of Nelson Mandela. Y'all must move forward. We will stop this lynching. Reverend Al Sharpton, I love you, my brother. Bianca Jagger, I love all of you. Y'all make sure that we continue to stand together. Reverend Jesse Jackson and know that this murder, this lynching will not be forgotten. I love you, too, my brother. This is genocide in America. This is what happens to black men when they stand up and protest for what is right and just. We refuse to compromise, we refuse to surrender the dignity for what we know is right. But we will move on, we have been strong in the past. We will continue to be strong as a people. You can kill a revolutionary, but you cannot stop the revolution. The revolution will go on. The people will carry the revolution on. You are the people that must carry that revolutionary on, in order to liberate our children from this genocide and for what is happening here in America tonight. What has happened for the last 100 or so years in America. This is the part of the genocide, this is part of the African [unintelligible], that we as black people have endured in America. But we shall overcome, we will continue with this. We will continue, we will gain our freedom and liberation, by any means necessary. Stay strong. They cannot kill us. We will move forward.

To my sons, to my daughters, all of you. I love all of you. You have been wonderful. Keep your heads up. Keep moving forward. Keep united. Maintain the love and unity in the community.

And know that victory is assured. Victory for the people will be assured. We will gain our freedom and liberation in this country. We will gain it and we will do it by any means necessary. We will keep marching. March on, black people. Keep your heads high. March on. All y'all leaders. March on. Take your message to the people. Preach the moratorium for all executions. We're gonna stop, we are going to end the death penalty in this country. We are going to end it all across this world. Push forward people. And know that what y'all are doing is right. What y'all are doing is just. This is nothing more than pure and simple murder. This is what is happening tonight in America. Nothing more than state sanctioned murders, state sanctioned lynching, right here in America, and right here tonight. This is what is happening, my brothers. Nothing less. They know I'm innocent. They've got the facts to prove it. They know I'm innocent. But they cannot acknowledge my innocence, because to do so would be to publicly admit their guilt. This is something these racist people will never do. We must remember, brothers, this is what we're faced with. You must take this endeavor forward. You must stay strong. You must continue to hold your heads up, and to be there. And I love you too, my brother. All of you who are standing with me in solidarity. We will prevail. We will keep marching. Keep marching, black people, black power. Keep marching, black people, black power. Keep marching black people. Keep marching black people. They are killing me tonight. They are murdering me tonight.

GARY GRAHAM, convicted of robbery and murder, Texas. Executed June 22, 2000

"After considering all of the facts, I am convinced justice is being done," said Texas governor George W. Bush after the final appeals for Graham were denied. Inside the execution chamber, strapped with more restraints than normally used, Graham called executions a "holocaust for black Americans."

Graham maintained his innocence despite his conviction for shooting fifty-three-year-old Bobby Grant Lambert outside a Houston supermarket. Along with hundreds of protesters in California and Massachusetts and outside Huntsville Prison, sitting in as witnesses to Graham's execution were Rev. Jesse Jackson, Rev. Al Sharpton, and Amnesty International representative Bianca Jagger. "There were no tears shed," said Jackson, who talked and prayed with Graham an hour before his execution. "He had a sense of inner peace. He feels he was being used as a kind of change agent to expose the system."

Since I have already said all I need to say to all my loved ones, I'm not going to say anything to y'all at this time. Y'all know I love you and y'all know where we're at. I will see y'all when you get there. So this is my statement. To all of the racist white folks in America that hate black folks and to all of the black folks in America that hate themselves: in the infamous words of my famous legendary brother, Nat Turner, "Y'all kiss my black ass." Let's do it.

BRIAN ROBERSON, convicted of murder, Texas. Executed August 9, 2000

Roberson was convicted in the stabbing death of James Boots, seventy-nine, and his wife, Lillian, seventy-five, who lived across the street from him in Dallas. Roberson was African American and his victims were Caucasian. Amnesty International issued a memo before the execution urging action and "expressing concern at the prosecutor's systematic exclusion of African Americans from the trial jury." Roberson claimed he was "juiced up" on PCP and liquor during the crime. His last words were alternately recorded as "You ain't got what you want."

Later that same year, Roberson's twin brother, Bruce, was arrested for allegedly threatening then President-elect George W. Bush. In a *New York Times* article, officers reported that Bruce wanted "to take him down." The piece continued: "Mr. Roberson told them that Mr. Bush 'stole the election and he's not going to get away with it.'" Bush had been governor at the time of Brian's execution.

Mr. Bryant, I have wronged you and your family and for that I am truly sorry. I forgive and I have been forgiven. Death is but a brief moment's slumber and a short journey home. I'll see you when you get there. I am done, warden.

DAVID GIBBS, convicted of murder, Texas. Executed August 23, 2000

Gibbs, a self-described country gentleman, confessed to the rape and murders of two mentally handicapped women. In the end, he expressed regret, apologizing to Mickey Bryant, brother of one of the victims. "I don't believe in hitting women," Gibbs insisted before he was executed.

Father, forgive them, they know not what they do.

She smiled at her spiritual advisers and attorneys and stuck out her tongue.

WANDA JEAN ALLEN, convicted of murder, Oklahoma. Executed January 11, 2001

Allen was convicted in the shooting death of Gloria J. Leathers, her lover. Her case gained national attention when Amnesty International and the National Coalition to Abolish the Death Penalty pleaded for clemency. Rev. Jessie Jackson led protesters in Oklahoma City, where he and others were arrested after crossing a police barricade at Allen's prison.

Allen had previously served time for the shooting death of a roommate. Documentarian Liz Garbus covered Allen's life story and death in 2002's *The Execution of Wanda Jean.*

I am so sorry for what y'all had to go through. I am so sorry for what all of you had to go through. I can't imagine losing two children. If I was y'all, I would have killed me. You know? I am really so sorry about it, I really am. I got to go sister, I love you. Y'all take care and God bless you. Gracie was beautiful and Tiffany was beautiful. You had some lovely girls and I am sorry. I don't know what to say. All right, Warden, let's do it.

DENNIS DOWTHITT, convicted of murder, Texas. Executed March 7, 2001

Auto salesman Dowthitt received a lethal injection for the murders of his son's sixteen-year-old former girlfriend, Grace Purnhagen, and her sister, nine-year-old Tiffany Purnhagen. Dowthitt's sixteen-year-old son, Delton, first admitted to the gruesome killings before recanting and revealing that his father had slashed Grace's throat and sexually assaulted her with a beer bottle and had strangled Tiffany with a rope. Delton led police to the evidence; he was convicted of murder and sentenced to forty-five years behind bars.

Tonight I dance on the streets of gold. Let those without sin cast the first stone.

JASON MASSEY, convicted of murder, Texas. Executed April 3, 2001

Massey boasted in a diary that he wanted to be the "greatest ever" serial killer. He abducted a thirteen-year-old girl, and her body was later found raped, stabbed, disemboweled, decapitated, mutilated, and shot in the back. The girl's stepbrother was found nearby, shot in the head. During his final statement, Massey told the girl's family where they could look for her missing remains and told them, "I want you to know that Christina did not suffer as much as you think she did."

Invictus
By William Ernest Henley

Out of the night that covers me,
Black as a Pit from pole to pole,
I thank whatever gods may be
For my unconquerable soul.

In the fell clutch of circumstance
I have not winced nor cried aloud,
Under the bludgeonings of chance
My head is bloody, but unbowed.

Beyond this place of wrath and tears
Looms but the Horror of the shade,
And yet the menace of the years
Finds, and shall find me, unafraid.

It matters not how strait the gate,
How charged with punishments the scroll,
I am the master of my fate:
I am the captain of my soul.

TIMOTHY MCVEIGH, convicted on eleven charges including murder and use of a weapon of mass destruction, Indiana. Executed June 11, 2001

McVeigh and two accomplices bombed the Alfred P. Murrah Federal Building in Oklahoma City, using a rented truck and a homemade explosive device weighing several thousand pounds. They killed 168 people and injured hundreds more. During his trial, witnesses were called to the stand to testify that McVeigh had been a nice child and a good soldier who returned from the Gulf War decorated but unhappy. After his discharge, McVeigh had drifted across the United States, meeting with various militia groups. Until his execution, he claimed the bombing was a "legit tactic" against a government responsible for attacks on civilians in Waco and Ruby Ridge.

"I'm sorry these people had to lose their lives," McVeigh wrote to his hometown newspaper. "But that's the nature of the beast. It's understood going in what the human toll will be."

He did not deliver any final words but instead left behind the poem "Invictus," written in 1875 by the British poet William Ernest Henley. *Invictus* means "unconquerable" in Latin.

For almost nine years I have thought about the death penalty, whether it is right or wrong and I don't have any answers. But I don't think the world will be a better or safer place without me. If you had wanted to punish me you would have killed me the day after, instead of killing me now. You are not hurting me now. I have had time to get ready, to tell my family goodbye, to get my life where it needed to be. It started with a needle and it is ending with a needle.

Carl, you have been a good friend, man. I am going to look for you. You go back and tell your daughter I love her. Tell her I came in here like a man and I will leave like a man. It's been good, dude. Thank you, Shorty. I appreciate you. I came in like a man and I will leave like a man. I will be with you. I will be with you every time you take a shower. If you leave crying you don't do me justice. If you don't see peace in my eyes you don't see me. I will be the first one you see when you cross over . . .

That is it. Ready, warden.

Later:

It's burning.

JEFFREY DOUGHTIE, convicted of robbery and murder, Texas. Executed August 16, 2001

Doughtie had a $400-a-day drug habit, which he financed by selling stolen property. He had once worked for the antique store in Corpus Christi where he sold much of his loot. One day, after shooting a mix of heroin and cocaine, Doughtie beat the store's proprietors to death with a piece of metal tubing. He confessed to the murders.

Yes, sir. Where's Mr. Marino's mother? Did you get my letter? Just wanted to let you know, I sincerely meant everything I wrote. I am sorry for the pain. I am sorry for the life I took from you. I ask God for forgiveness and I ask you for the same. I know it may be hard, but I'm sorry for what I did. To my family I love each and every one of you. Be strong. Know my love is always with you . . . always. I know I am going home to be with the Lord. Shed tears of happiness for me. I love each and every one of you. Keep on living.

Betty, you have been wonderful. You guided me to the Lord. You have been like a mother to me. Sean, Rusty, Jenny, Marsha, God Bless each and every one of y'all.

Jesus, I confess you as my Lord and Savior. I know when I die, I'll have life in heaven and life eternal everlasting. I am ready for that mansion that you promised me.

It's all right Sean, it's all right. I'm going to a better place.

GERALD MITCHELL, convicted of robbery and murder, Texas.

Executed October 22, 2001

In his young life, Mitchell had been arrested for burglary and taking a pistol to school, served time in a juvenile detention center, and allegedly fathered seven children with six women prior to his death sentence. Shortly after robbing one man and killing another, Mitchell shot a third man to death, saying, "Raise your hands white boy, you don't want to die with your hands down." While he was on death row, Mitchell's father was shot to death, his brother was pinned for a felony bank robbery, and his mother was put on probation for drugs. On death row, Mitchell said, "I was full of hate, full of rage. I really can't explain why. I was attracted to the wild side, the street life where you're trying to make a name for yourself."

OK. I guess I'll address the Morgan family. Mrs. Morgan, the sister from the trial. Thirteen or fourteen years ago, I had a non-caring attitude at the time. I'm sorry for shooting your son down at that particular robbery. Politicians say that this brings closure. But my death doesn't bring your son back—it doesn't bring closure. I wish that I could do more, but I can't. I hope this brings you peace. Ursula, Manon, and Irene, I love y'all—take it easy. They've gotta do this thing. I'm still warm from the pepper gas. I love you. I'm ready to go. Call my mom and tell her that this particular process is over. Tell all the brothers to keep their heads up, eyes toward the sky.

EMERSON RUDD, convicted of murder, Texas. Executed November 15, 2001

When Rudd was eighteen years old, he and three others entered a seafood restaurant, intending to rob it. After the manager, Steve

Morgan, handed over eight hundred dollars, Rudd shot him in the abdomen. He died the next day.

Tell my family I love y'all. Watch out for Momma. Don't want to talk too much, I will cry. I'll just cry everywhere. I'm sorry, Teach, for not being a better son and not doing better things. It wasn't your fault. You raised me the way you should; at least I won't be there no more. I miss you, too. I see you there, you doing all right? I sent you a letter. Neckbone, there's a sheet. I got your name on it. Keep on writing, now . . . You people over there. You know what these people are doing. By them executing me ain't doing nothing right. I don't weigh 180 pounds and 5′7″. Take care, love y'all. Did Roger come up here yet? Tell Pat and them I love them. I'm gonna go ahead and let them do what they're gonna do. Help your sister. See ya later, Pat. Love ya, Becca. Do what you do, warden.

VINCENT COOKS, convicted of murder, Texas. Executed December 12, 2001

Cooks stood 6′3″ and weighed three hundred pounds. Witnesses of a robbery in which a police officer was killed identified a significantly shorter, slimmer man as the perpetrator. However, Cooks stood trial and was convicted of murder.

If I had a million lives, I couldn't say I'm sorry enough . . . And what happened in that case changed me so much. I'm not the same person I was 25 years ago . . . In our society, we hear and say "What would Jesus do?" You

can believe I don't believe Jesus would do this . . . It allows no room for redemption.
[The death penalty] dragged the victim's family and my family through living hell. It's incredibly sad that we live in a society that feels it has to kill people.

To four friends at the execution:
Leave this thing without any bitterness, any hatred, any anger.

RONALD KEITH SPIVEY, convicted of murder, Georgia. Executed January 24, 2002

In 1976, Spivey shot and killed a man over twenty dollars in a poolhall fight in Macon, and while on the run he later shot an off-duty security guard. He spent twenty-five years on death row, the second-longest time in Georgia history. Spivey agreed to have his scheduled electric-chair execution videotaped to help efforts to abolish the death penalty. However, the state declared it unconstitutional shortly before the date. He was given the needle instead.

My last full statement is being released in a way other than me right here. All I want to say, I love you all. Approximately 28 years ago, I remember looking down at a bassinet, I saw an angel. I am looking at her right now. I love you, Colleen. Let's get going. The road goes on forever, and the party never ends. Let's rock and roll. Let's go warden. Me and you, all of us. Remember Wet Willie—keep on smiling, keep on smiling. I love you. It's on the way; I can feel it. It's OK, baby. We have a party to go to. I can feel it now.

RANDALL HAFDAHL, convicted of murder, Texas. Executed January 31, 2002

A painter and mechanic by trade, Hafdahl was convicted in the shooting death of an off-duty police officer who had stopped to help at the scene of a one-car accident involving Hafdahl and two friends. Hafdahl had been drinking and taking hallucinogenic mushrooms that day. Previously, he had faced kidnapping, drug, and weapons charges.

... I'm fixing to die, but not for my mistakes. My trial lawyers, they are the ones who are killing me. . . . I want to thank you [to the victim's mother]. It meant a lot to me. Tell my mother I love her too. I didn't call her because I just couldn't. I am fine. I am happy. See you on the other side.

JOHNNY JOE MARTINEZ, convicted of murder and robbery, Texas. Executed May 22, 2002

When Martinez was twenty, he stabbed a Corpus Christi convenience-store clerk to death over the $25.65 in the store's cash register. After Martinez's sentencing, the mother of the victim appealed to the Texas Board of Pardons and Paroles, pleading with them to give him a life sentence. "Please do not cause another mother to lose her son to murder," she wrote. In spite of her efforts, Martinez was executed.

The act I committed to put me here was not just heinous, it was senseless. But the person that committed that act is no longer here—I am. I'm not going to struggle physically against any restraints. I'm not going to shout, use profanity or make idle threats. Understand though that I'm not only upset, but I'm saddened by what is happening here tonight. I'm not only saddened, but disappointed that a system that is supposed to protect and uphold what is just and right can be so much like me when I made the same shameful mistake.

If someone tried to dispose of everyone here for participating in this killing, I'd scream a resounding, "No." I'd tell them to give them all the gift that they would not give me . . . and that's to give them all a second chance.

I'm sorry that I am here. I'm sorry that you're all here. I'm sorry that John Luttig died. And I'm sorry that it was something in me that caused all of this to happen to begin with.

Tonight we tell the world that there are no second chances in the eyes of justice . . . Tonight, we tell our children that in some instances, in some cases, killing is right.

This conflict hurts us all; there are no sides. The people who support this proceeding think this is justice. The people that think that I should live think that is justice. As difficult as it may seem, this is a clash of ideals, with both parties committed to what they feel is right. But who's wrong if in the end we're all victims?

In my heart, I have to believe that there is a peaceful compromise to our ideals. I don't mind if there are none for me, as long as there are for those who are yet to come. There are a lot of men like me on death row—good men—who fell to the same misguided emotions, but may not have recovered as I have.

Give those men a chance to do what's right. Give them a chance to undo their wrongs. A lot of them want to fix the mess they started, but don't know how. The problem is not in that people aren't willing to help them find out, but in the system telling them it won't matter anyway. No one wins tonight. No one gets closure. No one walks away victorious.

NAPOLEON BEAZLEY, convicted of murder, Texas. Executed May 28, 2002

Beazley, a teenager from an upper-middle-class African American family, was a star athlete and the president of his senior class. But he also dealt drugs and carried a gun. In 1995, he told a friend he wanted to experience what it was like to steal a car and murder someone. He and two accomplices (who received life sentences) followed John and Bobbie Luttig to their home and shot at them both, killing John.

I'd just like to say I'm sailing with the Rock and I'll be back like "Independence Day" with Jesus, June 6, like the movie, big mother ship and all. I'll be back.

AILEEN WUORNOS, convicted of murder, Florida. Executed October 9, 2002

Wuornos was labeled a serial killer for murdering seven men in less than twelve months. The life of Wuornos, from her abusive childhood to her life as a teenage prostitute, became the focus of the 2003 film *Monster* and two documentaries by Nick Broomfield. On the day of her execution, she told Broomfield that the police framed her and used sonic waves to control her. State psychiatrists decided that she was mentally competent for execution. Charlize Theron won an Oscar for her portrayal of Wuornos in *Monster*.

Written:

There are many things I would like to say, but none more important than how I feel toward Mr. and Mrs. Kenney, and Ms. Arnot. I would like to apologize and say I'm sorry but words seem so hollow and cheap.

Their death should not have happened, but it did. I'm so sorry that all of this took place. Now I have devastated my family as well, but my heart has grown in the last few minutes because I was forgiven by the family of Mr. and Mrs. Kenney, and Ms. Arnot. Thank you. You have given me more hope than I have had in a long time. If I could change things I would, not for my sake but for all those who have loved me over the years, and for those who have forgiven me. Thank you for all that you have given me.

SAMUEL GALLAMORE, convicted of murder, Texas. Executed January 14, 2003

Gallamore was convicted of beating and stabbing Clayton Kenney (eighty-three), his partially paralyzed wife, Juliana (seventy-four), and her daughter, Adrienne Arnot (forty-four). Gallamore had once cared for Juliana in a nursing home. He confessed to police, saying that he and an accomplice had robbed the Kenney family in order to buy drugs. Refusing to say any last words, Gallamore had his written statement distributed after his execution.

I would just . . . [speaks in French] I love all of you. I love you Lundy, Levi, my dad. I have no grudges against anyone, or any of the things that have gone wrong. I would like to say to the world, I have always been a nice person. I have never been mean-hearted or cruel. I wish everybody well.

GRANVILLE RIDDLE, convicted of murder, Texas. Executed January 30, 2003

In his murder confession, Riddle said that while he did beat Ronnie Hood to death with a tire iron, he did it in self-defense. Riddle was also charged with robbing Hood's house, stealing Hood's wallet and pickup truck, which was found burned in a ravine. Prior to his arrest, Riddle had broken out of Potter County Jail during a substance abuse class. He was recaptured two days later with a .22 rifle, which he picked up from a previous robbery.

Written:

The death penalty in Texas is broke. When an attorney can be forced to represent you, who is not qualified to represent you under Texas laws, the system does not work. When an attorney can dismiss your appeal process, by missing a filing deadline or for failing to file documents on behalf of a client, that's not due process of law as guaranteed under the United States Constitution; the system does not work. When officials of any state, such as the state of Texas, has so much confidence in their justice system, mistakes will be made, and innocent people will be executed. Texas has executed innocent people, and tonight, Texas has shown just how broke and unfair its system is. There is no clemency in Texas, a process that needs to be reviewed, and fixed. Most importantly, the Texas justice system needs to be fixed. I hope the politicians such as Elliot Naishtat, Harold Dutton, Rodney Ellis, and others, continue to do their part in trying to fix the Texas justice system, and until so is done, continue to work for a moratorium on the death penalty in Texas.

Spoken:

To my family and friends . . . who has always been there for me and done everything in their will and power to help me and stand by my side, I love you dearly, and you will always be in my heart forever. Please continue to struggle and fight against the death penalty, as its only use has been for revenge, and it does not deter crime. It's time for a moratorium in the state of Texas.

HENRY DUNN JR., convicted of murder, Texas. Executed February 6, 2003

Convicted armed robber Henry Dunn and two companions kidnapped, tortured, and shot a gay man. Dunn confessed, was charged with a hate crime, and was sentenced to death.

Yes. I would just like to say to my family that I am sorry for all the grief I have caused. I love you all. Tell Mama and the kids I love you; I love all of you. And I would like to clear some things up if I could. Tommy Perkins, the man that got a capital life sentence for murdering Kinslow—he did not do it. I did it. He would not even have had anything to do with it if he had known I was going to shoot the man. He would not have gone with me if he had known. I was paid to shoot the man. And Martin, the younger boy, did not know what it was about. He thought it was just a robbery. I am sorry for that. It was nothing personal. I was trying to make a living. A boy on Eastham doing a life sentence for killing Jamie Kent—I did not do it, but I was with his daddy when it was done. I was there with him and down through the years there were several more that I had done or had a part of. And I am sorry and I am not sure how many—there must be a dozen or fourteen, I believe, all total. One I would like to clear up is Cullen Davis—where he was charged with shooting his wife. And all of these it was never nothing personal. It was just something I did to make a living. I am sorry for all the grief I have caused. I love you all. That is all I have to say.

BILLY VICKERS, convicted of murder, Texas. Executed January 28, 2004

Vickers had multiple convictions for robbery, arson, and gun possession dating back to 1967. In his final statement, he confessed to the murders of more a dozen men other than the grocery store owner he was executed for shooting to death during a botched robbery in 1993.

Yes I do. Sir, in honor of a true American hero, "Let's roll." Lord Jesus receive my spirit.

DAVID HARRIS, convicted of murder, Texas. Executed June 30, 2004

Harris's final statement was a reference to the words of Todd Beamer, a passenger who helped fight the hijackers on United Airlines Flight 93 on 9/11. Harris was sentenced to death after shooting a man to death as Harris tried to abduct the man's girlfriend. Harris is best known for his false testimony that helped convict Randall Dale Adams of killing a police officer; he retracted his statement after the 1988 documentary *The Thin Blue Line* proved Adams innocent. Harris was never charged with the crime. Adams was released from prison in 1989, but by that time Harris had been on death row for three years.

There was a lot of people that got me to this point and I can't thank them all. But thank you for your love and support. They have allowed me to do a lot more than I could have on my own. . . . I have overcame a lot. I am not angry but I am disappointed that I was denied justice. But I am happy that I was afforded you all as family and friends. I love you all. Please just keep the struggle going. . . . I am just sorry and I am not as strong as I thought I was going to be. But I guess it only hurts for a little while. You are all my family. Please keep my memory alive.

DOMINIQUE JEROME GREEN, convicted of murder, Texas.
Executed October 26, 2004

Green and three accomplices robbed and shot Andrew Lastrapes Jr. to death, prosecutors said, in a parking lot. Many of Lastrapes's relatives opposed the execution, and his widow, Bernatte Luckett Lastrapes, wrote to the Texas governor and parole board in support of Green: "All of us have forgiven Dominique for what happened and want to give him another chance at life. Everyone deserves another chance." Green was the subject of Thomas Cahill's book *A Saint on Death Row*.

Yes sir. I would like to ask you to forgive me. I made a mistake and I am sorry for what I did. All I can do is ask you to forgive me. I love you and I will see all of you in Heaven. I love you very much. Praise Jesus. I love you. Our Father, who art in Heaven, hallowed be thy name. Thy kingdom come, Thy will be done, on earth as it is in Heaven. Give us this day our daily bread, and forgive us our trespasses as we forgive those who have trespassed against us. And lead us not into temptation, but deliver us from evil. Amen.

TROY KUNKLE, convicted of murder, robbery, and abduction, Texas.
Executed January 25, 2005

On their way from San Antonio to Corpus Christi in 1984, Kunkle and three companions offered Stephen Horton a ride. They robbed him of his wallet, which contained thirteen dollars, and Kunkle shot him in the head, after which he sang lines from "No Remorse," a song by heavy metal band Metallica: "Another day, another death, another sorrow, another breath." Kunkle, age thirty-eight at the time of execution, spent half his life on death row.

I would like to say I apologize to Carol Skjerva, the girl that I murdered, her family and her friends. This is the punishment that I deserve. I'm taking responsibility for my actions. I want everybody to know I'm not a volunteer but this is my responsibility I have to take.

Written:
I unjustly took the life of Carol Skjerva. I have made my peace with my God and go now to face His judgment.

GLEN OCHA, convicted of murder, Florida. Executed April 5, 2005

An intoxicated Ocha brought Carol Skjerva into his home and had sex with her. After she threatened to tell her boyfriend what happened, Ocha tried three times to strangle her with a rope. He finally hung the rope from his kitchen doorframe and drank a beer while she died. Ocha had a long history of drug and alcohol abuse. He pleaded guilty to the crime and waived a jury trial.

Yes sir, warden. OK I've been hanging around this Popsicle stand way too long. Before I leave, I want to tell you all. When I die, bury me deep, lay two speakers at my feet, put some headphones on my head and rock and roll me when I'm dead. I'll see you in heaven someday. That's all warden.

DOUGLAS ROBERTS, convicted of kidnapping, robbery and murder, Texas. Executed April 20, 2005

His first dose of cocaine had been at age ten, Roberts said. He was "stoned out of [his] mind" when he stole a car and robbed and killed a man. After the murder, Roberts called police from a pay phone and waited for them to pick him up. He refused all appeals after his first failed, as he saw his execution as a way out of the "23 hours a day in a cement box." "So if you've got to spend the rest of your life like this, and if you're like me and know the Lord, then today's a good day to go," Roberts said.

Everybody has to die sometime, so . . . let's get on with the killing.

KEVIN CONNER, convicted of murder, Indiana. Executed July 27, 2005

Dubbed "Iceman" because of his cold demeanor, Connor requested that his friends sell souvenir T-shirts emblazoned with an ice block and a knife. He spent eighteen years on death row for an alcohol-fueled triple murder of friends, and he ultimately asked not to be reprieved. To Indiana governor Mitch Daniels he wrote: "Killing a person is far more honest and humane than imposed repression under the guise of justice in the penal system."

A life for a life, let it be done and justice will be served.

HERMAN ASHWORTH, convicted of murder, Ohio.
Executed September 27, 2005

A deputy coroner said the injuries Daniel Baker incurred during his beating from Ashworth were similar to those of a high-speed traffic accident or a plane crash. Ashworth beat Baker with his fists and a six-foot board, took forty dollars off the unconscious man, left to go to another bar, but then returned to kill Baker to avoid identification. Ashworth claimed Baker had made a pass at him and he "freaked out." He pleaded guilty to the charge, offering no mitigating evidence or appeals, and did not ask for clemency.

I go forward now on wings built by the love and support of my family and friends. I go with a peace of mind that comes from never having taken a human life. I forgive those who have hardened their hearts to the truth and I pray they ask forgiveness for they know not what they do. This is not a death, it is a lynching.

MARLIN GRAY, convicted of murder, Missouri. Executed October 26, 2005

Gray and three companions raped two girls, then shoved them off the Chain of Rocks Bridge in St. Louis in 1991. The girls' cousin was told to jump or be pushed off the bridge; he survived the jump and testified against the killers. Gray was executed first out of the group; another accomplice was also sentenced to death; a third received life without parole; and the fourth was sentenced to thirty years. Gray appeared to mouth the words "I love you" to witnesses shortly before the needle was injected into his arm.

After a nurse took more than ten minutes to put the needle into his arm:
You doing that right?

STANLEY "TOOKIE" WILLIAMS (AKA BIG TOOK), convicted of murder, California. Executed December 13, 2005

Williams spent his time on death row writing children's books with peace and antigang messages, donating the proceeds to antigang promotion charities. He was nominated for the Nobel Prizes for Literature and for Peace, but Williams's life before prison had been exactly the opposite. In 1971 he cofounded the violent street gang the Crips, and in 1981 he was convicted for the murders of four people. Williams never admitted to the crimes, prompting Gov. Arnold Schwarzenegger to refuse clemency despite appeals from people including Rev. Jesse Jackson and Jamie Foxx, who portrayed Williams in the TV movie *Redemption*.

I sincerely apologize to the families of Josie Curry, Michael Gregory, and James Riddle. I am very sorry for the pain that my actions caused to them. Hopefully, my decision to have this sentence carried out, without delay, will help you understand the sincerity of my apology, and will provide you with some closure. To those of you who have expressed forgiveness to me, I thank you. For those of you who have been unable or unwilling to forgive me, I pray that today will provide you with the peace you deserve.

DAVID MARK HILL, convicted of murder, South Carolina. Executed June 6, 2008

Hill, according to a South Carolina Supreme Court filing, "was convicted of three counts of murder after he walked into the Aiken County Department of Social Services office building on September 16, 1996, and shot and killed three employees," after losing custody of his children.

The next morning, according to the document, Hill "was found lying on the railroad tracks behind the building with his gun nearby. He had a bullet hole through the roof of his mouth and an exit wound in the top of his skull. Although he was seriously injured, [Hill] was able to speak" and "admitted to the shootings."

After being carried into the execution chamber:
I want everyone to know I did not walk to this because this is straight-up murder. I am not going to play a part in my own murder. No one should have to do that . . . I do not know all of your names and I don't know how you feel about me. And whether you believe it or not, I did not kill them . . . You have to move past it. It is time to move on.

As the lethal injection started:
This is some nasty.

LAMONT REESE, convicted of murder, Texas. Executed June 20, 2006

Admitted drug dealer Reese, twenty-eight, protested his own execution by not walking to the death chamber. He did say, however, that he was glad it was now instead of "10 or 20 years" in jail, according to the *Associated Press*. A triple murder charge had resulted in Reese's death sentence.

After he delivered his final words, he gasped. At that moment, the *AP* reported, "his mother, Brenda Reese, began pounding with her fists on the chamber window and began screaming repeatedly, 'They killed my baby.'

"She kicked two holes in the death chamber wall and eventually was removed from the chamber. She sobbed loudly as she walked from the prison and nearly collapsed as she reached the prison administration building across the street."

I want to ask if it is in your heart to forgive me. You don't have to. I know I allowed the devil to rule my life. I just ask you to forgive me and ask the Lord to forgive me for allowing the devil to deceive me. I thank God for having patience with me. I don't deserve to cause you pain. You did not deserve this. I deserve what I am getting.

ANGEL RESENDIZ, convicted of murder, Texas. Executed June 27, 2006

Last-ditch appeals delayed Resendiz's execution after he told psychiatrists that he was half-man, half-angel, and as such couldn't die. Serial killer Resendiz was linked to at least thirteen murders, but he may have committed up to twenty-four, earning him a spot on the FBI's most-wanted list. The *Fort Worth Star-Telegram* reported, "The start of the execution was delayed almost two hours while the U.S. Supreme Court considered several last-day appeals."

I'm sorry for what I done. I'm sorry for killing your mama. I'm not asking you to forgive me. Not a day goes by that I'm not trying to forgive myself. Don't let your anger and hate for me destroy your lives.

After apologizing to his parents for the "embarrassment and shame" brought on the family:

As Gary Gilmore said, "Let's do it."

ROCKY BARTON, convicted of murder, Ohio. Executed July 12, 2006

After a domestic dispute, Barton shot his wife, then turned the gun on himself. Barton said he deserved execution and gave up his appeals shortly before his death. He was the first to receive a new technique of lethal injection in Ohio, with two veins instead of one used to administer the drug.

I want to thank the guards here on death row who have been like family to me, and their lives have been a blessing to me. I've had a good life here on Earth. It's been a blessing. It's been a blast. I want to thank my savior Jesus Christ for all he's done for me. I look forward to being with him now and for eternity.

ERIC PATTON, convicted of robbery and murder, Oklahoma. Executed August 29, 2006

Patton asked to borrow money from Charlene Kauer, for whom he had done some painting, and when she refused, he stabbed her. He claimed that he was under the influence of cocaine during the murder and that Kauer was a demon. Patton and his lawyers challenged the use of lethal injection, calling it cruel punishment because a condemned convict could be awake when the chemicals were injected. The lawsuit was thrown out.

However, as the Reuters news service reported: "Most states inject a large dose of a sedative to render a condemned prisoner unconscious before the prisoner is given chemicals that stop the lungs and heart. Even though Patton's lawsuit failed, Oklahoma doubled the dosage of sedatives that Patton and future condemned prisoners receive."

The state of Florida is killing an innocent person. The state of Florida is committing a crime, because I am innocent. The death penalty is not only a form of vengeance, but also a cowardly act by humans. I'm sorry for what is happening to me and my family who have been put through this.

ANGEL DIAZ, convicted of murder, Florida. Executed December 13, 2006

It was Diaz's death that brought a temporary statewide halt to executions by Florida's then-governor, Jeb Bush. Diaz's death took thirty-four minutes instead of the typical fifteen. After the initial dose, Diaz's lawyer said his client was still conscious, moving his mouth for twenty minutes. It took a second dose to end Diaz's life. Gov. Bush appointed a panel to investigate whether lethal injection could be considered "cruel or unusual punishment," and all death sentences were put on hold.

Diaz had been convicted and sentenced to death for killing Joseph Nagy, a strip-club manager, with two accomplices.

Jennifer, where are you at? I'm sorry, I did not know the man but for a few seconds before I shot him. It was done out of fear, stupidity, and immaturity. It wasn't until I got locked up and saw the newspaper. I saw his face and

his smile and I knew he was a good man. I am sorry for all your family and my disrespect—he deserved better. Sorry Gus. I hope all the best for you and your daughters. I hope you have happiness from here on out. Quit the heroin and methadone. I love you dad, Devin, and Walt. We're done warden.

JONATHAN MOORE, convicted of murder, Texas. Executed January 17, 2007

In 1995, Moore was one of three who, while attempting to burglarize a home, were spotted by Officer Fabian Dominguez. Moore shot Dominguez in the face as he approached their car; he then retrieved Dominguez's firearm and shot him three more times in the head. Moore was pursued by police and confessed to the murder upon his arrest.

You know, once upon a time diamonds were priceless. I never knew until I ran across my own. I just want Eve to know that. One of these days I'm going to return and get that for myself. Thank you to my family, I love you. Each and every one of you. This is not the end, but the beginning of a new chapter for you and I together forever. I love you all. Remember what I told you Brad. Ms. Irene, God bless you, I love you. See you on the other side. Warden, murder me. Sodom and Gomorrah which is Harris County.

JAMES JACKSON, convicted of murder, Texas. Executed February 7, 2007

Jackson killed his two stepdaughters and their mother, whom he was attempting to win back despite their impending divorce.

I do, I would like to tell everybody that I'm sorry about the situation that happened. My bad—everybody is here because of what happened. I'd like to thank everybody that's been here through the years. The little kids overseas—they really changed me. Sister Doris, mom, brothers, sister, dad; I love y'all. My brother . . . where's my stunt double when you need one? My Lord is my life and savior, nothing shall I fear.

VINCENT GUTIERREZ, convicted of murder, Texas. Executed March 28, 2007

Gutierrez was convicted of killing Capt. Jose Cobo, an air force officer, during a carjacking with an accomplice. According to the Associated Press, "Gutierrez was 18 at the time. Just two weeks before the shooting, he had been released from a two-month stint at a prison boot camp for a burglary conviction. He acknowledged shooting Cobo—and expressed no remorse—saying he fired at the military officer because he didn't want to go back to jail for another robbery."

When the Browns are in the Super Bowl in the next five years, you'll know I'm up there doing my magic. . . . I know I flipped some worlds upside down. For me, it's fine, but the state needs to learn this ain't the answer. This is no deterrent to crime. Some are falsely convicted, railroaded. The state needs to wake up. Maybe they will follow the Europeans. God is the only one who knows.

JAMES FILIAGGI, convicted of murder, Ohio. Executed April 24, 2007

In a wide-ranging final statement, Filiaggi touched on subjects including his love for his daughters, football's Cleveland Browns, and capital punishment. Filiaggi faced lethal injection for the murder of his ex-wife, Lisa, after a long history of domestic violence and intimidation. The *Columbus Dispatch* noted: "While Filiaggi never apologized directly for killing his ex-wife, he said in an interview earlier this year that he didn't intend to do it. 'I was planning to put my brains on her wall. With depression, you don't think straight,' he said."

Go Raiders.

ROBERT COMER, convicted of murder, Arizona. Executed May 22, 2007

Comer killed Larry Pritchard at a campground after inviting the man to dinner and drinks with his girlfriend, Juneva Willis. After the murder, Comer and Willis stole from the dead man, then kidnapped and assaulted another camping couple. During his execution, Comer lay on the gurney holding a picture of his daughter as the lethal drugs took effect.

Yes, boy, I could sure go for some beef stew and a chicken bone. That's it.

Written:

If I could take it back, I would. To my family, I love you and I'm sorry.

CHRIS NEWTON, convicted of murder, Ohio. Executed May 24, 2007

Newton murdered fellow prison inmate Jason Brewer over chess. "He kept giving up," said Newton. "Every time I put him in check, he'd give up and want to start a new game . . . I just got tired of it." At 265 pounds, Newton proved to be difficult to execute: it took two hours and ten needle sticks before the proper veins were found. During the delay, Newton talked and laughed with the staff; he was even given a bathroom break.

Yes, I do. I thank the Lord for giving me my friends, for getting me the ones I love. Lord reach down and help innocent men on death row. Lee Taylor needs help, Bobby Hines, Steve Woods. Not all of us are innocent, but those are. Cleve Foster needs help. Melyssa, I love you girl. I know I wasn't going to say anything, but I've got to. Jack, Irene, Danny, Doreen, I love you guys. I said I was going to tell a joke. Death has set me free. That's the biggest joke, I deserve this. And the other joke is I am not Patrick Bryan Knight, and y'all can't stop this execution now. Go ahead, I'm finished. Come on, tell me Lord. I love you Melyssa, take care of that little monster for me.

PATRICK KNIGHT, convicted of murder, Texas. Executed June 26, 2007

Knight solicited jokes from the general public so he could tell one at his execution for the double abduction and murder of Walter and Mary Werner. He received more than thirteen hundred suggestions after a friend set up a MySpace.com profile named "Dead Man Laughing." Knight, however, opted for more serious subjects and then claimed he was not "Patrick Bryan Knight." His fingerprints, taken before the execution, confirmed his identity.

I want you all to know, everyone with all my heart, soul, mind and strength. Thank you for being here today to honor Felecia Prechtl, whom I didn't even know. To celebrate my death. My death began on August 2, 1991 and continued when I began to see the beautiful and innocent life that I had taken. I am so terribly sorry. I wish I could die more than once to tell you how sorry I am.

I have said in interviews, if you want to hurt me and choke me, that's how terrible I felt before this crime. I am sorry, it is her innocence and her life which began the remorse. Every [day] since December 1, 1991, I have embraced life. Thank you for being a part of my life. I love you. May God be with us all. May God have mercy on us all. I am ready. Please do not hate anybody because . . .

KARL CHAMBERLAIN, convicted of murder, Texas. Executed June 11, 2008

An Associated Press writer reported that Chamberlain was "unable to finish as he slipped into unconsciousness." The August 2 date he referred to was the date of his crime, when he raped and murdered neighbor Felecia Prechtl, whose body was later found by her five-year-old son. (News accounts differ on the spelling of the victim's first name.)

Tell my family and friends I love them, tell the governor he just lost my vote. Y'all hurry this along, I'm dying to get out of here.

CHRISTOPHER SCOTT EMMETT, convicted of murder, Virginia. Executed July 24, 2008

The *Washington Post* reported: "Emmett fatally beat his roofing company co-worker, John F. Langley, with a brass lamp in a Danville, Va., motel room in 2001. He then stole Langley's money to buy crack." He later lost an appeal in Virginia claiming that the state's lethal injection protocol constituted "cruel and unusual" punishment.

Asked if he'd like to make a final statement:

For what? You motherfuckers haven't paid any attention to anything I've said in the last 22½ years, why would anyone pay any attention to anything I've had to say now?

RICHARD COOEY II, convicted of murder, Ohio. Executed October 14, 2008

Cooey entered death row at age nineteen after his conviction for killing two college students with an accomplice in 1986. Before his death, his lawyers unsuccessfully argued that Cooey, by then age forty-one, was morbidly obese and medically unfit for execution.

Written:

I, Marco Chapman, only have a few things to say as my last words on Earth. First and foremost I have to say I'm truly sorry to Carolyn and Courtney Marksberry for the crimes and sins I've committed to them and with all my heart and soul I'm sorry with ending the life of two beautiful children Cody and Chelbi Marksberry.

I know the ending of my life will never bring them back and let them have the life they deserve but hopefully with my death it will give some sort of peace to Carolyn and Courtney Marksberry. I don't know why I did the things I did and I know the hate of me over that night must be overwhelming but Carolyn and Courtney you have to know that wasn't who I was or am. I am not a monster even though I did a monstrous, evil thing.

That is why I give my life willingly as well as quickly in hopes that you know how truly sorry I am. I hurt and ache daily for the loss I've created in the Marksberry's family, but I hurt as well. After all before that dreadful night I thought Carolyn as a friend and Courtney, Cody and Chelbi like nieces and nephews cause I did and still care for them very deeply.

I'm sure to Carolyn and Courtney what happen that night was your worst nightmare imaginable but it is also mine and for that I have to say I'm sorry again. I have no right to ask for forgiveness and don't intend to but I want you to know that I believe wholeheartedly that Cody and Chelbi are safe in Heaven. I don't know if I deserve Heaven after what I did but I pray with all my heart that I find some sort of peace and happiness after my last breath.

I pray daily but not just for me but for Carolyn and Courtney that even though they have the right to hate me I just hope they don't live with hate in their hearts. With that said I close my eyes in prayer that Carolyn and Courtney find a type of peace they can live with and can find love and happiness in their lives.

As for my family and loved ones just know I will miss and love each and every one but I know its right to give my life for the lives I've shattered and ended. I hope and pray with all that I am that you remember who I was and not what I did. Don't be sad over my death but relieved that I have found peace.

Just know I'm with you all each and every day in my heart and I will see you all again someday. Bye for now but never forever.

With all my love and sorry,
Marc Chapman
I'm Sorry To Everyone

MARCO ALLEN CHAPMAN, convicted of murder, Kentucky. Executed November 21, 2008

Chapman killed two small children after raping and stabbing their mother, Carolyn Marksberry. Marksberry and a third child survived the attack. Chapman consistently misspelled the last name of his victims as "Marksbury," in addition to misspelling two of his victims' first names as "Kourtney" and "Shelby." Punctuation, grammar, and other errors have been corrected in this printing.

Warden Tom Simpson read Chapman's statement, and afterward "Chapman looked toward the room where Marksberry and family members were scheduled to view the execution, and apologized again. His voice shook, and he had tears in his eyes," reported the *Lexington Herald-Leader*. "Chapman could not see into the room reserved for families of victims because of two-way glass."

Is the mic on? My only statement is that no cases ever tried have been error free. Those are my words. No cases are error free. You may proceed Warden.

DALE DEVON SCHEANETTE, convicted of murder, Texas.
Executed February 10, 2009

Scheanette faced the death penalty for the Christmas Eve death of Wendie Prescott, age twenty-two. The Associated Press reported: "Scheanette, 35, became known as the 'Bathtub Killer' after two women at the same apartment complex in Arlington in 1996 were found dead in half-filled bathtubs, strangled, raped and bound with duct tape. The slayings terrorized the Dallas-Fort Worth area and went unsolved for more than three years, until Scheanette was arrested for a burglary and his fingerprints were tied to the killings. DNA strengthened the confirmations and pointed to his involvement in the other rapes."

The Polunsky dungeon should be compared with the death row community as existing, not living. Why do I say this? The death row is full of isolated hearts and suppressed minds. We are filled with love looking for affection and a way to understand. I am a death row resident of the Polunsky dungeon. Why does my heart ache? We want pleasure love and satisfaction. . . . The walls of darkness crushed in on me. Life without meaning is life without purpose. But the solace within the Polunsky dungeon, the unforgivenness within society, the church pastors and Christians. It is terrifying. Does anyone care or who I am? Can you feel me, people? The Polunsky dungeon is what I call the Pit of Hopelessness. The terrifying thing is the U.S. is the only place, country that is the only civilized country that is free that says it will stop murder and enable justice. I ask each of you to lift up your voices to demand an end to the death penalty. If we live, we live to the Lord. If we die we die to the Lord. Christ rose again, in Jesus' name. Bye Aunt Helen, Luise, Joanna and to all the rest of y'all. You may proceed Warden.

JOHNNY JOHNSON, convicted of murder, Texas. Executed February 12, 2009

The Polunsky Unit—which Johnson referred to as "the Polunsky dungeon"—is the home of death row inmates in Livingston, Texas. Johnson was sent there for killing Leah Joette Smith, forty-one, though court documents said he was tied to at least "five rape-slayings" in Texas.

According to prison records, after Johnson finished his final words he began singing.

To the Timbrook family, you definitely have the wrong person. The truth will come out one day. This here, killing me, there's no justice about it.

EDWARD NATHANIEL BELL, convicted of murder, Virginia. Executed February 19, 2009

Bell, a native of Jamaica, was sent to death row for the shooting death of police officer Ricky Timbrook in 1999. Bell maintained his innocence throughout trial. The case became "a flash point in the debate over Gov. Timothy M. Kaine's views on the death penalty," reported the *Washington Post*. ". . . The case had particular resonance for Kaine, a Catholic who personally opposes the death penalty but has said he will enforce the law."

I just hope God's will be done and everybody finds the peace they need. I'm good.

JIMMY LEE DILL, convicted of murder, Alabama. Executed April 16, 2009

Dill killed Leon Shaw during a robbery of money and cocaine in 1988. The victim's son, Leon Shaw Jr., attended Dill's execution with his mother and two of Dill's nieces.

"I told him I forgave him," Leon Shaw Jr. said afterward. "I see him as a victim, a victim of his raising, a victim of the circumstances. I see my dad as a victim, too, and it's continuing."

Don't cry, it's my situation. I got it. Hold tight. It's going to shine on the golden child. Hold tight. I love you, I'm through with my statement.

DERRICK JOHNSON, convicted of murder, Texas. Executed April 30, 2009

Johnson faced the death penalty for the murder of LaTausha Curry, age twenty-five, whom he robbed, raped, and beat with a two-by-four and suffocated with her own clothing. The crime took place "during what authorities determined was part of a two-week crime spree in January 1999 involving Johnson and a companion. During the binge, numerous women were robbed or raped from Dallas to south of Waco," according to the Associated Press.

During his execution, Johnson tried to comfort his mother, telling her not to cry.

I wish to apologize to the people who I have hurt and I ask for their forgiveness. I don't deserve it, but I do ask for it.

JACK TRAWICK, convicted of murder, Alabama. Executed June 11, 2009

Trawick was a self-professed serial killer who faced the death penalty for kidnapping, stabbing, and strangling twenty-one-year-old Stephanie Gach in 1992. He claimed to have killed at least four other people and was serving a life sentence for one of those murders.

After the execution, Gach's sister Heather expressed surprise at Trawick's last words. "The Jack Trawick I've seen has been kind of unremorseful, reveling in the attention he got for being a serial killer. But he gave no indication of that tonight."

Written:

I cannot wait to finish paying this debt I owe so I can apologize to the souls of Mr. Morgan and Mr. Bullard, and ask them to forgive me for my taking their lives. To the familiar of my victims all I can say is I'm sorry for

the pain I've caused you. I hope my death will bring you some peace.

MICHAEL P. DELOZIER, convicted of murder, Oklahoma. Executed July 2, 2009

DeLozier declined to give any oral statement before his execution but had his attorneys release the above statement. DeLozier, with two accomplices, had killed Orville Lewis Bullard and Paul Steven Morgan during a 1995 campsite robbery, after which he burned the camp and his victims' bodies. After the execution, the victims' families released a statement that read in part, "We have waited nearly 14 years for this day. We feel that justice has finally been served."

A NOTE ON ACCURACY
AND SOURCES

Whenever possible, last words of the condemned were taken from prison records, eyewitness statements, newspaper accounts, period diaries, and written statements.

Newspapers such as the *New York Times, Washington Post,* and *Chicago Tribune* were invaluable sources of information—but even these fine news sources didn't always agree on last words or had incomplete case histories. So the greatest possible care was taken to cross-reference information with other sources, notably the prison archives at San Quentin and Texas's vast Department of Criminal Justice Web site. The rather large number of books in the bibliography and scholars I've thanked in the acknowledgments also helped sharpen the entries.

But it should be noted here that records are kept by fallible humans, so the historical record cannot be counted on as completely accurate.

For instance, in the earliest accounts, last words often came from pamphlets or chapbooks published by local printers after an execution. They have titles such as "A Chronicle of Welch's Confession and Last Words" (1754) and "Last Words and Dying Speech of Edmund Fortis" (1794). Some appear to be written by the condemned, while others had more questionable origins. More than a few contained religious or sensational overtones and seemed to be more concerned with saving souls or selling copies than with historical fidelity. Quotes from these more dubious publications did not make it into this volume.

Convicted murderer Wharton Ransdale, hanged in Virginia in 1818, even used his last words to warn people against such false reporting. An article in the *Alexandria Herald* reported: "The prisoner requested . . . to declare to the people, that 'if any thing should be hereafter published as his confession, or acknowledgment of guilt in himself or his associates, it would be false, that he had nothing to confess, but to his God—to him he confessed that he was a sinner and begged his forgiveness.'"

When the state or clergy did not record final words, newspaper reporters would take them down in prison interviews. Some statements come from the death chamber or gallows, others from the final holding cell. In cases where the recording of last words was less formal, the accounts come from eyewitness conversations just before the execution.

More often than not, newspaper accounts of executions disagree by a few words and sometimes a whole passage. In these cases, the most reputable eyewitness descriptions were favored, though where disagreements exist, it's noted in my account.

I've also preserved the peculiar grammar, spelling, and dramatic capitalization from early newspapers, except in instances where modern editing could clear up confusion. Newspapers and prisons themselves often censor profanity. Prison press releases and Web sites also contain spelling and small factual errors, which have been corrected in this volume.

But it's important to remember that except in a few cases (notably Georgia), last words are not electronically recorded. For most of history, statements were taken with pencil and paper just before an execution. Imagine a newspaper reporter straining to hear someone's parting speech from the scaffold, furiously scribbling in shorthand as the wind carries half the words away.

Other factors come into play. The prison bureaucracy can sometimes be a filter. According to Rev. Carroll Pickett—who attended ninety-five men during their executions in Huntsville, Texas—one warden wanted final statements to be short. "No Gettysburg Addresses" was Pickett's order when taking last words. When I inter-

viewed Pickett for this volume, I asked about the process of taking
last words. In Pickett's experience, he and the prison often knew
what the last words would be, because they'd be taken an hour before execution. "I hate to use the word *rehearsed*, . . . so many of
them would have a less than college education," he said. "My warden always wanted me to find out what they were gonna say so
he . . . would not stop the world from hearing their last words by
starting lethal injection too quick or cutting them off. So we would
normally go through their last words between 10 and 11 o'clock at
night. We basically knew what the last words were going to be before it happened."

Still, news reporters would often hear the words incorrectly, as
Ted Koppel did in a *Nightline* report in the 1995 execution of Mario
Marquez. Koppel reported the words as "I hold nothing against
anyone, not even the prosecutors. I just want to come home to Him.
Thank you, Lord Jesus."

The prison recorded: "Thank you for being my Lord Jesus and
Savior and I am ready to come home. Amen."

Pickett said he alerted Koppel to the discrepancy, and he explained the matter this way: "So many people hear what they want
to hear or hear only a portion, and also because they're very emo-
tionally involved. It's difficult to watch. I'm not criticizing the press;
it's difficult to watch somebody dying . . . who doesn't speak real
loud even though we got a microphone ten inches from them." But,
Pickett added, even official prison releases are sometimes imperfect.
"There's no way for it to be totally accurate," he said.

Pickett explained how last words were recorded in his facility:
An assistant warden sits outside the death chamber, which "is separated by a big heavy door, and he's there listening and he's on a telephone . . . and he's repeating it to a secretary who's trying to write
it down as he speaks. And it's just very difficult. And I always felt
sorry for both of those people, because so often you just can't keep
up with them."

He continued: "And I don't like criticizing the prison, because
since they allow no tape recorders, nothing but paper and pencil,
it's difficult to write down in a traumatic situation what is going on
right in there."

1608   George Kendall is accused of plotting to betray the Brit-
        ish to the Spanish. He is shot near modern-day Jamestown,
        Virginia, in the first recorded instance of capital punish-
        ment in precolonial times.

1636   The first death-penalty statutes are recorded in the form of
        the Capital Laws of New-England. The statutes are accom-
        panied by Old Testament verses.

1692   In the series of events known as the Salem Witch Trials, 185
        people are accused of witchcraft in Salem, Massachusetts.
        Fifty-nine of them are tried, 31 convicted, and 19 executed.

1787   Benjamin Rush, regarded as the father of the anti–death-
        penalty movement in the United States, delivers a talk at
        Benjamin Franklin's house calling for a justice system that
        rehabilitates rather than punishes.

1833   Rhode Island becomes the first state to outlaw public hang-
        ings.

1846   Michigan becomes the first state to officially abolish capital
        punishment, although it leaves an exception open for trea-
        son against the state. The state has not executed anyone
        since 1830.

1890   William Kemmler becomes the first person to be executed
        in the electric chair when he is put to death for murder in

Auburn Prison in New York. The state formally adopts the electric chair as a means of execution in 1898.

1924   Gee Jon is convicted of murder and executed by the state of Nevada. He is the first prisoner to be put to death in a gas chamber.

1935   Capital punishment peaks during this year, reaching a nationwide all-time high of 199 prisoners executed.

1936   The last public execution in the United States occurs when Rainey Bethea is hanged in Kentucky for rape and murder. Bethea's execution is also the first hanging performed by a woman.

1952   Julius and Ethel Rosenberg become the first U.S. citizens to be executed for espionage.

1966   Public support for the death penalty reaches an all-time low of 42 percent.

1967   Luis Monge is the last man to be executed for ten years.

1972   In the landmark case *Furman v. Georgia*, the Supreme Court rules 5–4 that the inconsistent administration of the death penalty makes capital punishment cruel and unusual. In the plurality opinion, Justice Potter Stewart describes the current use of capital punishment as "freakish and wanton," and elaborates, "These death sentences are cruel and unusual in the same way that being struck by lightning is cruel and unusual."

1976   In another landmark case, *Gregg v. Georgia*, the Supreme Court rules that capital punishment is constitutional if statutes are rewritten so as to avoid discrimination. Stewart writes the plurality opinion again: "In part, capital punishment is an expression of society's moral outrage at particularly offensive conduct. This function may be unappealing to many, but it is essential in an ordered society that asks its citizens to rely on legal processes, rather than self-help, to vindicate their wrongs."

1977

January 17   Gary Gilmore is shot by a volunteer firing squad in Utah after fighting for his execution for several months. He is the first person to be executed after a hiatus of ten years.

June 29 In *Coker v. Georgia*, the Supreme Court votes 7–2 that capital punishment is a disproportionate sentence for those convicted of rape. The plurality opinion reads, "Rape is without doubt deserving of serious punishment; but in terms of moral depravity and of the injury to the person and to the public, it does not compare with murder, which does involve the unjustified taking of human life."

1982 Charles Brook becomes the first prisoner ever to be executed by lethal injection. Lethal injection in the United States was first authorized by the state of Oklahoma in 1977.

1985 The Supreme Court rules in *Ford v. Wainwright* that the execution of the insane is unconstitutional. Justice Thurgood Marshall writes, "Whether its aim be to protect the condemned from fear and pain without comfort of understanding, or to protect the dignity of society itself from the barbarity of exacting mindless vengeance, the restriction finds enforcement in the Eighth Amendment."

1987 In *McCleskey v. Kemp*, the Supreme Court rules that the proof of a statistical pattern of discrimination—in this case, discrimination against black prisoners, who are executed at seven times the rate of white prisoners—is not grounds for overthrowing a death sentence. The Court writes, "Because discretion is essential to the criminal justice process, we would demand exceptionally clear proof before we would infer that the discretion has been abused."

1994 National support for the death penalty peaks at 80 percent.

1996 Bill Bailey becomes the last U.S. prisoner to be executed by hanging after he turns down the option of lethal injection. One day later, John Albert Taylor also refuses lethal injection and becomes the last prisoner to be executed by firing squad.

2000 Illinois governor George Ryan declares a moratorium on capital punishment in the state after thirteen people were exonerated by new evidence. "We have now freed more people than we have put to death under our system," Ryan said. "There is a flaw in the system, without question, and it needs to be studied." By contrast, Illinois had executed twelve inmates since 1977. Just before leaving office in 2003, Ryan commuted the sentence of everyone on death row to life in prison—167 convicts in all.

2001 The first federal execution since 1963 occurs with the death of Oklahoma City bomber Timothy McVeigh.

2002 The Supreme Court rules in *Atkins v. Virginia* that it is unconstitutional to execute a mentally retarded prisoner, with the plurality opinion noting, "Mentally retarded defendants in the aggregate face a special risk of wrongful execution."

2005 Kenneth Boyd is executed in North Carolina. He is the one thousandth prisoner to be executed since Gary Gilmore in 1977. Before he dies, Boyd says, "I'd hate to be remembered as [the thousandth execution]. I don't like the idea of being picked as a number."

2007 New Jersey abolishes the death penalty, becoming the first state to do so in forty years.

2008 The Supreme Court refuses to hear an appeal by death row inmate Troy Anthony Davis, who argues that the execution of a prisoner who is "actually innocent" violates the Eighth Amendment.

In April, the Supreme Court upholds Kentucky lethal injection protocol as constitutional.

In June, the Court overturns a law allowing capital punishment for those convicted of child rape.

ACKNOWLEDGMENTS

First, thanks to Studs Terkel for his unbelievable foreword and his support of this project. Studs, you continue to hold my gratitude and my awe. I miss you.

Were it not for the vision and enthusiasm of my editor Robert Devens, *Last Words of the Executed* would be a very different book. Thanks Robert, for believing in me.

I'm indebted to my former *Chicago Tribune* editors—among them Tim Bannon, Pam Becker, Maureen Hart, Lilah Lohr, George Papajohn, Scott L. Powers, and James Warren—for their support of my work.

Also, thanks to scholars James R. Acker, Scott Christianson, Charles S. Lanier, and David Protess for their thoughtful criticism and feedback. Mark W. Falzini at the New Jersey State Police Museum was particularly helpful in tracking down the last words of Bruno Richard Hauptmann. Associated Press reporter Matt Reed helped complete the entry for Richard Cooey II. Thanks to Brian Shovers at the Montana Historical Society for steering me toward valuable local sources.

I'm also indebted to Rob Warden, executive director of the Center on Wrongful Convictions, for directing me to the story of William Jackson Marion. To Flynn McRoberts: Thanks for your insight and encouragement. To Vernell Crittendon: For your service and thoughtful responses I am forever grateful.

Thanks to Steve James and Kate Anthony for their parts in inspiring this book. A special nod of gratitude goes to Willis Barnstone for his advice on the title.

Last Words of the Executed would not have been possible without the eagle eyes and research mojo of Shay Bapple, Gina Brown, Lilian Bürgler, Sheila Burt, Alexis Crawford, Kasia Dworzecka, Michelle Edgar, Jenifer Fischer, Drew Fortune, Megan Frestedt, J. Scott Gordon, Ruth Goring, Constance Grady, Jay Grooms, Kelin Hall, Matthew Hendrickson, Michael Hirtzer, Laurel Jorgensen, Jina Hassan, Sharon Kim, Alison Knezevich, Rikki Knutti, David Lanzafame, Gabriel Mares, Nomaan Merchant, Theodore Noble, Caroline Picard, Ryan Ptomey, Nate Radomski, Kristen Radtke, Zack Seward, Benjamin Summers, Chelsea Trembly, Mia Umanos, Jessica Victor, and Eugenia Williamson. Thank you—every one of you—for the late nights of fact-checking, research, and straightening out my dyslexia.

My good friend and collaborator Aaron Vetch did an amazingly detailed read of the manuscript for which I'm inexpressibly grateful.

Lastly, I couldn't have done this without my wife, editor, and best critic: Betsy Edgerton. She helped shape and edit most of this book while seven, eight, and nine months pregnant—with twins. The last draft of the book was edited when they were almost two years old.

Now that's love.

Robert K. Elder
Chicago
July 2009

BIBLIOGRAPHY

Abbott, Geoffrey. *The Executioner Always Chops Twice*. New York: St. Martin's, 2002.

Allen, Danielle S. *The World of Prometheus: The Politics of Punishing in Democratic Athens*. Princeton, NJ: Princeton University Press, 2000.

Allen, Harry E., and Clifford E. Simonsen. *Corrections in America: An Introduction*. 9th ed. Upper Saddle River, NJ: Prentice-Hall, 2001.

Andrews, William. *Old-Time Punishments*. London: Tabard, n.d.

Arriens, Jan. *Welcome to Hell: Letters and Writings from Death Row*. 2nd ed. Boston: Northeastern University Press, 2005.

Banner, Stuart. *The Death Penalty: An American History*. Cambridge, MA: Harvard University Press, 2002.

Baumann, Ed. *May God Have Mercy on Your Soul*. Chicago. Bonus Books, 1993.

Bean, J. P. *The Book of Criminal Quotations*. London: Artnik, 2003.

Beccaria, Cesare. *Of Crimes and Punishments*. New York: Marsilio, 1996.

Bedau, Hugo A. *The Death Penalty in America*. 3rd ed. Oxford: Oxford University Press, 1982.

Bessler, John D. *Death in the Dark: Midnight Executions in America*. Boston: Northeastern University Press, 1997.

Blank, Jessica, and Erik Jensen. *Living Justice: Freedom, Love, and the Making of "The Exonerated."* New York: Atria, 2005.

Boethius. *The Consolation of Philosophy*. Translated by Victor Watts. London: Penguin, 1999.

Bowers, William J. *Legal Homicide: Death as Punishment in America, 1864–1982*. Boston: Northeastern University Press, 1984.

Brian, Denis. *Sing Sing: the Inside Story of a Notorious Prison.* Amherst, NY: Prometheus, 2005.

Brown, Larry K. *You Are Respectfully Invited to Attend My Execution.* Glendo, WY: High Plains, 1997.

Cahill, Thomas. *A Saint on Death Row: The Story of Dominique Green.* New York: Nan A. Talese/Doubleday, 2009.

Capote, Truman. *In Cold Blood.* New York: Random House, 1965.

Cawthorne, Nigel. *Public Executions from Ancient Rome to the Present Day.* London: Arcturus, 2006.

Christianson, Scott. *Condemned: Inside the Sing Sing Death House.* New York: New York University Press, 2000.

Dobbs, Michael. *Saboteurs: The Nazi Raid on America.* New York: Alfred A. Knopf, 2004.

Donovan, Tom, *Hanging Around the Big Sky: The Unofficial Guide to Lynching, Strangling, and Legal Hangings of Montana,* bk. 1, *Legal Hangings.* Great Falls, MT: Portage Meadows, 2007.

Dow, David R. *Executed on a Technicality: Lethal Injustice on America's Death Row.* Boston: Beacon, 2005.

Drehle, David Von. *Among the Lowest of the Dead: The Culture of Death Row.* New York: Times Books, 1995.

Drimmer, Frederick. *Until You Are Dead: The Book of Executions in America.* New York: Citadel, 1990.

Duffy, Clinton T., with Al Hirshberg. *88 Men and 2 Women.* New York. Doubleday Permabook, 1962.

Duffy, Clinton T., and Dean Jennings. *The San Quentin Story.* Garden City, NY: Doubleday, 1950.

Engel, Howard. *Lord High Executioner: An Unashamed Look at Hangmen, Headsmen, and Their Kind.* Buffalo, NY: Firefly, 1996.

Eshelman, Bryon E., with Frank Riley. *Death Row Chaplain.* Englewood Cliffs, NJ: Prentice-Hall, 1962.

Fetherling, George. *The Book of Assassins: A Biographical Dictionary from Ancient Times to the Present.* New York. John Wiley and Sons, 2001.

Foucault, Michel. *Discipline and Punish: The Birth of the Prison.* New York: Vintage, 1995.

Fulker, John.. . . *And True Deliverance Make . . .* Francestown, NH: Marshall Jones, 1985.

Grant, George. *Killers.* London: Chartwell, 2006.

Green, James. *Death in the Haymarket.* New York: Pantheon, 1996.

Guthke, Karl S. *Last Words: Variations on a Theme in Cultural History.* Princeton, NJ: Princeton University Press, 1992.

Hearn, Daniel Allen. *Legal Executions in New Jersey: A Comprehensive Registry, 1691–1963.* Jefferson, NC: McFarland, 1997.

Hoffman, Yoel. *Japanese Death Poems Written by Zen Monks and Haiku Poets on the Verge of Death.* Boston: Tuttle, 1986.

Inbau, Fred E., John E. Reid, and Joseph P. Buckley. *Criminal Interrogation and Confessions.* 3rd ed. Baltimore: Williams and Wilkins, 1986.

Ingle, Joseph B. *Last Rights: 13 Factual Encounters with the State's Justice.* Nashville: Abingdon, 1990.

Hofstadter, Richard, and Michael Wallace. *American Violence: A Documentary History.* New York: Alfred A. Knopf, 1970.

Kurtis, Bill. *The Death Penalty on Trial: Crisis in American Justice.* New York. PublicAffairs, 2004.

Lawes, Lewis E. *Twenty Thousand Years in Sing Sing.* New York: Ray Long and Richard R. Smith, 1932.

Le Comte, Edward S. *Dictionary of Last Words.* New York. Philosophical Library, 1955.

Lesser, Wendy. *Pictures at an Execution: An Inquiry in the Subject of Murder.* Cambridge, MA: Harvard University Press, 1993.

Lockyer, Herbert. *Last Words of Saints and Sinners.* Grand Rapids, MI: Kregel, 1969.

Lynch, Thomas. *The Undertaking: Life Studies from the Dismal Trade.* New York: Penguin, 1997.

Lyons, Lewis. *The History of Punishment.* Guilford, CT: Lyons, 2003.

MacPherson, Malcolm. *The Black Box.* New York: Quill, 1998.

Masur, Louis P. *Rites of Execution: Capital Punishment and the Transformation of American Culture, 1776–1865.* New York: Oxford University Press, 1989.

Mauer, Marc. *Race to Incarcerate.* New York: New Press, 2006.

McAllister, Pam. *Death Defying: Dismantling the Execution Machinery in the 21st Century U.S.A.* New York: Continuum, 2003.

Mencken, August. *By the Neck.* New York: Hastings House, 1942.

Mitford, Jessica. *Kind and Usual Punishment: The Prison Business.* New York: Alfred A. Knopf, 1973.

Moran, Richard. *Executioner's Current: Thomas Edison, George Westinghouse, and the Invention of the Electric Chair.* New York: Vintage, 2002.

Morris, Norval, and David J. Rothman. *The Oxford History of the Prison: The Practice of Punishment in Western Society.* New York: Oxford University Press, 1995.

Norton, Mary Beth. *In the Devil's Snare: The Salem Witch Crisis of 1692.* New York: Vintage, 2002.

O'Hare, Sheila, Irene Berry, and Jesse Silva. *Legal Executions in California.* Jefferson, NC: McFarland, 2006.

Palmer, Louis J., Jr. *Encyclopedia of Capital Punishment in the United States.* Jefferson, NC: McFarland, 2001.

Robinson, Ray. *Famous Last Words.* New York: Workman, 2003.

Rommel, Bart. *Execution Tools and Techniques.* Port Townsend, WA: Loompanics Unlimited, 1990.

Santos, Michael G. *Inside: Life behind Bars in America.* New York: St. Martin's Griffin, 2006.

Smith, Gene, and Jayne Barry Smith. *The National Police Gazette.* New York: Simon and Schuster, 1972.

Solotaroff, Ivan. *The Last Face You'll Ever See.* New York: Harper Collins, 2001.

Swanson, James. L. *Manhunt: The 12-Day Chase for Lincoln's Killer.* New York: William Morrow, 2006.

Teeters, Negley, K. *Hang by the Neck.* Springfield, IL: Thomas, 1967.

Vila, Bryan, and Cynthia Morris. *Capital Punishment in the United States: A Documentary History.* Westport, CT: Greenwood, 1997.

Vollen, Lola, and Dave Eggers. *Surviving Justice: America's Wrongfully Convicted and Exonerated.* San Francisco: Voice of Witness, 2005.

Waller, George. *Kidnap: The Story of the Lindbergh Case.* New York: Dial, 1961.

Warden, Rob. *Wilkie Collins's "The Dead Alive": The Novel, the Case, and Wrongful Convictions.* Evanston, IL: Northwestern University Press, 2005.

West, John Foster. *The Ballad of Tom Dula.* Durham, NC: Moore, 1977.

INDEX

Abbott, Clinton, 226
Abyssinia, 89
AC (alternative current), 125
Academy Awards (Oscars), 185, 248
Acero, Fernando, 68
Adams, Allen J., 65
Adams, Aubrey, Jr., 168
Adams, John R., 41
Adams, Randall Dale, 252
Adams, Sylvester, 207
Addison, George, 22
Adkins, Orville, 96
African Americans, ix, 9, 3, 10, 26, 94,
  169, 182, 188, 237, 248
Afrika Korps, 97
Age of Science, 125
Aiken County Department of Social Ser-
  vices (SC), 257
Akipa, 41
Alabama, 129, 169–71
alcohol, 17, 63, 81, 143, 225, 254–55
Alexandria Herald, 274
Alfred P. Murrah Federal Building (Okla-
  homa City, OK), 240
Allah, 172, 191–92. *See also* Islam; Mo-
  hammed
Allen, John, 186

Allen, Sheryl, 103
Allen, Wanda Jean, 238–39
Allen, William, 27
Allender, Harvey, 79
Alta California, 53
America. *See* United States
American Civil Liberties Union, 187
Amnesty International, 167, 169, 237, 238
anarchists, 66–68, 127–28, 136–37
anarchy, 67, 136
Andrews, Henry F., 58
Andrews, Joseph, 20
Andrews, R. E., 49
Antichrist, 163
Antonio, Anna, 144–45
Apache, 83
Appel, George, 138
Arbeiter-Zeitung, 67
Arizona, 85, 92, 180, 189, 263
Arkansas, 77, 101, 108, 136, 149, 184,
  206, 228
Armstrong, Maxine, 179
Arnot, Adrienne, 249
arsenic, 130
arson, 2, 18, 26, 27, 252
Asher, Rosalie, 178
Ashworth, Herman, 255

Brown, Josephine, 51
Brown, Newt, 166
Bryant, Joseph, 147
Bryant, Mickey, 238
Buchalter, Louis (pseud. Louis Lepke),
   154
Buchanan, Robert, 130
Buck, Rufus, 77
Buckminster and Graves, 135
Bulliner family, 55
Bundy, Ted, 127, 168
Burger, Peter, 151
burglary, 58, 199, 204, 207, 213, 219, 220,
   230, 243, 262, 268
Burke, John, 34
Burness, Frank Henry, 132
Burns, Jennifer E., 210
Burroughs, George, 16
Burton, Burr, 45
Burton, Willard, 186
Bush, George W., 221, 237, 238
Bush, Jeb, 193, 260
Bushnell, Bennie, 123
Butterworth, Bob, 173

Cadotte, Joseph, 74
Cahill, Joseph, 83
Cahill, Thomas, 253
Calabrese, Joseph, 139–40
Caldwell, Janet, 211
Caldwell, Johnson William, 184
Calef, Robert, 16
California, 10, 30, 32, 34, 45–46, 52–53,
   68, 70, 73, 79–80, 84, 90–93, 95,
   101–2, 105, 114, 158, 176, 177, 180–89,
   193, 208, 215, 218, 220, 237, 256
California Police Gazette, 45
Cameron, John, 7
Campione, Frank, 87
Canada, 36, 91
Cannon, Joseph, 213
Cannon, Robert Lee, 176, 180
Cantu, Domingo, Jr., 220
capital punishment, x, 2–3, 6–7, 10, 78,
   90, 98, 102–3, 123, 125, 127, 133, 147,
   158–59, 161–63, 166, 169, 171, 176–77,
   177–79, 181, 187, 189, 192–93, 196,
   198, 200, 203, 205, 207–9, 211, 220,

223, 225, 227–28, 236, 238, 241, 245,
   250, 260, 262, 268–71, 277–80, 283
Capone, Louis, 154
Capote, Truman, 98–99
Cardinella, Sam, 87
Carey, Peggy, 17
Carey, William, 108
Carlson, Thomas, 224
Carpenter, Richard, 156
Carrisalez, Enrique, 200
Carter, Judith Ann, 161
Carter, Matilda, 59
Carter, Nash, 59
Carver, Alfred M., 9
Cassidy, James, 134
Castillo, David, 216
Catholic, Catholicism, 3, 9, 32, 54, 71, 72,
   91, 270
Celestine, Willie, 166
Center on Wrongful Convictions, 201,
   214, 281
Cermak, Anton J., 142
Chamberlain, Karl, 265
Chambers, Bryan, 207
Champion, Clarencio, 216
Cha Nopa Uhah, 73
Chapman, Marco Allen, 266–68
Chessman, Caryl, 177–78
Chicago, 28, 57, 66, 68, 72, 75–76, 115,
   139, 141–42, 150, 152
Chicago Daily, 53, 82
Chicago Daily Tribune, 53, 63, 66, 86, 119,
   140–42, 144, 157
Chicago Times, 54
Chicago Tribune, 1, 35, 55, 57, 66, 197,
   273, 281
Chimurenga, Ashanti, 235
Chinese, 149, 175
Chow, Yip, 149
Christ. *See* Jesus
Christian, 4, 7, 25, 70, 164, 168, 213, 269.
   See also Baptist; Catholic, Catholi-
   cism; Devil; Episcopal; First Corinthi-
   ans (New Testament); God; heaven;
   hell; Jesus; Lord; Paradise; Protestant;
   Sabbath
Christian, Scott, 154, 281
Christmas, 45, 113, 147, 166, 209, 268

Williams, Duncan, 64
Williams, Robert W., 159
Williams, Stanley "Tookie" (aka Big
    Took), 256
Williams, Willie Ray, 204
Willie, Robert Lee, 160
Willis, Juneya, 263
Wilson, Henry, 45
Wilson, James, 30
Wilson, Woodrow, 114
Windrath, Joseph, 76
Wineville Chicken Coop Murders, 92
Wing, George Chew, 148
Wingo, Jimmy, 166
Winn, Michelle, 202
Wisconsin, 204
Wishon, Ernest, 153

witchcraft, 15, 16, 277
Wood, Frederick, 158
Woods, Omer R., 117
Woods, Steve, 264
Woodward, Charles Francis, 82
Woolls, Randy, 196
Woolman, Jacob, 19
Wright, Harry, 146
Wuornos, Aileen, 248
Wynn, L. L., 145
Wyoming, 54, 62, 82, 83, 212

You Bet Your Life, 84
Young, Brigham, 101, 103, 109. *See also*
    Mormon

Zangara, Giuseppe, 142